Please remember that this is a library book,
and that it belongs only temporarily to each
person who uses it. Be considerate. Do
not write in this, or any, library book.

Criminality and violence among the mentally disordered
The Stockholm Project Metropolitan

In recent years it has become apparent that mentally ill people are at increased risk of committing crimes of violence. Most writing and research about crime and mental disorder has focused necessarily on the immediate problems which confront clinicians and law makers – assessing and managing the future risk of violence. In this important new book the authors attempt to step back from these immediate preoccupations and describe the criminality of the mentally ill and try to identify the complex chain of factors which cause it. As part of their analysis they examine a unique cohort composed of 15,117 persons born in Stockholm who were studied from birth to the age of thirty. While they conclude that we still do not understand exactly how and why persons with major mental disorders commit crimes, their findings make a valuable contribution to ongoing debates on mental health and criminal justice policy and practice.

SHEILAGH HODGINS is Professor at the Université de Montréal, Foreign Adjunct Professor of Psychiatry at the Karolinska Institutet, Stockholm, and Adjunct Professor at Concordia University, Montreal. Her recent books include *Violence Among the Mentally Ill: Effective treatments and management strategies* (2000) and with R. Müller-Isberner, *Violence, Crime and Mentally Disordered Offenders: Concepts and methods for effective treatment and prevention* (2000).

CARL-GUNNAR JANSON is Sociology Professor Emeritus at Stockholm University. In 1964 he started Project Metropolitan and is still analysing its data. He is the editor of *Seven Swedish Longitudinal Studies in Behavioral Sciences* (2000).

Cambridge Studies in Criminology

Editors:
Alfred Blumstein, *Carnegie Mellon University*
David Farrington, *University of Cambridge*

This series publishes high quality research monographs of either theoretical or empirical emphasis in all areas of criminology, including measurements of offending, explanations of offending, police, courts, incapacitation, corrections, sentencing, deterrence, rehabilitation, and other related topics. It is intended to be both interdisciplinary and international in scope.

Also in the series:

J. David Hawkins (editor), *Delinquency and Crime: Current Theories*
Simon I. Singer, *Recriminalizing Delinquency: Violent Juvenile Crime and Juvenile Justice Reform*
Scott H. Decker and Barrik Van Winkle, *Life in the Gang: Family, Friends, and Violence*
Austin Lovegrove, *A Framework of Judicial Sentencing: Decision Making and Multiple Offence Cases*
John Hagan and Bill McCarthy, *Mean Streets: Youth Crime and Homelessness*
Eduard Zamble and Vernon L. Quirsey, *The Criminal Recidivism Process*
Joan McCord (editor), *Violence and Childhood in the Inner City*
Malcolm M. Feeley and Edward L. Rubin, *Judicial Policy Making and the Modern State: How the Courts Reformed America's Prisons*
Don Weatherburn and Bronwyn Lind, *Delinquent-Prone Communities*
Alfred Blumstein and Joel Wallman, *The Crime Drop in America*
Denise Gottfredson, *Schools and Delinquency*
David Weisbund, Elin Waring and Ellen Chayet, *White-Collar Crime and Criminal Careers*
Terrie E. Moffitt, Avshalom Caspi, Michael Rutter and Phil A. Silva, *Sex Differences in Antisocial Behaviour: Conduct Disorder, Delinquency and Violence in the Dunedin Longitudinal Study*
Jerzy Sarnecki, *Delinquent Networks: Youth Co-offending in Stockholm*

Criminality and violence among the mentally disordered

The Stockholm Project Metropolitan

Sheilagh Hodgins

Carl-Gunnar Janson

CAMBRIDGE
UNIVERSITY PRESS

PUBLISHED BY THE PRESS SYNDICATE OF THE UNIVERSITY OF CAMBRIDGE
The Pitt Building, Trumpington Street, Cambridge, United Kingdom

CAMBRIDGE UNIVERSITY PRESS
The Edinburgh Building, Cambridge CB2 2RU, UK
40 West 20th Street, New York, NY 10011-4211, USA
477 Williamstown Road, Port Melbourne, VIC 3207, Australia
Ruiz de Alarcón 13, 28014 Madrid, Spain
Dock House, The Waterfront, Cape Town 8001, South Africa

http://www.cambridge.org

© Sheilagh Hodgins and Carl-Gunnar Janson 2002

First published 2002

Printed in the United Kingdom at the University Press, Cambridge

Typeface New Baskerville 10/13 pt.   *System* LATEX 2_ε [TB]

A catalogue record for this book is available from the British Library.

Library of Congress cataloguing in publication data

Hodgins, Sheilagh.
Criminality and violence among the mentally disordered: the Stockholm Project
Metropolitan / Sheilagh Hodgins, Carl-Gunnar Janson.
    p.   cm. – (Cambridge studies in criminology)
Includes bibliographical references and index.
ISBN 0 521 58073 0 (hardback)
1. Mentally ill offenders – Sweden – Stockholm Region.   2. Violent crimes –
Sweden – Stockholm Region – Psychological aspects.   I. Janson, Carl-Gunnar.
II. Title.   III. Cambridge studies in criminology (New York, NY)

RC569.5.V55 H635 2002
364′.087′4 – dc21

2002035098

ISBN 0 521 58073 0 hardback

Contents

Figures

Tables

Preface

This book illustrates how an investigation of a birth cohort followed for thirty years, which was designed principally as a study of inequality and social deviance, was used to examine the relation between the major mental disorders and criminality. The findings presented here, plus those found in many other publications from Project Metropolitan, demonstrate the wealth of knowledge that can only be gleaned from tracking individuals over their life-span. The present volume also illustrates how information routinely collected by governments can be de-identified and used in a cost-effective manner to study questions which have important implications for social policy and as well for advancing our understanding of human development. The results reported here also demonstrate how the data from such a project can be used to answer questions that were not even thought of at the time the project was designed. The Scandinavian tradition of supporting and maintaining longitudinal investigations of cohorts which integrate information from registers with information collected from the subjects themselves is to be praised. This tradition, now being slowly adopted elsewhere, has proven repeatedly to produce a wealth of knowledge that cannot be obtained in other ways. (See, for example, C. G. Janson (ed.), *Some Swedish Longitudinal Studies in the Behavioural Sciences*, 2000.)

The criminality of persons who suffer from major mental disorders is now a social problem confronting governments in the Western industrialised countries. The results from Project Metropolitan were the first published epidemiological data on criminality among persons who develop mental illness in the era of deinstitutionalisation. As described in this volume, they have subsequently been replicated by investigations of birth cohorts in three other countries and by numerous cross-sectional studies of samples of mentally ill patients and convicted offenders. In countries with relatively low crime rates, the crimes committed by the mentally ill, particularly violent crimes, represent a significant proportion of all crimes. Finding a humane way to prevent these crimes is urgent. The suffering of both the perpetrators and victims of these crimes, and of their loved ones is immeasurable. In addition to the human burden associated with these crimes, there are the financial costs to society. The findings from the Metropolitan study presented in this volume, we hope, contribute knowledge that will be useful in identifying both short- and long-term solutions.

Sheilagh Hodgins would like to thank Professor Carl-Gunnar Janson for the privilege of working on Project Metropolitan. This opportunity allowed me to study, in a scientifically valid manner, a problem that I thought was important. Collaborating with Professor Janson has been a rich learning experience. He was always generous with his time and with his knowledge and wisdom. I greatly appreciate his graciousness, willingness to debate, and integrity.

Sheilagh Hodgins would also like to thank numerous other persons who have contributed over the years to the studies described in this volume. Three students, Dr Anne Crocker, Dr Lynn Kratzer, and Dr Micheline Lapalme played key roles in studies using data from Project Metropolitan. Working with them was inspiring and a pleasure. My colleagues, Dr Gilles Côté and Dr Jean Toupin, participated in many hours of discussion on the meaning and implications of results. Their knowledge, competence, and support have always been greatly appreciated. Finally, three wonderful, patient, and talented women made sure that this volume was produced and that other manuscripts based on the Project Metropolitan arrived successfully at the publishers. Guylaine Bouchard, Sylvie Sylvestre, and Joëlle Chevrier are to be thanked for the masterful preparation of the manuscripts. The work presented in this volume was supported by grants from the Fonds pour la Formation de Chercheurs et l'Aide à la Recherche (Québec), the Social Sciences Research Council (Canada), and the Foundation Wenner-Grennska samfundet (Sweden).

Carl-Gunnar Janson would like to thank Professor Sheilagh Hodgins for stimulating and informative cooperation. She is to be commended for finding much more use for Project Metropolitan data than was originally intended. Belatedly, he would like to express his sincere gratitude to all members of the Project Metropolitan team who collected and coded the data and made the data ready for computer use in the first place: Ann-Marie Janson, Maria Feychting, Leif Andersson, Marie Torstensson, and Jan Andersson.

There would have been no Project Metropolitan without the unprecedented decision by the Bank of Sweden Tercentenary Foundation to support the project for the whole twenty-one year period, 1966–86, to collect and organise the data. Finally, Carl-Gunnar Janson wants to acknowledge support given by the Swedish Council for Planning and Coordination of Research (1986–92), the Commission for Social Research (1986–90), the Foundation Wenner-Grenska samfundet (1991), the Bank of Sweden Tercentenary Foundation (1991–96), the Swedish Council for Social Research (1992–95), and the Swedish Council for Humanistic and Social Sciences (1997–2002).

Chapters 1, 4, 5, and 7 were written by Sheilagh Hodgins and Chapters 2 and 3 by Carl-Gunnar Janson. Chapter 6 was written by Sheilagh Hodgins, Micheline Lapalme from the Université de Montréal, and Lars Bergman from the University of Stockholm.

Sheilagh Hodgins and Carl-Gunnar Janson

Introduction

Since the 1960s there has been a significant increase in documented criminality and violence among persons suffering from major mental disorders in Western industrialised societies. This criminality causes immeasurable suffering for the victims and their families, as well as for the perpetrators and their families. The mental disorders increase the risk of criminality and violence, even more among women than among men, and as many mentally ill women as men regularly assault others. However, the impact of the women's behaviours may be even more far reaching than that of the males, for many of these women carry children through pregnancy and then are responsible for their upbringing. A mother who is both mentally ill and anti-social or violent or both, may confer certain genetic predispositions on her child, affect the child's development with inappropriate behaviour during the pregnancy, and provide inadequate or inappropriate parenting. The measurable costs include not only this human suffering and damage to future generations, but also a considerable financial burden to the health and social services and criminal justice systems. These costs include psychological care and social services for the victims, the costs of police, lawyers, judges and expert witnesses, all necessary to process the perpetrator through the criminal justice system, and the further costs associated with psychiatric or custodial care, or both, for the perpetrator. While this increase in criminality and violence among the mentally ill has become evident since the policy of deinstitutionalisation was implemented in the mental health field, as will be discussed, other individual factors which are, not yet, clearly understood, also appear to be playing a causal role in determining these illegal behaviours.

1

Most writing and research about crime and mental disorder have focused necessarily on the immediate problem which confronts clinicians and law makers, that of assessing the risk of violence among persons with major mental disorders. This book attempts to step back from the immediate, day-to-day preoccupations with assessment and management, and to describe the phenomenon; the criminality and violence perpetrated by the mentally ill, and to try to identify the complex chain of factors which cause it. To accomplish this task, we examine a unique cohort of 15,117 persons who were studied from pregnancy through to the age of thirty.

Project Metropolitan includes all the persons born in Stockholm in 1953, and who were still living there a decade later. These persons grew up in a type of society which probably never existed previously and may not again. Sweden, at this time, was a true social-democracy, providing all of its citizens with extensive, high quality, health and social care, education and housing. The post-war economy was prospering and there was virtually no unemployment. Those with special needs received special services, the best there were on offer at the time, as well as housing, pensions and other social services adapted to their needs. A tradition of thorough record keeping and documentation on health, social services, schooling, criminal activities enabled the collection of extensive objective data on the cohort members and their families. Further, a sense of social responsibilities and an understanding of the importance of scientific research led to active participation by cohort members in completing various questionnaires and tests.

Project Metropolitan was not originally established to study mental disorder and crime. However, this book will demonstrate how it has been used to advance our knowledge of this problem. The findings described in this book provide concrete evidence of the value of longitudinal cohort studies like Project Metropolitan in which data are collected prospectively. As will be shown, such an investigation can be used to answer important questions, many of which were not even thought of at the time the study was originally designed and undertaken. The funds and manpower invested in such long-term endeavours are substantial, but as we hope to show, the benefits far outweigh the costs. Such investigations, if well conceived, include data which would traditionally be thought of as belonging to several different disciplines – sociology, criminology, psychology, psychiatry and medicine. The necessity of examining all these different types of data for the same individual and of collaboration between researchers with different training, experiences and traditions of research will also become evident as we proceed.

The book begins by describing the context – the knowledge base – that was used to develop the questions asked, and to interpret the findings.

On the one hand, there is an extensive literature on how and why certain persons become offenders while others do not. On the other hand, there are equally extensive, but completely distinct literatures on how and why each of the major mental disorders develops. Unfortunately, as yet, there is almost no knowledge of how and why some persons develop both a major mental disorder and persistently commit crimes. These knowledge bases, one focusing on antisocial or criminal behaviour and the other on the major mental disorders, have each produced typologies. That is, they have used descriptive data to identify homogeneous groups, each of which follow different development trajectories from conception to adulthood. The challenge for the scientists working in one or other of these areas is to identify the complex chain of biological, psychological and social factors and the continuous interactions among these numerous factors which determine the offending behaviour or the mental illness. Based on this knowledge, we have just begun, as will be seen, to develop a typology of mentally ill offenders and to attempt to identify the complex chain of factors and the interactive processes which lead to both offending and mental illness.

Chapter 2 describes the Metropolitan Study, the data we have used to answer our questions. The overall design of the study, the implementation and data collection phases are described. The records from which the data were extracted, are presented, the procedures used to conceptualize and code the data are described, and when relevant, the procedures used to combine data for the present analyses are presented.

Chapter 3 includes a brief introduction to the cohort members and their families and describes the social context in which they were born, raised, and began their adult lives. While the subsequent chapters focus mainly on the characteristics of the cohort members, an understanding of the social environment in which they grew up is important. Every person perceives, is influenced by, and influences his/her environment in unique ways. While we do not pretend to understand or even accurately describe the complexity of these person/environment interactions, we do think that it is important to at least describe the social reality in which the cohort members lived.

Data extracted from psychiatric and school records was used to classify cohort members into five groups. Three groups of subjects had been admitted to a psychiatric ward by age thirty: (1) those with diagnoses of major mental disorders; (2) those with alcohol and/or drug related disorders; (3) those with other disorders. A fourth group of subjects were mentally retarded, and the fifth group is composed of all those cohort members who had never been admitted to a psychiatric ward nor to a special stream in

school for retarded children. This latter group the most numerous, constitute our comparison group. Chapter 4 presents comparisons of the official
criminality of the five groups of cohort members, separately for men and
women. Our findings are then compared and contrasted with the results
from other birth cohort studies, from follow-up studies of the criminality
of patients with major mental disorders who have been discharged to the
community, and investigations of the prevalence of major mental disorders
among convicted offenders.

Chapter 5 critically reviews the principal explanations proposed in recent
years to explain the criminality of persons with major mental disorders. We
attempt to examine the extent to which findings from the present analyses as
well as those from other investigations concur with the various explanations.

Chapter 6 presents an alternate hypothesis to explain the increased risk of
criminality observed among men and women with major mental disorders.
It is hypothesised that there are two types of offenders with major mental
disorders. The early-starter displays a stable pattern of antisocial behaviour
from a young age, while the late-starter shows no evidence of conduct disorder until late adolescence or early adulthood when the symptoms of the
major mental disorders begin to develop. It is further hypothesised that the
developmental paths, and the causal factors involved in the criminality of
these two types of mentally ill offenders differ.

The final chapter discusses the implications of our research for further
scientific investigations and for mental health and criminal justice policies
and practices. While even at the end of this book it will be apparent that we
still do not understand precisely how and why persons with major mental
disorders commit crimes, our findings along with those from many other
investigations, do constitute a body of knowledge which can be used to
contribute to the development of programmes aimed at preventing crime
and violence among the mentally ill. Using this knowledge to revise current
mental health and criminal justice policies and practices would lessen the
suffering caused by these illegal behaviours and would reduce the associated
costs. Further, this new knowledge could be used to develop programmes
aimed at providing optimal parenting for the children of individuals who
suffer from major mental disorders. The changes to policies and practices,
which are suggested by our findings, are presented and discussed, and the
feasibility and costs of implementing such changes are assessed.

We think that the analyses presented here demonstrate the wealth of
knowledge that can be gained from prospective, longitudinal investigations
of unselected birth cohorts. Even though Project Metropolitan was not originally designed to study the relation between major mental disorders and

criminality, nor the development of mentally ill offenders, we hope this book demonstrates that it has been successfully used for this purpose. This new knowledge only adds to all the other contributions made by the project in other fields of study. Furthermore, Project Metropolitan demonstrates how information collected routinely by governments, when de-identified, can be used to advance knowledge about many different issues in a cost-effective manner.

CHAPTER 1

RESEARCH ON THE CRIMINALITY
AND VIOLENCE OF THE MENTALLY ILL

Scientists contribute to resolving the social problem of crime committed by mentally disordered persons in two very different ways. One, they conduct applied research designed to contribute information useful for amending laws and providing services for mentally ill offenders. Two, scientists pursue more basic research on the causes of violence among persons with major mental disorders. The research described in this book falls within the second category, but, as will be seen, it provides much useful information for those who are responsible for the planning and organisation of services for persons with major mental disorders, for developing effective treatment programmes and management strategies, and for creating legal dispositions which prevent crime and violence in this population in the most humane manner possible.

APPLIED RESEARCH ON MAJOR MENTAL
DISORDERS AND CRIMES

Applied research in this field is dominated by studies designed to improve the accuracy of assessing the risk of violent behaviour. These studies identify the characteristics of patients and their environments that are associated with violent behaviour in the future. They are conducted in clinical settings, with clinicians, and result in constant refinement of the procedures used to assess risk, improvements in the accuracy of these predictions, and more appropriate clinical and legal decisions about the placement and disposition of mentally ill offenders. Accurate selection of those who are likely to behave in an illegal or violent manner prevents abuses of the rights of those who are unlikely to hurt others. Further, these assessments 'of the risk of dangerousness' provide information on the conditions under which a patient is likely to behave aggressively and the conditions under which such behaviour is not likely, or is less likely, to occur. They are thus essential for decisions about where and under what conditions the patient can live safely in the community. This body of work has progressed at a tremendous rate over the past eighteen years and a great deal has been learned about the variables associated with aggressive behaviour in this population (see for example, Douglas and Webster, 1999; Quinsey, Harris, Rice, and Cormier, 1998; Menzies and Webster, 1995; Monahan and Steadman, 1994). Systematic procedures for assessing the violence of persons suffering from major mental disorders have been published (see for example, Webster and Eaves, 1995; Webster, Harris, Rice, Cormier, and Quinsey, 1994). These types of studies are of immediate relevance to clinicians and legal authorities who care for and manage the mentally disordered on a day-to-day basis.

For our purposes, it is essential to remember that prediction is not equivalent to explanation. Because a variable or set of variables predicts aggressive behaviour in the near future with relative accuracy does not necessarily mean that this variable or combination of variables are the determinants of the behaviour (for a further discussion, see Quinsey, 1995). Investigations of how to predict violence provide a great deal of information about the proximal determinants of violence among persons suffering from major mental disorders, and clues about the determinants farther removed in time. This results from the fact that most prediction studies are designed using information that can be readily collected in a clinical setting and they aim to provide information to clinicians that can be easily used. These investigations are not designed to uncover the etiology of violence among persons with major mental disorders.

Because mental health professionals are regularly required by law to assess the risk that a patient will behave violently or commit an illegal act in the future, it is not surprising that most of the research on crime and mental disorder has been limited to studies of how to make such predictions of 'dangerousness'. Inaccurate predictions can lead to horrific human tragedies or unwarranted confinement for the patient. Accurate predictions, on the other hand, can lead to placing patients in community treatment programmes that effectively prevent crime and violence. To date, the accuracy of these predictions has not been good (see for example, Bonta, Law, and Hanson, 1998; Borum, 1996). In order to increase the accuracy of these predictions, it is essential that they are based on results of empirical research. However, on what type of research should these procedures for clinical prediction be based? Presently, the literature on the prediction of 'dangerousness' among the mentally disordered consists of studies of variables that are easily ratable in a clinical situation, which were entered into a linear regression model and found to account for a 'significant proportion of the variance'. These types of studies are inadequate, both conceptually and methodologically, and consequently their results may be misleading. In order to improve the accuracy of these clinical predictions of dangerousness their scientific basis must be made sound. This requires abandoning variable oriented investigations which presume that the same predictors apply in the same way to all patients (Brown, Harris, and Lemyre, 1991) and developing prediction procedures based on a more general understanding of the development of individuals who as adults suffer from major mental disorders and commit crimes. The work presented in this volume attempts to contribute to advancing knowledge of these developmental processes.

It is not only criminal and violent behaviour on the part of persons suffering from major mental disorders that is difficult to predict. As noted by Magnusson and Stattin (1998):

> Given the complex, often non-linear interplay of mental, biological and behavioral subsystems within the individual and an environment, operating in a probabilistic, sometimes very uncertain and unpredictable way, it is unrealistic to hope for accurate prediction of individual functioning across environmental contexts of differing character or over the life span... the final criterion for success in our scientific endeavours is not how well we can predict individual behaviour across situations of different character or across the life course, but how well we succeed in explaining and understanding the processes underlying individual functioning and development. (p. 287).

The scientific goal as noted by these authors is: (1) to identify the factors operating in human functioning and ontogeny; and (2) to identify and understand the mechanisms. Thus, while the prediction of behaviour is necessary in clinical situations in order to prevent violent and other criminal behaviour, prediction is an inappropriate scientific goal. Rather, the procedures used to make predictions of behaviour in clinical situations will increase in accuracy only if they are based on a more fundamental understanding of the patients whose behaviour is in question.

A more fundamental understanding of such persons can be achieved by adopting the perspective of holistic interactionism. This perspective rests on four basic propositions:

(1) the individual functions and develops as a total, integrated organism;
(2) individual functioning within existing mental, biological and behavioural structures, as well as developmental change, can best be described as complex, dynamic processes;

(3) individual functioning and development are guided by processes of continuously ongoing, reciprocal interaction among mental, behavioural and biological aspects of individual functioning and social, cultural and physical aspects of the environment;

(4) the environment functions and changes as a continuously ongoing process of reciprocal interaction among social, economic, and cultural factors (Magnusson and Stattin, 1998).

This approach implies identifying homogeneous sub-types of individuals among our population of interest and identifying how each type interacts differently with both its immediate and larger social environments. Using this approach as will be shown, has allowed us to contribute knowledge that is essential to unravelling the processes which lead to criminality and violence among persons with major mental disorders. However, such knowledge, it can be argued, is also the basis for the development of effective treatment programmes and for accurate risk assessment.

In addition to the research on risk predictions, other applied research on crime and violence by persons with major mental disorders focuses on describing persons who receive various legal dispositions. Such studies are important for understanding how laws are being interpreted and applied, and for evaluating the functioning of criminal justice and mental health systems (see, for example, Brooke, Taylor, Gunn and Maden, 1996; Satsumi, Inada and Yamauchi, 1997; Steadman, Cocozza and Veysey, 1999). Other research is conducted within security hospitals and correctional facilities in an effort to identify predictors of aggressive behaviour and treatment and management strategies to reduce such behaviours (Cooke, 2000; Quinsey, 2000). Many studies are undertaken to document the characteristics which distinguish those who recidivate once discharged, and the circumstances in which these offences occur (see for example, Quinsey, Colemn, Jones and Altrows, 1997). Unfortunately, little research is conducted in an effort to identify treatment programmes that are effective in preventing crime and violence in the mentally ill (Müller-Isberner and Hodgins, 2000).

The evaluation studies that have been done, not surprisingly concur in showing that, institutionalisation limits criminality among the mentally disordered. Several different components of hospital treatment such as immediate and precise sanctions for inappropriate behaviours, staff with expertise in intervening to prevent aggressive behaviour, medications and isolation during periods of agitation may be responsible for limiting illegal and/or aggressive behaviours of in-patients. Community treatment programmes, specifically designed for mentally disordered offenders, have also been found to be effective in limiting offending even among high risk cases (Heilbrun and Peters, 2000; Hodgins, Lapalme and Toupin, 1999; Müller-Isberner, 1996; Wilson, Tien and Eaves, 1995). These programmes which have documented low criminal recidivism rates in the years following discharge from an inpatient unit have a number of features in common. Staff has accepted a double mandate, that is they see themselves as treating major mental disorders but also preventing criminality and violence. Staff has legal powers to rehospitalise the patients quickly, either because of an exacerbation of the symptoms of the disorder or in order to prevent crime. Further, these programmes acknowledge the multiple problems presented by mentally disordered offenders and attempt to provide interventions specific to each problem. While these latter programmes are highly structured and specifically designed for mentally disordered offenders, less specific outpatient treatment for the major disorder has been associated both with less aggressive behaviour (Swartz, Swanson, Hiday, Borum, Wagner and Burns, 1998 a and b) and with more aggressive behaviour (Swanson, Borum, Swartz and Monahan, 1996).

RESEARCH ON THE ETIOLOGY OF CRIMINALITY AND VIOLENCE AMONG PERSONS WITH MAJOR MENTAL DISORDERS

Research on the etiology of criminality and violence among persons with major mental disorders aims to describe the developmental pathways which lead to both major mental disorders and illegal behaviours. This research is conducted in the context of two larger research domains, one which focuses on the development of criminal and aggressive behaviour, and the other on the development of each of the major mental disorders. As will become evident in the course of reading this book, the links between each of these disorders and illegal behaviours are not presently known. For example, does schizophrenia cause or lead to the illegal or violent behaviour? Or alternatively, are the determinants of schizophrenia distinct from the determinants of the illegal behaviours? The answers to these questions are not currently known. Consequently, research is at the stage of asking what factors differentiate the development of individuals who in adulthood both have a major mental disorder and commit crimes and/or violence from the development of individuals who are either only antisocial and violent or only mentally ill. In order to proceed with this research, a detailed understanding of what is known about the development of adult offenders and of each of the major mental disorders is required. A brief review of some of the principal findings from these literatures follows. These findings have guided the formulation of questions asked in the present investigation.

FACTORS ASSOCIATED WITH THE DEVELOPMENT
OF CRIMINAL BEHAVIOUR

Important advances in understanding the etiology of criminality among non-disordered persons have been made in recent years. These advances in knowledge have resulted principally from a two-step strategy adopted by researchers. The first step involved examining descriptive data of age-related patterns of offending and developing a typology of offenders based on these age patterns. The second step in this strategy was to identify the characteristics of each of the types of offenders, and using prospectively collected data from longitudinal investigations to identify the distinctive developmental pathways, from conception to adulthood, followed by each type (DiLalla and Gottesman, 1989; Farrington, 1983; Kratzer and Hodgins, 1999; Loeber, 1988; Moffitt, 1994; Moffitt, Caspi, Dickson, Silva and Stanton, 1996; Patterson and Yoerger, 1993; Magnusson and Stattin, 1998).

Both steps one and two of this research strategy have been applied primarily to data from male subjects. Consequently, the typology provides a more accurate classification of male offenders, and the correlates and developmental trajectories descriptive of each type more accurately portray males than females. We have used this strategy to examine both male and female non-disordered offenders in the Metropolitan cohort (Kratzer and Hodgins, 1999), and in Chapter 6 we use it to examine the offenders with major mental disorders. Not only is this typology of offenders based on research on males, in fact almost all knowledge about the development of criminality has been derived from studies of men. While most crime is committed by men, and most offenders are male, the fact that so little is known about female offenders, as will be seen, sorely limits our understanding of mentally disordered women who commit crime. The gender gap so evident among non-disordered criminals is much smaller among mentally disordered offenders (Hodgins, 1992; Hodgins, Mednick, Brennan, Schulsinger and Engberg, 1996). This is especially true for violent crime. Longitudinal studies of cohorts have demonstrated the importance of distinguishing three types of offenders who have different developmental trajectories, different individual and family characteristics, and different determinants of their criminal behaviours (Lyons *et al.*, 1995; Moffitt, 1994).

Stable early-start offenders

The early-starter displays a stable pattern of antisocial behaviour from a young age and throughout his/her life. While the antisocial behaviours change with age, the persistence is remarkable. These individuals are at very high risk of becoming recidivistic adult offenders (Hodgins, 1994b).

Individuals like this, who display a stable pattern of antisocial behaviour from a young age through adulthood, have been identified in longitudinal prospective studies in Denmark (Høgh and Wolf, 1983), England (Farrington, 1983), Finland (Pulkkinen, 1988), New Zealand (Moffitt, 1990), Norway (Olweus, 1993), Poland (Zabczynska, 1977), Sweden (Janson, 1982; Stattin and Magnusson, 1991) and in the US (Cline, 1980; Blumstein, Farrington and Moitra, 1985; Patterson and Yoerger, 1993; Robins and Ratcliff, 1979). As these studies were conducted in different countries with very different cultures, judicial systems, mental health and social welfare policies and programmes, the consistency of the findings suggests that this type of individual is not the product of one social setting. Furthermore, the subjects in these investigations benefited from all of the available rehabilitation programmes and were subject to criminal justice system sanctions and yet, their antisocial behaviour persisted. This persistence of illegal behaviour despite various types of sanctions and attempts at rehabilitation underlines the lack of effectiveness of traditional strategies in modifying the behaviour of this type of antisocial individual.

Not only has the early-antisocial type been identified in several different societies, the prevalence among males has been consistently estimated at approximately 5% (Moffitt, 1992). The prevalence among females however, has consistently been reported to be very low (Moffitt, 1994). In the Metropolitan cohort, 6.2% of the males and 0.4% of the females who were neither mentally ill nor mentally retarded fitted the definition of stable early-start offenders. While only 6.2% of all males in the cohort, these early-start offenders were responsible for 70% of all crimes and 71% of all the violent crimes committed by males in the cohort. Similarly, the 0.4% of female cohort members who were early-starters committed 33% of all the crimes and 30% of all the violent crimes committed by females in the cohort (Kratzer and Hodgins, 1999).

Most research conducted to date on the early-start offenders has unfortunately treated them as if they are a homogeneous group, which, as recent evidence demonstrates, is not the case (Hodgins, Toupin and Côté, 1996; Rutter, 1996). Studies which have treated this group as if it were homogeneous have analysed results by comparing children with early-onset, stable antisocial behaviour to children without such behaviour. For example, mean scores obtained on IQ tests, neuropsychological tests, on tests of personality traits by children who have displayed a stable pattern of antisocial behaviour are compared to those obtained by children who do not display antisocial behaviour. This research strategy has led to the identification of a number of characteristics which clearly distinguish the early-antisocials from other children. They demonstrate mild impairment on neuropsychological tests, particularly those measuring executive and verbal skills. Many also have problems concentrating. There is evidence that these children have lower levels of intelligence, especially verbal intelligence (Lynam, Moffitt and Stouthamer-Loeber, 1993; Stattin and Klackenberg-Larsson, 1993, Kratzer and Hodgins, 1999) and that deficiencies in language development are apparent as early as six months of age (Stattin and Klackenberg-Larsson, 1993). These impairments are often coupled with particular personality traits such as impulsivity and sensation seeking. In addition, they have few prosocial skills and have a peculiar style of interaction labelled 'coercive' (Patterson and Yoerger, 1993), in that they demand, and find ways to get, immediate rather than delayed gratification. They are so aversive and/or non-rewarding that parents and teachers give up attempting to change their behaviour when they are still very young.

The parents of such children are also distinguished by their parenting practices and particularly their failure to adequately and appropriately sanction the child (Patterson and Yoerger, 1993; Patterson, Capaldi and Bank, 1991; Patterson and Reid, 1984). This means that they fail to reward the child's prosocial behaviour; they do not use effective punishments in response to the child's coercive behaviours; and they encourage coercive behaviour by consistently rewarding it. Observation studies have shown that children's relative rates of deviant behaviours are matched to the relative payoffs provided by the family – '... what works best is used the most' (Patterson and Yoerger, 1993, p. 142; Patterson, 1984; Snyder and Patterson, 1986; 1992).

With age, as the frequency of the child's antisocial behaviours increases, there is an increase in the severity of the behaviours (Patterson, 1982). When entering school these children are both antisocial and lacking in prosocial skills as compared to children of their own age. At school they reproduce the same patterns of behaviour which were evident in the home. They spend more and more time unsupervised by adults and quickly develop relations with antisocial peers (Bank and Patterson, 1992). Not surprisingly, it has been found that the parents of these early-onset stable antisocial children often meet criteria for antisocial personality disorder, alcohol and drug use disorders, and particular personality traits (Cadoret, Yates, Troughton, Woodworth and Stewart, 1995; Lahey, Piacentini, McBurnett, Stone, Hartdagen and Hynd, 1988).

Thus, the individual characteristics of the child – cognitive impairment, impulsiveness, a lack of prosocial skills – interact with those of his/her environment – inadequate and inappropriate sanctions – so that the child arrives at kindergarten ill prepared to follow the rules and accede to the demands of a structured learning environment. The extra effort which would be required, both on the part of the child and that of the teachers, in order to overcome the child's cognitive difficulties and to facilitate learning, is thwarted by the child's consistent disobedience. As the child becomes more and more frustrated at his/her inability to learn and perform academically as easily as other children (Stattin and Magnusson, 1993), teachers become less and less optimistic about the possibilities for modifying the child's behaviour (for a further discussion, see Moffitt, 1992; 1993; Patterson and Yoeger, 1993; Stattin and Magnusson, 1991).

However, as noted, recent evidence suggests that this group of early-onset antisocial children is not homogeneous. The characteristics identified by comparing their average test scores with those obtained by children who do not show antisocial behaviour do not necessarily apply to all of these children. Within this group of early-onset antisocial children are a number of distinctive sub-groups of children. It is important to identify these sub-groups because the determinants of the antisocial behaviour probably differ, as do the temporal course of the antisocial behaviour and the adult outcomes. Interestingly, all of the sub-groups are composed of far more males than females. Sub-groups identified to date include: children characterised by severe attention deficits and hyperactivity (who would likely meet criteria for Attention Deficit and Hyperactivity Disorder) who as adults are at high risk for violent crime and alcohol abuse (Achenbach, Klinteberg, Andersson, Magnusson and Stattin, 1993; Farrington, Loeber and Van Kammen, 1990); mentally retarded children whose antisocial behaviour persists into adulthood and is evident in a pattern of repetitive criminal offences (Crocker and Hodgins, 1997); children who will be diagnosed as psychopaths in adulthood and who as adults will obtain IQ scores and neuropsychological results well within normal limits, but who will commit more crimes and crimes of violence than any other type of offender (Hodgins, Côté and Toupin, 1998); children who inherit a form of alcoholism and certain specific biological peculiarities in the serotonergic systems of the brain (Virkkunen et al., 1994a and b); and as will be seen, children who have inherited a vulnerability for one or other of the major mental disorders which will develop after puberty.

The group of early-onset antisocial children often also include aggressive children. These children show a stable pattern of aggressive behaviour from a young age and through adulthood, but not other forms of antisocial behaviour (Huesmann, Lefkowitz, Eron and Walder, 1984; Olweus, 1991; Tremblay, Loeber, Gagnon, Charlebois, Larivée and Leblanc, 1991). Neither the longitudinal cohort studies which have followed subjects prospectively from childhood through adulthood, nor the DSM diagnoses of childhood disorders adequately distinguish aggressive and antisocial children. Yet, empirical investigations have demonstrated the importance of differentiating these two types of individuals (Achenbach, 1993). Not only do the determinants of stable aggressive behaviour differ from those of stable antisocial behaviour (Cadoret *et al.*, 1995), so do the adult outcomes (Ferdinand and Verhulst, 1995). In our attempt to understand the criminality of persons with major mental disorders, it may be of importance to verify whether they displayed patterns of antisocial behaviour or aggressive behaviour or both in childhood.

Adolescence-limited offenders

Research has identified a second type of offender, the individual who commits crimes only during adolescence, but who evidences no antisocial behaviour either before or after this period of life. It has even been argued that delinquency limited to adolescence is normative adolescent behaviour. In fact, self-report studies find that almost all adolescents commit at least one illegal act, and that approximately one-third commit offences only during adolescence (Moffitt, 1992). Not surprisingly then, many girls as well as boys are delinquent during this time in their lives. In the Metropolitan cohort using official criminal records as opposed to self-reports of offending, we found that 9.9 per cent of the boys and 2.2 per cent of the girls who were neither mentally retarded nor developed a major mental disorder offended before the age of eighteen but not after. This type of offender usually commits non-violent crimes of a minor nature. His/her behaviour is not consistent across situations; for example, while shoplifting or using soft drugs he/she will behave in an acceptable manner at school and/or at home (Kratzer and Hodgins, 1999).

Adolescent-limited offenders, as they are called, do not present the individual and family characteristics which distinguish the early-onset stable antisocial type of offender (DiLalla and Gottesman, 1989; Moffitt, 1992; Patterson and Yoeger, 1993). With good social skills the adolescent-limited offenders are intensely involved with their peers, and often offend with others. It has been proposed that they may be particularly sensitive to family crises precisely because they are generally socially attuned to others. Delinquency and association with deviant peers may be an effort to distance themselves from such a crisis (Patterson and Yoerger, 1993). In the Metropolitan cohort, the adolescence-limited offenders had presented more problems during childhood than the non-offenders, and as well they had obtained lower scores on an intelligence test at age thirteen (Kratzer and Hodgins, 1999). However, while individual characteristics dominate in distinguishing early-onset stable antisocial individuals, it is primarily social characteristics such as family and peer influences, that distinguish the adolescent limited delinquent (DiLalla and Gottesman, 1989). The extent to which adolescents who are developing a major mental disorder get caught up in this type of delinquency is not yet known. And if they do, it is not known if the delinquency ends, as it does for the non-disordered adolescents as they enter adulthood?

Adult-start offenders

The third type of offender begins his/her criminal career in adulthood. Little is known about this type of person. Among the non-retarded, non-mentally ill subjects in the Metropolitan cohort, 12.8% of the males and 3.5% of the females began offending after age eighteen. These were the largest offender groups among both the males and the females. Thirty per cent of these male and female adult-start offenders committed three or more offences between the ages of eighteen and thirty. While the adult-start males were responsible for 13% of all the offences and 17% of the violent offences committed by male subjects in the cohort, the adult-starter females were responsible for 45% of all the offences committed by women in the cohort and 41% of the violent offences. These offenders were found to show, on average, more difficulties during childhood than the non-offenders, but many fewer than the other offender groups. They had also obtained slightly lower intelligence test scores at age thirteen than had the non-offenders (Kratzer and Hodgins, 1999).

Summary

Research on the development of criminal behaviour has identified a typology of offenders based on age-related patterns of offending and shown that the principal factors associated with the development of offending differ by type of offender. Most of this research has been conducted with male subjects and consequently, the typology is a more accurate description of male than of female offenders. A number of longitudinal prospective cohort studies conducted in different countries have identified a small group of boys who display a stable pattern of antisocial behaviour from a young age throughout their adult lives. Some small number of girls fit this type, as well. While this early-start stable antisocial type of offender is distinguished primarily by individual characteristics which are reinforced and even exaggerated by particular patterns of parenting, the adolescence-limited offender is distinguished primarily by his/her choice of peers and social activities. The third type of offender, the adult-starter, remains largely unknown.

THE MAJOR MENTAL DISORDERS

As noted in the Introduction, the terms 'major mental disorders' and 'mental illness' are used to refer to the most severe and chronic mental disorders schizophrenia, bipolar disorder and major depression. Also included in this category are other, non-drug induced psychoses and delusional disorder. Little is known about this latter disorder as the paranoid symptoms of the disorder limit contact of afflicted persons with either researchers, clinicians and even with family or significant others.

Schizophrenia

Schizophrenia affects approximately one per cent of both men and women. It onsets in late adolescence or early adulthood in men, and on average, a decade later among women. The manifestations of schizophrenia can be viewed as five independent categories of problems, each having a distinct cause and necessitating a specific treatment.[1] The first problem is that of positive symptoms – hallucinations, delusions, certain forms of thought disorder and some bizarre behaviours. The second problem is that of negative symptoms – restricted affect, diminished emotional range. The assumption is made that negative symptoms, when present, are enduring features of the illness whereas positive symptoms may fluctuate dramatically over time (Carpenter, Heinrichs and Wagman, 1988). The third category of problems is a lack of social skills. These skills include participating in routine social situations, asserting oneself as necessary, requesting information, refusing inappropriate or abusive requests, and developing and maintaining interpersonal relationships. The fourth problem is a lack of life skills. These skills include personal hygiene, health care, reading and writing, obtaining housing, buying and eating nutritious foods, dressing appropriately for the weather and using public transportation. The fifth problem is aggressive behaviour towards others. It is not as yet clear whether a greater proportion of individuals who suffer from schizophrenia, as compared to those who do not, behave aggressively towards others, however, it is clear that this type of behaviour is frequently observed among schizophrenics (Kallmann, 1938; Kety, Rosenthal, Wender and Schulsinger, 1968; Landau, Harth, Othnay and Sharthertz, 1972; Lewis and Bälla, 1970; Lindelius, 1970; Mednick, Parnas and Schulsinger, 1987; Ortmann, 1981; Robins, 1966; Silverton, 1985).

Individuals who suffer from this devastating disorder describe horrific suffering. They report being unable to control their heads, hearing voices haranguing them twenty-four hours a day, being anxious and afraid in everyday situations, being dependent on others to fulfil even simple needs. In addition, many live with a sense of failure, a realisation that they have not 'amounted to much', that they have not lived up to their own expectations nor to those of their families. Antipsychotic medications are used primarily to control the positive symptoms, delusions and hallucinations of the disorder. However, many of those who suffer from schizophrenia find the side effects of these medications disagreeable and stop taking them once the positive symptoms abate. This leads to an exacerbation of the positive symptoms which usually requires hospitalisation to treat. Consequently, most persons suffering from schizophrenia require many short stays on psychiatric wards when they are actively psychotic, and multi-faceted care and supervision of medication when they are in the community.

As noted previously, women develop schizophrenia later in life than do men. This finding is not due to a greater tolerance for symptoms in women. Investigations have shown that women are first hospitalised for schizophrenia at a later age and also that symptoms are first noted at a later age. In addition, short-term outcome (ten years) differs for males and females. Women who develop schizophrenia are hospitalised, on average, less often than men and spend less time in hospital (for a review see Goldstein, 1988). Women show better social functioning (Léveillée, 1994). Female schizophrenics generally have better premorbid functioning than the males, and their social skills may account for their better prognosis. The later age of onset in women and the more favourable course of schizophrenia suggests that some protective factor, be it biological (see for instance Seeman, 1985) or psychosocial (better life skills and social skills), is at work.

If recovery is defined as presenting no cognitive/perceptual symptoms associated with schizophrenia and living as an autonomous adult (capable of looking after oneself financially and otherwise), no study has demonstrated that individuals who succumb to schizophrenia recover. Outcome varies widely, as do the characteristics of individuals who are affected by the disorder, and the family and community resources available to them (for reviews of the European studies see Harding, 1988; for reviews of the North American studies see McGlashan, 1988; for reviews and comments see McGlashan and Carpenter, 1988 and Shepherd, Watt, Falloon and Smeeton, 1989; Leary, Johnstone and Owens, 1991; for a meta-analysis of the outcome literature see Hegarty, Baldessarini, Tohen, Waternaux and Oepen, 1994; for a typology of outcome see Marengo, 1994). Probably the most important conclusion to be drawn from these investigations was made by McGlashan (1988). 'Long-term follow-up studies have yet to demonstrate clearly any effect of treatment on the natural history of schizophrenia.' (p. 515)

The factors involved in the development of schizophrenia have provoked controversy for many decades. Research completed in the last twenty years however, has produced compelling evidence that this disorder results from structural damage to the developing foetal brain. Whether or not this damage results from the genes associated with the disorder or from insult or from an interaction between these two factors is still unknown. The inherited factor may be necessary, but it is far from being sufficient to cause the disorder. Twin and adoption studies suggest that the genes are not associated directly with schizophrenia but rather with a disturbance of personality which renders the individual socially withdrawn, suspicious, eccentric, and a bit bizarre (a diagnosis of schizotypal personality disorder). Additional factors, such as adverse events occurring during the perinatal period, separation from the mother in early life, difficult family functioning interact with the predisposition to lead to the development of the disorder in late adolescence or early adulthood (Hodgins, 1996; McNeill, Cantor-Graae and Isamail, 2000; Torrey, 1994; Walker, Lewine and Newman, 1996).

Major depression

Major depression denotes the severest form of depressive episode characterised by the following symptoms present for at least two weeks: a depressed mood consistently (twenty-four hours a day) every day, diminished interests and pleasure in all or almost all activities (even those that were once considered pleasurable), significant weight loss or gain, insomnia or hypersomnia nearly every day, psychomotor agitation or retardation, fatigue or loss of energy nearly every day, feelings of worthlessness or excessive or inappropriate guilt, diminished ability to think or concentrate, and often, recurrent thoughts of death (American Psychiatric Association, 1994).

The most recent findings indicate that 12.7% of men and 21.3% of women develop at least one episode of major depression (Kessler et al., 1994). These prevalence rates are derived from diagnostic assessments of 8,098 adult subjects who composed a representative sample of US citizens. In a study of a cohort of 21-year-olds in New Zealand, one year prevalence rates for major depression were estimated at 22.6% for women and 11.2% for men (Newman, Moffitt, Caspi, Magdol, Silva and Stanton, 1996). These alarmingly high prevalence figures for major depression among adolescents concur with those observed in other recent investigations (Cichetti and Toth, 1998). The current rates of major depression observed in these recent investigations are considerably higher than those obtained a decade earlier in the ECA study. This latter study determined the prevalence of major depression to be 2.6% among adult men, and 7.0% among adult women (Weissman, Bruce, Leaf, Florio and Holzer, 1991). While the Kessler *et al.*, (1994) investigation was carried out from 1990 to 1992, the ECA diagnoses were made a decade earlier. To date, no adequate explanation for the differences in the prevalence rates for major depression obtained in the two studies has been proposed. They could be due to variance in the two samples that were studied, to differences in the two diagnostic instruments, or to both. Alternatively, the increase could be a real one. There is further evidence of an increase in the prevalence of major depression among persons born after 1940 as compared to those born between 1900 and 1940 from studies conducted in Sweden, (Hagnell, Lanke, Rorsman and Öjesjö, 1982), Switzerland (Angst,1985), and the US (Gershon, Hamovit, Guroff and Nurnberger, 1987; Lavori *et al.*, 1987; Warshaw, Klerman and Lavori, 1991; Wickramaratne, Weissman, Leaf and Holford, 1989).

Klerman and Weissman reviewed the extant literature in 1989. Their conclusions continue to apply to more recent findings.

> Several recent, large epidemiologic and family studies suggest important temporal changes in the rates of major depression: an increase in the rates in the cohorts born after World War II; a decrease in the age of onset with an increase in the late teenage and early adult years; an increase between 1960 and 1975 in the rates of depression for all ages; a persistent gender effect, with the risk of depression consistently two to three times higher among women than men across all adult ages; a persistent family effect, with the risk about two to three times higher in first-degree relatives as compared with controls; and the suggestion of a narrowing of the differential risk to men and women due to a greater increase in risk of depression among young men. These trends, drawn from studies using comparable methods and modern diagnostic criteria, are evident in the United States, Sweden, Germany, Canada, and New Zealand, but not in comparable studies conducted in Korea and Puerto Rico and of Mexican-Americans living in the United States. These cohort changes cannot be fully attributed to artifacts of reporting, recall, mortality, or labelling and have implications for understanding the etiology of depression and for clinical practice.   (p. 2229)

In the ECA project, it was found that the age of onset of major depression in adults peaked at fifteen to nineteen years in females and at twenty-five to twenty-nine years in males (Burke, Burke, Regier and Rae, 1990; Burke, Burke, Rae and Regier, 1991). The recently observed increased rates among adolescents suggests that the average age of onset may now be lower.

Most persons who suffer from major depression do not seek treatment. This conclusion is based on studies conducted in the US (Weissman *et al.*, 1991) and in Sweden (Rutz, Von Knorring, Pihlgren, Rihmer and

Wallinder, 1995). Around 12% to 20% of those who develop a major depression never recover from the episode (Keller *et al.*, 1992), and among those who recover most relapse at least once (Bland, 1997; Klerman and Weissman, 1992; Tohen *et al.*, 2000). While it has been thought that antidepressant medication speeded up recovery from an acute episode (McNeal and Cimbolic, 1986) a recent meta-analysis indicates that placebos have comparable effects (Kirsch and Sapirstein, 1998). Between the acute episodes of major depression, the level of psychosocial functioning of afflicted persons is significantly reduced (Coryell, Scheffner, Keller, Endicott, Maser and Klerman, 1993; Hodgins, 1996) limiting their autonomy, work and family life. As noted by Klerman and Weissman in 1992, 'Major depression is an episodic condition with relapses, recurrences, and some chronicity.' (1992, p. 833).

Much more is known about the causes of schizophrenia than about the cause of major depression. Research to date suggests that the etiology of major depression is different from that of more minor depressions and of the depressive symptoms that many persons experience now and again. Family studies and twin studies indicate that a hereditary factor is associated with the disorder. As with schizophrenia, all the accumulated evidence suggests that this factor is not sufficient, in and of itself, to cause the disorder. Rather it leads to a vulnerability which in interaction with certain non-genetic factors leads to the disorder. One of these non-genetic factors may be stress on the mother during pregnancy (Machon, Mednick and Huttenen, 1997; Watson, Mednick, Huttenen and Wang, 1999). The vulnerability for major depression may be reflected by certain personality traits which limit the individual's ability to adapt easily to the stresses and unpredictable problems which are an inevitable part of daily life. While most people resolve these difficulties as they arise, individuals who are vulnerable to major depression appear to over-react emotionally when faced with daily hassles, and consequently fail to resolve them. The unresolved problem doesn't go away, but usually gets worse, setting up a vicious circle where the unskilled problem solver is required to solve more and more difficult problems. The over-reaction to stress, it has been hypothesised, results from an inherited vulnerability and a series of adverse events in early childhood, which permanently alter the functioning of the neuroendocrine system (Post, Weiss and Leverich, 1994). As a result, the afflicted individual constantly feels stressed, and his/her body reacts as if it is stressed.

Bipolar disorder
Bipolar disorder is characterised by extreme changes in mood, behaviour and thought patterns, which occur as distinctive episodes, at regular

intervals, throughout the adult lives of afflicted persons. These individuals suffer periods of mania and severe depression, interspersed with periods of relative 'normality' in which the excesses of the manic and depressive periods are fully appreciated, and their return is feared. During these periods in which they are free of symptoms, bipolar patients are able to describe with great precision the horrors of the disorder. Many of them have written eloquently about the disease, their fears of future episodes, of causing further embarrassment to loved ones, and of passing on the disease to their children (Anonymous,1984; Endler, 1982; Logan, 1976; Lowell, 1977).

Manic episodes are characterised by heightened mood, elation, grandiosity, generally a pleasant and good feeling that anything is possible. Speech increases in speed until it becomes incomprehensible. Thoughts race until it is impossible to concentrate on one idea at a time. The individual moves faster and faster, not stopping to eat or to sleep. Finally, irritability sets in, accompanied sometimes by paranoid ideas, and the individual may lose contact with reality. Before medications were available for the treatment of the disorder, individuals were known to die from exhaustion during a manic episode.

In the early 1990s, lifetime prevalence rates for bipolar disorder were estimated to be 1.6 per cent for men and 1.7 per cent for women (Kessler *et al.*, 1994). These figures are slightly higher than what had been found in the early 1980s, that 1.2 per cent of men and women develop bipolar disorder during their lifetime (Weissman *et al.*, 1991). Three studies have shown that the prevalence of bipolar disorder is rising. First, Angst (1985) examined all admissions to the regional psychiatric hospital near Zurich from 1920 to 1980. He found an increase in the rates of mania and depression, with the ratio of mania to depression remaining constant. Second, in the US, Gershon and colleagues (Gershon, Hamovit, Guroff and Nurnberger, 1987) found an increase in bipolar disorder among those born after 1940, as compared to those born between 1910 and 1939. Third, using the ECA data, Weissman and colleagues (Weissman, Livingston-Bruce, Leaf, Florio and Holzer, 1991) have also identified a similar increase in the prevalence of bipolar disorder, and suggest that the increase is due to a decreasing age of onset. No methodological artefacts have been found that might explain the findings. It appears to be a robust and valid result.

Bipolar disorder onsets in most cases by the age of twenty (Goodwin and Jamison, 1990). At the First International Conference on Bipolar Disorder held in June 1994, M. Thase concluded: '... the results of both controlled clinical trials and naturalistic follow-up studies conducted over the past decade indicate that the prognosis of many patients with manic depression is surprisingly poor. Moreover, rates of sustained remission of finite

periods of time, such as 3 or 5 year intervals seldom exceed 50% despite pro-
phylactic treatment.' (Thase, 1994, p. 229). This conclusion is supported by
the few follow-up studies which have been published. For example, Tohen,
Waternaux and Tsuang (1990) followed seventy-five bipolar patients for four
years after discharge from an inpatient ward. Only twenty-one (28 per cent)
did not relapse during the follow-up period.

The etiology of bipolar disorder continues to elude us. The importance
of the hereditary factor associated with bipolar disorder is much greater
than that associated with schizophrenia or with major depression. However,
twin studies suggest that other non-genetic factors are necessary to cause the
disorder. Sub-cortical brain structures which are involved in regulating vege-
tative functions and bodily rhythms are most likely involved in determining
this disorder. Psychosocial factors do not appear to have much influence
either as triggers of depressive or manic episodes, nor as determinants of
the disorder itself.

Levels of impairment associated with the major mental disorders

The suffering inflicted by the major mental disorders on both those who
develop the disorders, and on their families, is unmeasurable. These disorders seriously limit all aspects of an individual's functioning. Findings from
the World Health Organization – World Bank Global Burden of Disease
Study – indicate that mental disorders rank high among the leading causes
of disability worldwide (Murray and Lopez 1996; Walker and Howard, 1996).
Persons with schizophrenia are unable to develop social relationships, even
though they report wanting such relationships (Léveillée, 1994). Consequently, they do not maintain intimate relationships and only infrequently
have children. Few are able to obtain or to maintain employment.

Among persons suffering from major affective disorders, 12 per cent may
never recover to a non-symptomatic state (Keller *et al.*, 1992), and most relapse (Klerman and Weissman, 1992; Lewinsohn, Zeiss and Duncan, 1989).
These individuals endure a special horror; in between acute episodes, they
realise that the symptoms are likely to return and that there is little that
can be done to prevent a relapse (see, for example, Endler, 1982). In addition, persons suffering from the major affective disorders have difficulty
maintaining stable relationships as is evidenced by high rates of divorce and
separation (Weissman, Bruce, Leaf, Florio and Holzer, 1991); however, they
may have as many children as do non-disordered persons (Slater, Hare and
Price, 1971).

It is often assumed that the major affective disorders are cyclical or
even non-recurrent, and that consequently they have little or no impact

on psychosocial functioning during periods of remission. However, recent empirical data seriously challenge this assumption. Psychosocial impairment associated with the major affective disorders is often severe and chronic (see for example, Harrow, Goldberg, Grossman and Meltzer, 1990; Klerman and Weissman, 1992; Stoll *et al.*, 1993; Tohen, Waternaux and Tsuang, 1990). For example, researchers from the US National Collaborative Project on Depression have concluded: 'The psychosocial impairment associated with mania and major depression extends to essentially all areas of functioning and persists for years, even among individuals who experience sustained resolution of clinical symptoms.' (Coryell, Scheftner, Keller, Endicott, Maser and Klerman, 1993, p. 720). Current findings indicate that depression will be the second leading cause of disability in the year 2002 (Murray and Lopez, 1996).

Premature death associated with the major mental disorders

We are currently examining a Danish birth cohort composed of 324,401 persons (Hodgins, Mednick, Brennan, Schulsinger and Engberg, 1996). Among subjects who were never admitted to a psychiatric hospital, 2.9% of the men and 1.7% of the women died before the age of forty-five, as compared to 16.6% of the men and 9.2% of the women who had been admitted to a psychiatric hospital with a diagnosis of a major mental disorder. These figures are similar to those reported by others (see, for example, Baldwin, 1979; Black, Winokur and Nasrallah, 1987a and b; Goodwin and Jamison, 1990, ch. 6; Gottesman and Shield, 1982). The increased rates of premature death are due in part to increased rates of death from particular diseases (see, for example, Baldwin, 1979), and in part to suicide. Among those suffering from schizophrenia, close to 13% take their own lives (Johns, Stanley and Stanley, 1986). The numbers of persons suffering from the major affective disorders who commit suicide are difficult to establish. This is partly due to the fact that the majority of persons with these disorders are never treated. A recent Finnish investigation examined all suicides during a twelve-month period. In a random sample diagnosed using the suicide autopsy procedure, 26% of the males and 46% of the females met the criteria for major depression (Henriksson *et al.*, 1993). Among the fifty-three adolescents (forty-four boys and nine girls) who committed suicide in this period, 45% of the boys and 44% of the girls were judged to have suffered from major depression (Marttunen, Aro, Henriksson, and Lönnqvist, 1991). In a study of consecutive admissions to a Belgian hospital, 29% of men and 44% of women who had seriously attempted to kill themselves met criteria for major depression (Linkowski, de Maertelaer and Mendlewicz, 1985). These findings are similar to older US figures which indicated that 46% of persons who committed suicide suffered from a recurrent major affective disorder (Robins, Murphy, Wilkinson, Gassner and Kayes, 1959). There are no studies of suicide among persons suffering from bipolar disorder which overcomes the problem of documenting suicide among non-treated cases. However, after an extensive review, Goodwin and Jamison (1990) concluded that the ' . . . mortality rate for untreated manic-depressive patients is higher than it is for most types of heart disease and many types of cancer' (p. 227). Bipolar disorder may also be associated with adolescent suicide. One study has reported that 22 per cent of a sample of adolescents who killed themselves suffered from bipolar disorder (Brent *et al.*, 1988).

Mental disorders occurring co-morbidly with the major disorders

Personality disorders and other non-major mental disorders are more prevalent among individuals who suffer from one of the three major disorders, than among samples of the general population. For example, after diagnosing three different samples of persons suffering from schizophrenia, we have calculated that the prevalence of antisocial personality disorder is thirteen times more prevalent among those with schizophrenia than in the general population (Hodgins, Toupin and Côté, 1996). While there are few published studies of personality disorders among persons with major depression, all available findings indicate that individuals suffering from major depression are more likely than the general population to manifest other disorders (see, for example, Kessler *et al.*, 1994). A study of a cohort of female twins, (a cohort which includes cases of major depression regardless of whether or not they have received treatment) indicated that major depression is associated with high rates of phobias and anxiety disorders. High rates of personality disorders have also been documented (Charney, Nelson and Quinlan, 1981). Goodwin and Jamison (1990) found only four studies which examined personality disorders among persons suffering from bipolar disorder. All four reported elevated rates of borderline personality disorder and antisocial personality disorder. In children and adolescents suffering from depression, rates of co-morbidity are very high. In a review of the literature on this issue, Angold and Costello (1993) concluded that rates of co-morbid conduct disorder/oppositional defiant disorder ranged from 21% to 83%, co-morbidity with anxiety disorder ranged from 30% to 75%, and comorbidity with attention deficit disorder ranged from 0% to 57.1%. A recent retrospective study of childhood mental health records showed that a third of a sample of bipolar patients had been seen as children, most for externalizing disorders (Manzano and Salvador, 1993). A prospective study has now shown similar results (Carlson and Weintraub, 1993).

Substance use disorders occurring co-morbidly with the major mental disorders

Even experienced clinicians using structured diagnostic interview protocols fail to reliably diagnose alcohol and drug use disorders among individuals suffering from major mental disorders (Bryant, Rounsaville, Spitzer and Williams, 1992). Despite this fact, it is clear that the prevalence of substance abuse and/or dependence has skyrocketed in recent years among persons suffering from major mental disorders. As discussed elsewhere, prevalence rates of co-morbid substance abuse estimated in different studies are not comparable (Côté, Hodgins, Toupin and Proulx, 1995).

Among persons suffering from schizophrenia, the prevalence of alcohol and drug use disorders varies from one study to another, but in all studies it is very high (for a review of this work see a special issue of *Schizophrenia Bulletin*, 16, 1990, especially Drake *et al.*, 1990; Mueser *et al.*, 1990; for a review of studies concerning schizophrenic subjects who abuse alcohol and/or drugs see Ridgely, Goldman and Talbott, 1986). For example, in a US study of 115 schizophrenic subjects discharged to the community, 45% were using alcohol, and 22% were abusing alcohol (Drake, Osher and Wallach, 1989). In the ECA study, the prevalence of schizophrenia among those subjects who met the criteria for an alcohol use disorder was four times greater than that for the general population (Helzer and Przybeck, 1988). In three samples of schizophrenic subjects in Montreal, one recruited from the penitentiaries, a second from psychiatric and forensic hospitals, and a third from general hospitals, the prevalence of alcohol use disorders varied from 74% to 23%, the prevalence of drug use disorders varied from 68% to 23% (Côté and Hodgins, 1990; Dubé, 1992; Hodgins *et al.*, 1996).

In the Epidemiological Catchment Area study, 27% of subjects who had experienced at least one episode of major depression met criteria for a lifetime diagnosis of either an alcohol use disorder, a drug use disorder, or both. The prevalence of other drug use disorders was 18.0% among subjects with a lifetime diagnosis of major depression and 6.1% among the general population (Regier *et al.*, 1990).

Substance abuse is very common among persons suffering from bipolar disorder. In the ECA study, 56.1% of bipolar patients received an additional diagnosis for alcohol and/or drug use disorders: 43.6% received additional diagnoses of alcohol abuse and/or dependence, and 33.6% received diagnoses of drug abuse and/or dependence (Regier *et al.*, 1990). Three other investigations (Estroff, Dackis, Gold and Pottash, 1985; Freed, 1969; Morrison, 1974) have reported that 60% to 75% of bipolar patients abuse alcohol.

Homelessness and infectious disease among persons with major mental disorders

Rates of homelessness and infectious diseases among persons suffering from major mental disorders, particularly hepatitis, tuberculosis and AIDS, are difficult to document. Homeless persons don't readily agree to participate in diagnostic interviews for research purposes. However, all indicators suggest that many of the homeless suffer from a major disorder and that many develop infectious diseases (Belcher, 1989; Gelberg, Linne and Leake, 1988; Tessler and Dennis, 1989). No doubt the rates vary from region to region, even within the same country.

Summary

The major mental disorders which occur in late adolescence in most cases are chronic. Individuals suffering from these disorders usually require care throughout their adult lives. The types and intensity of care required varies considerably. Schizophrenia and bipolar disorder affect equal proportions of men and women. The prevalence of schizophrenia is just less than 1% and that of bipolar disorder is 1.6%. Major depression affects many more women than men. While prevalence rates vary, recent evidence from the US suggests that as many as 21% of women and 13% of men experience at least one episode of major depression. The level of psychosocial impairment associated with these disorders varies by disorder and also across individuals with the same disorder. However, in almost all cases, the impairment is extensive, affecting educational attainment, career and work, family and social relationships. While specific hereditary factors confer a vulnerability for one or other of the major mental disorders, these factors are insufficient to cause the disorders. Other non-genetic factors interact with these hereditary factors in the development of each of the disorders.

CONCLUSION

The research presented in this volume aims first to describe patterns of offending among individuals who develop major mental disorders, and second to explore pathways which lead to mental illness and criminality. This work straddles two research domains, one which focuses on the description and development of criminality and the other which focuses on the description and development of each of the major mental disorders. The research described in this book has been largely oriented by these two bodies of knowledge, and influenced to a lesser extent by more traditional research in forensic psychiatry, which focuses primarily on risk assessment, and to a much lesser extent on treatment effectiveness. As will become evident, however, all of these areas of research, which unfortunately remain distinct, are of relevance to understanding the criminality of persons who suffer from major mental disorders.

NOTE

1. This conceptualisation of the manifestations of schizophrenia was originally presented by Strauss, Carpenter and Bartko, 1974. The fifth category – aggressive behaviour – has been added to take account of recent findings (for a review see Hodgins, 1993).

CHAPTER 2

THE LONGITUDINAL APPROACH

PROJECT METROPOLITAN

The present study is empirically based on data collected within a long-term research project called Project Metropolitan in Stockholm, Sweden. The project was originally planned as a joint Scandinavian enterprise with cohorts in four Scandinavian capitals, but for various reasons only the Copenhagen and Stockholm sub-projects got off the ground. Here we are concerned with the Stockholm branch only.

The aims of Project Metropolitan

The general questions asked in Project Metropolitan are: in what ways and to what extent the social situations and behaviours of Scandinavian metropolitan adolescents and young adults reflect their social origins, early personal resources and childhood experiences? Thus, the project seeks to describe, in outline, the social positions, compositions and characteristics of the parental families as well as childhood, adolescent and young-adult social situations, abilities, resources and behaviours of young Stockholmers themselves within the substantive areas under consideration. Of the original fields of interest two have come to dominate the project. The first is deviance, and the second is social stratification and social mobility, with special focus on the role of selection to higher education.

Obviously, the project is about differential change and development of the type in which each individual passes through a sequence of phases. All phases have their dependent variables, which are related to dependent variables of earlier phases and to other variables, either changing or constant over time.

In order to study such phenomena empirically, we need data describing how individuals and their situations change and develop or stay the same over these phases, that is, we need lengthways (*longitudinal*) individual data.

The project is longitudinal in the strict sense of a long-term study of micro-units, individually compared over time, and with observations covering a given period of time. It could also be called a *panel*, but we prefer the longitudinal label. One reason for this is that a panel typically covers a fairly short period, such as an election campaign, and most often consists of a series of waves of surveys. A more important reason is that we want the reader to keep in mind that individual-level comparisons over a given time presuppose that data belonging to the same individual are linked together, even if they refer to different points in time. Obviously, without the linking of the individual's data, comparisons would generally not be possible on an individual level, but would be limited to an aggregate level. Survey waves using the same sample would still be unconnected at the individual level.[1] Problems of drawing individual-level conclusions from aggregate-level data ('the aggregate fallacy') are well known. For instance, recording change in the same sample from one survey to the next only gives net change in the margins.

The cohort

Some longitudinal studies follow samples of populations, others follow *cohorts*. A 'cohort' was a unit within the Roman army, but in demography and other social sciences it simply means 'an aggregate of individuals who were born (or who entered a particular system) in the same time interval and who age together' (Riley, Johnson and Foner 1972: 9).[2]

By definition, in a given year, the members of a cohort are of the same age, and as time goes by the age of the members increases. Hence, there is a relation between cohort, age and time. If C is the year the cohort was born and A is the age of the cohort (or rather of its members) at time P (P as in 'period'), then

$$A = P - C$$

For instance, the surviving cohort of Stockholmers born in 1953 will be forty-seven years of age in 2000. Thus, if one knows two of the three figures, the third one follows from them. This is to say that cohort, age and period are not mutually independent. To map all possible combinations of them one does not need three dimensions but only two.[3]

Project Metropolitan examines a birth cohort: the cohort of all boys and girls born in 1953 and living in the Stockholm Metropolitan Area in 1963:

7,719 boys and 7,398 girls. The period covered runs from (pregnancies in) 1952/53 to the end of 1983.

DESIGNING A LONGITUDINAL PROJECT

Defining the cohort

Observing individuals over such a long period as thirty years tends to take time (not necessarily thirty years, as will soon become clear) and thus to turn the study into a protracted project. Several difficulties originate here, such as funding problems, case attrition, and fading relevance. Besides, it is nice for the research team (not to mention the people at the grant giving agencies), if most of them outlive the project and manage to see the main results, preferably before they retire. There are various ways of making a long story shorter as far as the data-collection phase goes, without shortening the period under observation. One is to put together a synthetic cohort by joining shorter periods for different cohorts and substitute the composite for the genuine article. This would certainly be better than cutting the total period down to the size of a component period and clearly better than just having a cross-section, but it would carry a considerable qualitative cost.

Instead the project team decided to start gathering data as soon as possible after the cohort reached the age of ten,[4] thus gaining ten years. As already mentioned, the Stockholm cohort was limited to those who lived in the Stockholm area at age ten. Thus, the design is *prospective* from age ten and *retrospective* before that.[5] This meant that the project did not study those who left Stockholm or died before age ten. Instead we included those who were born outside the Stockholm area, but moved there before age ten. In fact, three per cent of the cohort members were born abroad to non-Swedish parents. At the time, those we lost seemed less central to the project than those we added, so the sacrifice, if any, was not felt to be great.

It should be underlined that the retrospective design for the early years does not imply that those years were examined with retrospective data. On the contrary, great efforts were made to get simultaneous or non-retrospective data even for these years and to avoid retrospective ones. 'Retrospective' in reference to data is often taken to mean that data were collected well after the events or circumstances they refer to. If so, it would now be impossible for anyone to base a study of, say, some early nineteenth-century political crisis, on non-retrospective data, whatever contemporary documents were dug up. In discussing quality of data it is more relevant to define retrospective data in relation to the time when they were produced: a retrospective item of information is an item produced after the time to which it refers. Information from an interview is produced when the question asked is answered. If the question asked is about the present time, the information is non-retrospective. If the question is about past time, the information is retrospective. Similarly, by this definition documents would be non-retrospective, if they were produced at the time of the events they referred to. They would remain non-retrospective, even if the documents were collected by a project much later. In this way Project Metropolitan collected non-retrospective data also concerning the cohort's first years.

When the project was planned in the early 1960s, with father – son intergeneration social mobility, as well as boys' deviance in focus, only boys were to be included. However, in Stockholm it was decided, after all, to bring in the girls, a decision not as obvious then as it appears now, but never regretted. Motives for the decision were partly practical: when making a questionnaire survey in schools classwise, it seemed a waste (and rather unpractical) to include only about every second pupil, when one could get data for the whole class. More important, gender was such a basic variable that in most analyses one should have a control for it, even though fields central to the project were much more concerned with males than with females. However, in the early 1960s changes in gender roles and gender concept seemed likely to occur, and if so, to be of great interest, both in everyday discussions, to sociology generally and to the project. Thus, foreseeable analyses should still be controlled for gender, but simply leaving females out would probably result in missing intriguing gender interactions.[6]

We started collecting data in 1964 by delineating the metropolitan area, drawing the cohort members from a population list and gathering some documentary data. In 1965 we prepared the first major grant application. The metropolitan area should extend beyond Stockholm City, as far as neighbouring municipalities had a suburban character. A set of criteria was set up,[7] and twenty-two suburban municipalities were found to qualify. With their 322,100 inhabitants added to 347,400 in the central city and 461,100 in suburban areas within the city limits, the metropolitan area had a total population of 1,160,600. In 1980 the population within these boundaries had increased to 1,321,900.

Surveys

In the spring of 1966 the cohort members in the metropolitan area filled out questionnaires at school. Practically all schools in the area with pupils born in 1953 cooperated, even most of the few private schools. The study was cleared with the principals, the teachers' unions, the National PTA, and the National Board of Education. At the time of the survey the cohort members were about thirteen years old and most of them were in sixth grade; some 7 per cent were still in fifth grade, and about 2 per cent already in seventh grade. Within each grade the pupils are divided into 'classes'. In the sixth and lower grades each class had a teacher assigned to it.[8] On a given day in each sixth-grade class of a given school all pupils spent three teaching hours filling out two questionnaires. Their teacher, who had received detailed written instructions and general information on the project in advance, supervised the questionnaires. In each school cohort members not in sixth grade completed the questionnaires guided by interviewers from Statistics Sweden, who also met the teachers before the interviews to answer questions. The teachers were asked to tell their pupils in advance about the study and inform them that they were to participate in a research project until they reached the age of thirty. The study would not have any consequences for them as participants. Each student put his or her questionnaires in an envelope and sealed it to be handed over to the interviewer from Statistics Sweden.

At this time of continuous school reforms both pupils and teachers seemed used to taking part in this type of study. Only 11 per cent of the cohort members did not participate in the School Study. This non-response rate includes 2 per cent of the cohort who were no longer in the metropolitan area by May 1966. The remaining 9 per cent of non-response includes those absent from school on the day of the interviews, those in a few classes that, for various reasons, did not participate, and those outside the general school system in the area, in most cases because they were in social care or severely handicapped.

The first questionnaire was constructed by Professor Kjell Härnqvist, University of Göteborg, who himself was drawing a 10 per cent national sample of pupils born in 1953 for a similar survey within his *Individual Statistics Project*. The questionnaire contained three tests of components of intelligence, three attitude scales about education and school, five scales measuring leisure interests, and several questions on plans for future education, on school work and leisure activities. The second questionnaire consisted of additional items on interests, evaluations of various occupations, and three sociometric questions, in each of which we asked for three classmates.

Two more surveys were conducted. The first of them took place two years after the School Study, at approximate cohort age fifteen. A stratified sample of 4,021 mothers (again with 9 per cent non-response within the area) were interviewed by interviewers from Statistics Sweden. The same sample was used for a mail-questionnaire study, delayed until just after the end of the period of observation, in 1985, at approximate cohort age thirty-two, but now the questions were put to the cohort members themselves. Some respondents answered by telephone, but this time the non-response rate became as high as 24 per cent. No data from the sample surveys were used in the present investigations.

Register data

All other data on the cohort members and their families were taken from governmental files. Registers were used in two important ways: first, to identify the cohort and the samples and to keep track of the cohort members over the years; and second, to get data on the cohort's members. The extensive population registers available for behavioural research in Sweden may generally be the Swedish behavioural researcher's greatest asset. Both knowing where the individuals live (cf. Table 2.1) and obtaining factual and reliable information from registers make research less cumbersome and can greatly improve its possibilities. For the registers to be of any use to research it is, of course, not enough that they are there, extensive, and reliable, they must also be accessible.

There is a constitutional right for every citizen to have access to documents and data held by authorities, *the principle of right-of-access*. The purpose of the principle is to protect the mass media and to keep the general public

Table 2.1. *Project Metropolitan percentage regional cohort distribution 1953–84*

	Metropolitan area	Other parts of county	Outside county	Not in Sweden	All deceased
1953	82.2	1.5	13.6	2.7	—
1960	93.0	0.7	5.5*	0.8*	—
1963	100.0	—	—	—	—
1970	93.9	0.7	4.7	0.7	0.2
1975	87.3	1.8	8.9	2.0	0.7
1978	82.8	2.7	12.1	2.4	1.0
1979	80.6	2.9	13.7	2.8	1.1
1980	79.4	3.0	14.7	2.9	1.1
1981	78.4	3.1	15.1	3.4	1.2
1982	77.3	3.3	15.8	3.6	1.3
1983	76.8	3.3	16.2	3.7	1.4
1984	76.9	3.7	15.4	4.0	1.4

* estimated

County: Stockholm County, which includes the Stockholm Metropolitan Area and some additional municipalities.

informed of the activities of all public agencies. (State, county and municipal). According to the Constitution a wide range of documents at such agencies must be shown to anyone who so requests, unless secrecy acts explicitly
stipulate otherwise. The identity of the person who asks for a document is
protected. With a simplification that will make constitutional experts wince,
one may say that the general picture is that all documents received by or
sent from a government office fall under this law. And so do all documents
produced in the office (except work notes), as soon as the case they refer to
is closed. Other documents may, but need not, be handed over on request.
Secrecy rules important for research concern the protection of privacy and
apply to personal data that might mean prejudice or damage to the individual, such as criminal records, social-assistance records, and medical records.
Information on assessed income and taxes paid is not considered to be of
this kind, so it is public for anyone to see. Data collected for statistical social research at non-private research institutes, such as state universities, are
protected, as they would otherwise be open to the media and the public.

When social and epidemiological researchers started to apply for access
to protected sensitive individual data, such as a person's criminal, welfare,
or medical record, the authorities in charge of the data considered whether
giving access to the data would cause damage or prejudice to the recorded
persons. In cases of strictly statistical investigations, the conclusion usually
was that access could be permitted under specified rigorous conditions.
Records must be kept completely confidential, so that individual identities
are never revealed to unauthorised persons, not even indirectly from the way
results are reported, and records must be used only for research purposes.
Thus, one of the first and most influential longitudinal studies, Boalt's analysis of the selection to secondary education in a Stockholm cohort (Boalt,
1947) could be based exclusively on documentary data.

The Swedish Data Act of 1973 and the way it was interpreted by the Data
Inspection Board (DI), the new national board it created, complicated the
use of computers as well as the use of computerised governmental micro
data on identifiable persons. According to the Act, the running of data on
identifiable individuals ('a person register') on a computer would require
a licence issued by the DI (except when the register was ordered by government or required by law). For most everyday administration in banks,
other businesses and personnel departments this was soon pared down to a
routine matter, but research files turned out to be more problematic. Generally, registered persons had the right upon request to see what information
had been filed on them and to have possible errors corrected. Furthermore, as to research registers, the DI extended the principle of *informed*

consent to information drawn from existing governmental micro files, whereas epidemiologists and behavioural scientists wanted research files to be exempted from the demand of a licence.

This led to some conflicts and compromises between the DI and researchers. Except in rare circumstances longitudinal projects need identifiers when new data are to be linked to data already recorded. That is, as long as new data are added, longitudinal projects are more problematic than, for instance, cross-sectional projects, which generally can do with non-identified data. Obviously, longitudinal projects relying on register data as thoroughly as Project Metropolitan does, would be especially vulnerable.

The Project had started before the Data Act and the increasing fear of computers behind the Act, but from the mid-1970s we had to comply with the DI's policy for research registers. After a while we were permitted to continue collecting register data on the cohort, until we had covered the period up till cohort age thirty (in fact up till age thirty-two). Age thirty was where the period of observation had been designed to end, and when we and the DI wanted us to stop running a 'person register'. So the clever thing to do would be to destroy the key-tape with the identifiers and then report *fait accompli* to the DI. But suppose the key-tape could be deposited in long-term storage at the National Archives, as Statistics Sweden did with some of its files, then younger researchers would later have a chance to negotiate with the cohort members and the DI to get the tape out and continue the project. For various reasons I was convinced such a deposit in connection with the de-identification would be acceptable to the DI. I was mistaken. The key-tape had to be destroyed, in May 1986. Thus, all Project Metropolitan data are irrevocably de-identified, so nobody can follow the cohort further into middle and old age. Moreover, while the matter was prepared within the DI, it reached the media and, for almost three months, made the Project a major media villain.[9] The deposit must have been one of my brightest ideas so far.

DATA FROM REGISTERS

Data from government registers were of several types. From population registers, various items of population book-keeping were recorded, such as addresses, marital status, occupations, emigration and deaths, causes of death (including suicide), and number of children born to or living with the cohort members. In addition we had access to two main categories of registers. First, we obtained information from registers or lists of decisions or evaluative statements on events or situations, by various authorities or experts:

decisions by local Social Welfare Committees and Child Welfare Committees (social assistants), schools (teachers and local school committees); tax authorities, public prosecutors and courts and hospitals (physicians). Second, we were permitted to extract information from surveys more extensive than we would ever have been able to afford and surveys we would never have been authorised to carry out ourselves. Among such surveys were the 1960, 1970, 1975 and 1980 Censuses of Population and Housing. Another such survey file consisted of the examinations by the medical board of the Recruitment and Replacement Office of the Armed Forces (Eastern District of the male cohort members eligible for military service). In this category of files one may also place research registers put together by The National Social Board on the female cohort members' deliveries, and by the Stockholm County Council on patients discharged from the hospitals in Stockholm County.

A list of the main data in the Project Metropolitan database obtained from government registers would be as follows.

REGISTER DATA ON THE FAMILY OF ORIGIN

- Social class, nationality and citizenship in 1953 and 1963; from population lists.
- Number of years the family received social assistance and amounts received in 1953–72, for all years the family lived in the metropolitan area; from 'social registers', run by the social authorities in each municipality.
- Father's prison record up to 1972; from the National Prison Board.
- Composition, marital status, occupations, employment, housing conditions in 1960 and 1970; from the Census of Population and Housing in 1960 and 1970; composition in 1963; from population list.
- Parents' education in 1960 and 1970; from the Census of Population and Housing in 1960 and 1970.
- Parents' assessed income in 1963 and assessed income of head of household in 1971; from population lists.

REGISTER DATA ON THE COHORT MEMBER 1953–1972

- Childbirth and delivery conditions; from delivery records in hospitals' delivery wards in the area in 1953; note that practically all deliveries took place in hospitals.
- Decisions by the Child Welfare Committees as to the child, due to family conditions or to child's behavioural problems, for example glue sniffing, shop-lifting, incorrigibility, or depression, when the family lived in the metropolitan area; from metropolitan Social Registers.

- Grade, in elementary school, spring semester of 1966; for sixth and ninth grades: year of grades, placement in class for pupils needing special attention, grade school average (GPA), marks in Order and Conduct, hours of absence and truancy; program of study in ninth grade; from local school records in the metropolitan area.
- Applications to senior secondary school *(gymnasium)*, acceptance of application, completion of senior secondary school, final grade point averages if completing senior secondary school; from local school records and from Statistics Sweden (nationally).
- Offences known by the police/public prosecutors and referred to the Child Welfare Committees 1966–68; from the National Police Board.
- Psychological and physical tests, psychiatric and somatic diagnoses from psychological and physical examinations of conscripts (boys only) before they entered their military service; from the National Conscript Bureau's Eastern District, 1971–72.

REGISTER DATA ON THE COHORT MEMBER 1968(1969)–1983

- Own (and possible cohabitant's) occupation, social class, employment, marital status and housing in 1980; from the 1980 Census of Population and Housing.
- Assessed income and marital status 1979–83; from population lists.
- Courses taken at universities; from Statistics Sweden.
- Days and periods of sick-leave 1980–83; the National Social Insurance Board.
- Social assistance received by the cohort member's own family of procreation in 1982 and 1983; from Social Registers.
- The female cohort member's child births and deliveries 1970–83; from a research file run by the National Social Board.
- Number of children living with the cohort member in 1980; from population lists.
- Main and secondary discharge diagnoses following in-patient care in hospitals in Stockholm County in 1969–83, dates of admission and discharge; from the Stockholm County In-patient Care Register.
- Presence of injection scars on cohort members held overnight at the Stockholm Police Headquarters; from a research file run at the Department of Social Medicine at *Karolinska Institutet.*
- Offences committed and criminal sanctions received according to decisions by public prosecutors and court sentences 1968–83; from the National Police Board.

Range in space and time

As seen from the above lists, most early data, for the years when all or most cohort members lived in the metropolitan area, were collected for the metropolitan area only: deliveries, parental and juvenile social register records, and comprehensive school records. Records from the 1960 Census of Population and Housing also referred only to those living in the metropolitan area at the time. Thus, the cohort is truncated in steps from the left, as shown in Table 2.1. The area held the great majority of the cohort members in the years the regional data sets refer to: 82% in 1953, 93% in 1960, around 90% in 1972, and of course, 100% in 1963. Then, as cohort members move out of the area, local school and social register data for 1964–72 are missing. Also three of the later series of data were regionally delimited. The conscript data covered 90% of the male cohort, and obviously the injection-scar sample was local. By far the most important regional set consists of the data on the hospital in-patients. It covered only the Stockholm County, the most populous part of which is the metropolitan area. At the end of the period, in 1975 89% of the cohort lived in the county, in 1980 a good 82%, and in 1983 80%.

All other series covered the whole of Sweden, within which 96% of the cohort were still registered in 1983.

Like the three surveys of our own, our census and military data sets refer to a given point or a short period in time, and so do the delivery and school data sets, as well as sick-leave and income data sets for the adult members. Other sets, those from the social registers on social dependency, juvenile problems and delinquency, and those on tertiary education, crime and hospital care, cover substantial periods, although the last-mentioned three sets were censured at the end of 1983, which we decided to see as the end of young adulthood. Thus, the later part of the cohort members' educational, criminal and hospital careers was not covered by the project. Especially, the in-patient data set covers only a part of the young cohort's medical history.

For the minority who exited from the area in question before the end of the period of observation, careers were not followed beyond exit time, although another set of careers were followed if their subjects were still alive in Sweden. This means that the samples were 'selected' rather than 'truncated' (Breen, 1996, p. 44). A Tobit model might apply. Also, if the record wanted for the member consisted of a course of events, either the missing part might be filled in by imputation or the record might be excluded, totally or from exit time. Which alternative to follow would depend, for instance, on the recorded information and what range was missing. Assume that, instead, the member's record consisted of notations whether certain events happened within the period of observation. Such events might be 'sentenced to imprisonment' or 'diagnosed as schizophrenic'. If so, a member's exiting after the event occurred and was recorded would not change this record, although it might prevent the recording of other instances of investigated events. Then the problem whether to use Tobit analysis, to exclude, or to apply imputation on incomplete records would rather rest with cases for whom no events of the type searched for were recorded before the member exited.

MORE ABOUT TWO CRUCIAL DATA SERIES

Offenders and offences

Two data sets require more detailed comments: the set of offences on which the dependent variables of the analyses will be based, and the set of in-patient psychiatric diagnoses from which the primary independent variables will be constructed.

The source of the offence set is the register of offenders at the National Police Board. It contains all violations of law that in the criminal judicial process have been handled by public prosecutors and could lead to sanctions other than a fine. The violations are mainly against the Code of Penal Law but also include offences against some special laws: the Road Traffic Offences Act, the Narcotics Drug Act, some customs regulations, and the Tax Offence Act. Thus, trivial violations, breaches of local ordinances, such as getting a parking ticket, and other petty misdemeanors are not included. Drunkenness in public places was not included even before it was decriminalised in 1977. For each offender, types, dates and numbers of offences, as well as dispositions of cases, are documented. The age of criminal responsibility is fifteen, but until 1968 the register also included under-age perpetrators. There were rules of rehabilitation, according to which offenders had their records deleted after five years without new offences. The register was searched several times from 1966 for the project's cohort members.

In 1966–68 3,606 offences by 793 under-age boys and 221 offences by 123 under-age girls were found. From age 15 to the end of 1983 24,811 offences leading to 7,716 convictions of 2,686 offenders were recorded (Andersson, 1993, pp. 10–20). Tables 2.2 and 2.3 present the cohort's recorded offenders and their offences, respectively, by type of offence.

When a suspect has been identified in a criminal case, the public prosecutor's office takes over and from then on directs all further investigations.

Table 2.2. *Registered offenders according to gender, period, and type of offence; each offender counted once for each type of offence committed and period*

Type of offence	Males			Females		
	1964–74	1975–83	Total	1964–74	1975–83	Total
Violence	395	324	599	46	40	79
Thefts	1,281	459	1,482	243	133	328
Fraud	275	257	474	66	88	135
Vandalism	317	190	453	16	18	31
Traffic offences	866	560	1,193	29	78	99
Narcotic offences	207	228	337	39	53	78
Other	748	435	1,018	46	40	78
Total	4,089	2,453	5,556	485	450	828

Note: Robbery and aggravated robbery, rape and sexual assault have been placed under 'violence'. The property-offence label 'fraud' contains the categories of fraud, fraudulent conduct, embezzlement, crimes in connection with debts, and falsification. The label 'thefts' covers all other property offences except those placed under 'violence' or 'vandalism'. The latter label includes offences inflicting damage, and arson. The 'other' category contains all offences not placed in any other category. Note that pimping is an offence, but prostitution is not.

If the suspect was below fifteen years of age at the time of the offence, he or she would just be handed over to the municipal Child Welfare authorities for possible action. If the suspect was between fifteen and eighteen years of age, the judicial and the social welfare systems share responsibility, and

Table 2.3. *Registered offences according to gender of offender, period and type*

Type of offence	Males			Females		
	1966–74	1975–83	Total	1966–74	1975–83	Total
Violence	750	887	1,637	72	82	154
Thefts	9,678	2,630	12,308	527	500	1,027
Fraud	766	1,312	2,078	196	534	730
Vandalism	507	293	800	16	28	44
Traffic offences	2,322	1,080	3,402	53	157	210
Drug offences	650	897	1,547	67	226	293
Other offences	1,795	1,244	3,039	80	150	230
Total	16,468	8,343	24,811	1,011	1,677	2,688

the prosecutor would check with the social agency what actions, if any, they were considering. Often the prosecutor would decide to suspend prosecution. This happened to boys in 513 cases and to girls in 49 cases. Prosecution might be suspended in other age groups too, and that happened in cases with sixty-two men and nineteen women. In minor cases in all age groups, the prosecutor often resolved to impose a fine as a summary punishment on the alleged offender. If the fine is paid, the case is closed. Such summons were used for 492 male offenders and 81 females in the cohort.

Plea-bargaining was not permitted (nor is it now).

In court, 1,083 prison sentences were imposed on men and 66 on women. Of the sentences 73 per cent were for less than 7 months and 5 per cent were for more than 23 months.[10] In addition five men received indefinite sentences; while sixty-seven boys aged eighteen–twenty-one were sent to youth prison. In a total of thirty-six times, twenty-five men and one woman were sentenced to in-patient psychiatric care. A form of probation, that might include a prison term, was meted out 1,175 times, 962 times to men and 360 times to women. There were 497 conditional sentences imposed on men and 107 on women; in a total of 260 times, 245 boys and 15 girls were sentenced to social care under to the Child Welfare Law. Finally, 2,552 fines, assessed on the basis of the defendant's daily income, were imposed on 2,066 men and 266 women.

As a sentence might contain more than one sanction, for example both probation and assessed fines, the figures just given add up to more than the total number of sentences given. Note also that several cohort members received sanctions on more than one occasion. Offenders in the period 1966–83, that is from cohort year 13 to cohort year 30, were filed to the extent that offences were reported before the end of 1984. Few early offences were committed long before they were recorded, but the first few offences in our file occurred in 1964. Note that the register is national, that is, all cohort members were under risk as long as they remained in the country.

Unfortunately, there are no self-report data on offences among our data sets. It was not possible to include self-report questions in the 1966 School Study at cohort age thirteen. A survey was planned for the Family Study sample in 1973, primarily on the members entering the labour market, and it might have included some self-reports if it had not been cancelled.

Our data on officially sanctioned offences have the advantages of being complete in a certain sense. They cover all sanctioned offences of some seriousness by all cohort members within the country during a whole period of eighteen years. In practice, it would not have been possible to cover such a long period with self-reports for the whole cohort, probably not even for, say, the Family Study sample.

The great disadvantage of our data on recorded offences is, of course, that in another sense they are incomplete: all unreported offences and all reported offences for which no offenders were found, are missing. Thus, the recorded offenders constitute only a non-random sample with a commonly alleged bias due to some of the selective processes in the judicial system. Note, however, that offences for which prosecution was suspended, are also included in our data. Furthermore, most offences were of a fairly simple kind that does not give much room for intricate judicial manoeuvring, especially not in the rather straightforward Swedish system. Whatever strings 'important' citizens might have been able to pull successfully to save their family members from severe penal consequences of their recorded offences, it would have been very difficult for them also to get the record erased before the regular time of record rehabilitation.[11]

The flaws in good police records (and our data are the closest one can get to police records in the Swedish system after records of *suspects*) are more serious in analyses of incidence than in analyses of prevalence (participation). If the risk of getting caught for an offence incident of a given kind is small, then the proportion of recorded incidences of that offence is equally small, and a correspondingly small proportion of a pattern of offending is recorded. Furthermore, serial clearing of offences increases chance variations. For prevalence, on the other hand, the more active offender (who often also is the more serious offender) has a higher risk of being recorded at least once than the risk of getting caught for a single incident. Obviously, getting caught at least once is the opposite of getting away every time.[12] Furthermore, *ceteris paribus*, more serious offences tend to have higher rates of apprehension than less serious ones, since stronger efforts are usually made to clear them up. Hence, active offenders generally run greater risks of apprehension than more occasional offenders and thus tend to get criminal records. This means that police records have a higher concentration of active offenders than self-report data (Hindelang, Hirschi and Weis, 1979). Even given this expected difference between acceptable police and self-report data, the two data types tend to be alike enough to come out on a par (Elliott and Ageton, 1980; for late period: Tittle, Villemez and Smith, 1978). They agree with some results of victim studies (Hindelang, 1981). As to race (which is not an issue in this study), Hindelang (1978) found arrest records more in agreement with victim studies than self-reports.

The use of register data on delinquency and crime is controversial. For good reasons many mainstream criminologists are sceptical of the usefulness of such data, because of the selective processes in the judicial system. At the same time they may be surprisingly tolerant in evaluating self-report surveys, accepting large selective non-response. Modern self-reports have developed remarkably since the 1960s and early 1970s (take Elliot *et al.*, 1989 as a case), but still there are difficulties with severe offences, and long periods of recall. Most seriously, perhaps inevitably, there is selective non-response, with a tendency for the members with the highest propensity to crime to be missing. It is well known that a small percentage of the population commits a large percentage of the offences. This may make even a fairly low non-response rate, 27 per cent, say, mean that a substantial percentage of the most active offenders are missing.

Both self-reports and official records on convictions in a wide sense should be evaluated in their context. There are reasons to believe that sentence records tend to be more valid in the kind of community described in the next chapter than in a more heterogeneous and more segregated community with an adversarial judicial system.

In-patient psychiatric diagnoses

The psychiatric diagnoses refer to discharged hospital cases in Stockholm County in 1969–83 as recorded in the Stockholm County In-patient Care Register (ICR). In the register, dates of admission and discharge, main and secondary diagnoses are recorded for each in-patient and for each admission. Cases are not entered until they are discharged from the ward. If moved to another ward the patient is recorded as a new case. Out-patient are not included as such. Both psychiatric and somatic diagnoses are recorded.

The ICR started in 1969 and was gradually computerised from 1971. In 1969 some 6 per cent of the discharges were missing, in the mid-1970s missing discharges were estimated to be some 3 per cent, and at the end of our period coverage was up to 99 per cent. In 1969–83 the ICR had data from all hospitals in the county except[13] the Maria Alcohol Clinic, which did not join until 1985. Nor does the register include psychiatric youth clinics and nursing homes. The *Karolinska Hospital* participated, although this state hospital came under county administration only in 1982. The validity of ICR schizophrenia diagnosis has been examined with positive results (Frändén, 1992: 10–19).

When the ICR records in 1969–83 were searched for the project's cohort members, 8,198 members were found, of whom 355 male and 329 female members had at least one psychiatric diagnosis. Several patients had been admitted more than once, and some got different diagnoses on different occasions. If each patient was counted once for each three-digit diagnosis given, the 355 male psychiatric patients would become 535 cases, and the 329 females would become 508 cases. In addition, fifteen female cohort

Table 2.4. *Psychiatric in-patients distributed according to diagnoses given at least once 1969–83, by gender*

Diagnosis	Males	Females	Total
291 Alcohol psychosis	8	2	10
293 Psychosis connected with cerebral condition	3	1	4
294 Psychosis associated with other physical condition	8	9	17
295 Schizophrenia	46	25	71
296 Affective psychosis	9	25	34
297 Paranoid states	8	4	12
298 Other psychosis	24	40	64
299 Unspecified psychoses	55	40	95
300 Neurosis	85	159	244
301 Personality disorders	31	31	62
303 Alcoholism	100	46	146
304 Drug dependence	140	85	225
305 Physical disorders of presumptive psychogenic origin	2	6	8
306 Special symptoms not classified elsewhere	2	16	18
307 Transient situational disturbances	9	18	27
308 Behaviour disorders of childhood	2	—	2
309 Mental disorders not specified as psychotic associated with physical conditions	1	1	2
Total cases	533	508	1,043

Note: Several in-patients were admitted more than once with the same diagnosis. Of the drug addicts only 39 males and 33 females had just one admission each with the 'narcomania' diagnosis, but 44 males and 24 females had the diagnosis five times or more. The highest number of narcomania discharges was 33. Together the 140 males addicts were discharged 692 times and the 85 female addicts 373 times.
Source: Janson (1989).

members had the diagnosis of anorexia nervosa but were not included in the present study. Numbers of patients given specific diagnoses at least once are shown in Table 2.4.

To some extent specific diagnoses may depend on the psychiatric orientations at the time in the area. Comparisons with a not quite comparable set of psychiatric diagnoses given to Copenhagen young males (Ortmann, 1981), suggest (Janson, 1989) that the Stockholm psychiatrists at the time were more reluctant than their Copenhagen colleagues to use the pathological-personality diagnoses (code 301) and less hesitant to find the patient neurotic[14] (code 300).

Since the CRI is regional, not national, it cannot be a complete record of all in-patient psychiatric discharge diagnoses given to cohort members in 1969–83. As already pointed out, with time an increasing number of members came to live outside Stockholm County. Disregarding members not living in Sweden, one finds that, on average, during 1969–83 some 775 males and 850 females lived in other counties. If we assume that they ran the same risk of getting in-patient psychiatric diagnoses as did cohort members still in Stockholm County, we would expect about forty additional males and an equal number of females to have been so diagnosed in other counties.

On the other hand, it might be argued that our file should be pruned of possible psychiatric cases that were discovered because the patient committed an offence. If we want to use psychiatric hospital records to analyse the propensity to crime among persons with such records, clearly a person's psychiatric and criminal records should be independent of each other.

First, an offender might be sentenced to psychiatric hospital care. As already mentioned, this happened to twenty-five men and one woman in the cohort a total of thirty-six times, but only eleven of the remittals were to CRI hospitals. Second, an offender might be referred to psychiatric hospital care without a court decision, as were six more men and four women. Third, for twenty-one members the district attorney suspended prosecution one or more times, because the offender was already in psychiatric care. That added five men and two women to the ones of the first and second judicial categories. Of the above, forty-three criminal in-patients – twenty-four men and six women – were found in our file as psychiatric in-patients on other occasions, whereas three men had the judicial remittal as their only psychiatric hospital episode. In addition, courts sent twenty-five more men and three women to undergo psychiatric examination before sentencing them, mostly to hospitals not in the CRI. Of them, thirteen men and two women were known in the county register as psychiatric in-patients, while the others were not known as such patients.

The decision was to make no changes in the ICR file because of judicially received cases. As already mentioned, the patients of the Maria Clinics were heavy drinkers and young drug users. The clinics worked in close cooperation with the Child Welfare Committee and other social care agencies. When persons, especially youngsters, picked up by the police or needed medical or social care because of being heavily intoxicated or confused from drugs, they were often brought to the clinics. As using drugs (as distinct from selling or possessing) was not a misdemeanour until 1977, and because possessing drugs for one's own use was not prosecuted until about the same time, the police often did not see the drug users as high-priority cases but more as problems for the social agencies as long as other offences were not involved. Of 208 drug abusers treated for the first time at the youth clinic in 1979–80, 10% came to the clinic through the police, some 30% through social care agencies, less than 10% from health care agencies, and around 40% on their own or their family's initiative. Some 20% were in social care. Most patients spent some time as in-patients, but were also treated in units outside the clinic (Carpelan, 1992). According to our excerpts from the social registers, thirty-eight boys and twenty-one girls in our cohort were treated at the youth clinic some time between 1969 and 1972, whether as in-patients or only as day patients is not known. Of them, eleven boys and twelve girls were also found in the CRI as in-patients at CRI hospitals at some other occasion. Of the patients at the Maria Alcohol Clinic we have no record. Most were day patients, except for short detoxification periods, few were under the age of thirty and, of course, even fewer were under twenty-one.

The fact that some rather special categories of psychiatric cases at the Maria Clinics were left out by the CRI, raises the question of how representative the CRI cases are. Leaving the Maria Clinics out, as well as nursing homes, treatment centres and approved institutions for detentional treatment of alcoholics and addicts, may somewhat reduce the risk of detected offences themselves leading to registered hospital diagnoses. However, it reinforces the possibility that CRI cases, on average, might have a higher propensity to crime than psychiatric cases left out. CRI *narcomania* patients are found to have an especially very high crime rate, even disregarding narcotics offences. This might be what some Swedish researchers would expect, as drug addicts often are assumed 'sooner or later to get in touch with police, courts, and criminal care, either because of narcotics offences or because of other offences they commit in order to get the money for their drug habit' (CAN and Folkhälsoinstitutet, 1995, p. 92f; see also Bejerot, 1975). Of course, there may be different opinions on how soon 'sooner or later' would be, but empirical results seem to indicate that known offences may cumulate into high rates rather fast (cf. Torstensson, 1987, Table 6.12). Nevertheless, a possible selection bias in CRI cases should be given to narcomania.

First, we find that the fifty-nine cohort teenagers treated at the Maria Youth Clinic had a crime rate of the same order as the CRI narcomania patients. Second, of the cohort draftees at the military muster, eighty were given the diagnosis 'narcomania' with the strongest levels of functional impairment; six others got the same diagnosis but their impairments were estimated to be only moderate.[15] Fourteen of the seriously impaired boys were found in the CRI with the same diagnosis (some with additional diagnoses as well). The functionally impaired narcomania cases were found to have a crime rate of the same order as the CRI narcomania males. These two findings do not support the selection bias hypothesis.

THE GENERAL PURPOSE OF ALL THIS

There are always problems associated with the use of data, which have been collected for other purposes. In order to exploit them appropriately it is essential to know a good deal about the way the files were originally constructed. Project Metropolitan's set of government data is extensive. By necessity and purpose it is overwhelmingly concerned with actual events and behaviours. To paraphrase Nelson Goodman's well-known quip: there are more things in heaven and earth than are dreamt of in our files, while we are concerned, rather, that there should not be more things dreamt of in our files than there are in heaven and earth (Goodman, 1983, p. 34).

Possibilities and limitations differ between types of data source. Files documenting decisions are precise and allow little choice on the part of those who extract the information. Social reports on which decisions are based, however, are usually less precise, and consequently more open to interpretation and judgement in selecting excerpts, although one has to stick with what there is. Such problems did not arise with the censuses. With one exception, the items there seemed more or less given. The exception was the socio-economic classifications, of which only the one in the 1980 census was of much use to us. For measures of parental social class we used occupational titles in parish registers and population lists of 1953 and 1963 as well as questions in our 1968 survey. Besides, when gathering data some twenty years before one's analyses it might be dangerous to get tied too closely to current and fashionable classifications. If some things are left open to be decided later, further theoretical developments can be taken into account. In the censuses we preferred detailed occupations to ready-made classifications.

The Metropolitan database has been extensively used, but its possibilities are far from exhausted. There have been studies on child development as a function of birth weight and gestation age (Lagerström et al., 1991, 1994), on twins (Ahlin-Åkerman and Fischbein, 1990; Fischbein and Ahlin-Åkerman, 1993), on sibling position, intellectual capacity and educational career (Walldén, 1990, 1992, 1994), on achievement-related behaviours of early adolescents (Martens, 1981, 1982) and on selection to higher education (Wolf-Seibel, 1980; Smith, 1994), on suicide and para-suicide (Frändén, 1992), on coping of young males as a function of their mother's child-rearing principles and of family background (Timms, 1991, 1995,

1996), on the inheritance of welfare dependency (Stenberg, 1994), on delinquency careers (Wikström, 1987; Farrington and Wikström, 1994), on the effects of incapacitation (Andersson, 1993), on delinquency and housing (Wikström, 1989), on delinquency as a function of social background (Janson, 1982; Wikström, 1989; Smith, 1991; Janson and Wikström, 1995), on delinquency and school context (Lindström, 1995), on drug abusers (Torstensson, 1987), on mental disorders and crime Hodgins (1992, 1993, 1994), Hodgins, Kratzer and McNeil (2001 and forthcoming), Crocker and Hodgins (1997), and by Kratzer and Hodgins (1997; 1999).

One may question what, on balance, are the advantages of this elaborate and protracted longitudinal approach in comparison with an 'ordinary' cross-sectional survey, or an instant retrospective oral-history study. A short list of succinct answers may be given, taking the most important points first.

1. If we want to analyse development, change, or constancy of individuals empirically, we need individual diachronous data of some sort. If we want to go beyond an age-cohort-period type of analysis, we need diachronically-linked individual data (cf. Janson, 1994), that is, we need to be able to connect information on each person at one time to information on the same person at another time.
2. With retrospective information one risks recall problems, which limit the time span over which such information can be reliably gathered. Equally important as a source of error is the hindsight involved in retrospective estimations and evaluations (cf. Janson, 1990).
3. In order not to miss cases who leave the cohort during the period under observation, thus withdrawing from observation or indicating a negative outcome, we prefer a prospective rather than a retrospective design. Furthermore, a prospective protracted design extends the categories of information on which we can get non-retrospective data.
4. The longitudinal design may facilitate causal interpretation in analyses of mechanisms, to the extent the time order of variables is made clear. Moreover, diachronous covariance of changes is often closer to the causal concept than covariance of synchronous states. Thus, comparing before-and-after changes for two alternative treatments is somewhat more convincing then just comparing the after treatment scores.
5. In longitudinal analyses of a given situation and its proximal antecedents, one may control for *observed*, presumably relevant earlier factors in a way that is not possible in projects with a shorter time span.
6. Even in analyses of change during an interval, longitudinal data provide some control for variations of *unobserved* variables. This is because uncontrolled factors may vary (1) between individuals, (2) within individuals

during the interval studied and (3) within individuals before the interval. But this third kind of variation does not influence the change.

7. And finally, analyses which are possible with cross-sectional data, are also possible in the longitudinal set, if the latter is large enough, but the reverse is not true.

There are also some risks of disadvantages involved in longitudinal approaches. Foremost of them would be the risk for heavy case-attrition and the risk of getting caught in a project of fading relevance due to a design laid out long before the time is ready for main analyses (Janson, 1981). We have passed the attrition test and were lucky to include data still relevant on several still relevant problems. Of course, in hindsight there are things we would have done differently (after all we must have learnt something over the years), but we were not heavy on detailed theories to begin with and kept things pretty much open. Thus, we were able to modify our design, as the data-collecting process went on to its finish some sixteen years ago, and in some cases we were really lucky, for example when including information that turned out to be more useful than we thought it would be.

Longitudinal data are necessary for the efficient study of individual development and change. Also other aspects of data quality and design are highly desirable. Obviously, however, no method (or theory) is a sufficient condition for a successful study. The Metropolitan team started with the conviction that the protracted longitudinal study has important advantages, and that, on balance, the project was worth doing. As Mae West is said to have said: 'Everything worth doing is worth doing slowly'. I still believe it was worth it, but I would not do it again, even if I were younger. I would leave that to somebody else.

NOTES

1. Thus, longitudinal analyses deal with individual (or individual-level) data from different points in time ('*diachronous*' data), whereas strictly cross-sectional analyses deal with data referring to the same point in time ('*synchronous*' data). However, in a strict longitudinal analysis it is not sufficient that data are diachronous and refer to the same set of individuals, as sometimes occurs in a panel. They also must be linked over time.

2. As to the place of the cohort concept in longitudinal analyses see Riley (1992).

3. Note that, since $P = A + C$, cohort and period effects cannot be separated from each other, if one has only one cohort.

   The time and age unit need not be 'years', but can be any unit deemed relevant in the context, for instance 'day', as in 'days of in-patient care'. Instead of birth cohorts one may have cohorts of members entering, leaving, or staying somewhere at the same time, for instance, students in medical school or cohorts of employees. The relation between time, age, and cohort still holds.

4. In fact, we started drawing the cohort members and collecting some register data in 1964.

5. This definition of the cohort corresponded to that used in one of the earliest Swedish longitudinal studies (Boalt, 1947). There, the cohort was defined as those boys and girls who left fourth form of elementary schools in the City of Stockholm in 1936, most of them born in 1925. In the Danish Project Metropolitan the cohort was defined as boys born in Zealand in 1953. In practice the difference between using 1953 or 1963 in defining the 1953 cohort was not important, since obviously members leaving the cohort before age ten could not be studied after that age.

6. In sub-projects researchers were able to analyse impacts of the combined factors of social class and gender.

7. The criteria concerned rates of agglomeration (urban population), agriculture, and commuting to the City of Stockholm.

8. The participating schools had 619 sixth-form classes containing at least one cohort member, most often between 18 and 33 cohort members. In many classes there were also pupils who did not belong to the cohort, the majority of them because they were born in 1952. Most classes had about the same number of boys and girls. Three per cent of the classes were for pupils who needed special attention due to reading or general learning disabilities, impaired vision or hearing or other disabilities. These classes had a maximum of fifteen members.

9. After tensions between the DI and the researchers came to a head in 1986, the situation improved. The DI has held on to its principle of *informed consent*, but under less belligerent commissioners it has become more flexible in its applications. From 1999 there was a new Personal Data Protection Act. Instead of 'person register' the new act is about 'processing of personal data which is largely computerised'. Its field will be extended to include manual processing, but only 'if the data is to form part of a proper register'. No licence will be required. Instead a 'controller' shall be responsible for the processing of personal data and shall notify the DI.

10. In the period studied, prison terms exceeding two months were conditionally suspended, when two thirds, but not less than two months, of the time, had been served.

11. The great majority of behavioural complaints received by the CWC did not lead to decisions to take the child into social care or to other actions. After being investigated many complaints were taken *ad acta*, that is, just filed.

12. Let us assume that the risk of getting apprehended for a criminal act of a given kind is p. If so, the chance of getting away with the offence is $1 - p$. To simplify, let us assume that each criminal act of the given kind has the same risk p as long as the perpetrator has not been apprehended before (if he has, the risk may get higher). Then, committing the same type of offence in the same way n independent times, he has the risk

$$P = 1 - (1 - p)^n > p$$

of being apprehended at least once, that is, of getting a record. For instance, if $p = 0.2$ and $n = 10$, then $P = 0.89$, and if $p = 0.1$ and $n = 20$, then $P = 0.88$.

Suppose somebody stops each day on his way home from the office to have a few shots at the bar and then drives home a bit stoned. He does this for a year (200 times a year). Each time he runs a very small risk of being stopped by the police (p = 0.001). However, under the same assumptions as above, the risk of his being stopped at least once during the year would be P = 0.87.

13. Also a private hospital without a psychiatric ward did not participate.
14. In the military board's examination of the Stockholm conscripts, however, the frequency of the pathological-personality diagnosis was more in accord with the Copenhagen report.
15. Since severe impairment would mean exemption from military service, some conscripts may have tried putting some drug or alcohol habits to use here.

CHAPTER 3

SWEDISH SOCIETY AND STOCKHOLM: THE COHORT AND ITS CONTEXT

INTRODUCTION

Every empirical study can be seen as based on a sample of observations in time and space. The phenomena under study occur in a context, which is a more or less unique in time and place, making findings linked to the circumstances of that situation on that occasion. Their meanings and the mechanisms behind them may be generalisable over either wide or narrow ranges of various dimensions, most of them rather vaguely conceptualised.

Swedish Society, albeit narrowed down to the Stockholm community at the time of the cohort, provides the context for many of the studies based on Project Metropolitan data. The general message of this chapter is that certain features of the cohort and its society should be kept in mind, since they may be relevant to the validity, meaning, interpretations and generalisations of the findings of the present investigation. This chapter is an attempt to back up these messages by presenting selected aspects, presumably relevant, of that context. Finally, the cohort itself is briefly described.

POPULATION

Ethnic composition

In their contacts with non-Nordic Europe, Sweden and the other Nordic countries have generally been receiving rather than giving ideas and competence. Urbanisation and industrialisation started late, in Sweden around 1850, but proceeded fast. Also, in about 1850 the huge European, mostly transatlantic, flow of emigration started to be felt in Sweden too. Here it culminated in 1880–93 and subsided after the turn of the century, but the

1930s was the first decade with a small immigration surplus. Sweden then was an ethnically homogeneous country with a homogeneous, if regionally somewhat varied, culture. The same could be said about all the Nordic countries, which were and are culturally similar, although the Finnish language is not related to the Scandinavian languages.

From the 1930s Sweden has been a country of immigration. At times, the heavy inflow of immigrants and refugees has cumulatively changed the homogeneous population of the 1930s to the modern day ethnically heterogeneous population. However, the process has been gradual, and at least during part of the time covered by the Project, the population retained much of its ethnic and cultural homogeneity. The great transition to a 'multicultural' society came with the refugees from the Middle East and other non-European countries in the second half of the 1980s.

During the Second World War and again at its end, Sweden received about 200,000 refugees, with the majority of them returning to their home countries. But of the 30,000 refugees from the Baltic states, many settled in Sweden. In 1954 a common Nordic labour market was created. Until 1985 around 450,000 Finns, including family members, entered Sweden. Of them, some 280,000 eventually returned to Finland. In addition, from the late 1940s non-Nordic labour-force immigrants were brought in, but after 1972, with a few exceptions, only family members of those who had already arrived, were admitted. Labour-force immigration peaked in the boom years of 1969–70, when 142,000 persons entered. Among them were 80,000 from Finland, of whom around 45,000 returned in the next few years.

In the 1970s about half of the immigrants came from non-Nordic countries, almost all from European countries. From the 1950s refugees were received, for instance Hungarians (1956), Greeks, Poles, Czechs, Chileans and Turks. In the 1980s most new arrivals were refugees or close relatives, in the second half of the decade more than half came from non-European countries. In 1980 non-citizens comprised 5% of the population, almost 3% coming from the Nordic countries. Adding foreign-born Swedish citizens would increase the immigrant part of the population to 8%, 43% of whom were Finnish and 16% Scandinavian. In the 1980s 5% of the Swedish labour force were non-Swedish citizens, of whom about half were Nordic citizens. At the end of 1986, those born abroad and non-citizens together constituted 10% of the Swedish population, 5% coming from the Nordic countries.

In 1982 foreign-born persons formed 7.5% of the population, whereas those born in Sweden with at least one foreign-born parent constituted 4.5%. In 1980 54% of those foreign-born had come from the Nordic countries, 31% from other European countries, and 15% from non-European countries.

Stockholm attracted more immigrants than other parts of the country. In 1982 Stockholm County had 13.7% foreign-born persons and non-citizens, of whom 7.5% originated in the Nordic countries and 4.8% in other European countries.[1]

The inflow of non-Nordic immigrants caused some minor changes in the religious structure of Swedish society, which, however, remained culturally secular. In 1983 95% of the citizens still belonged to the Lutheran State Church, the role of which was mostly ceremonial, while the membership of the 'free', that is, non-conformist churches had gone down from 6.9% in 1955 to 4.5%. The Roman Catholic Diocese had grown to 1.4% of the population (or 27% of the non-citizens). The first Swedish mosque of some size was founded (in Malmö) in the mid-1980s.

In the first decades the labour-force immigrants paid more taxes than they received in social benefits, but this surplus shrank, as the immigrants grew older and their families grew in size. To receive refugees was seen as a strong obligation. The general attitude of the authorities and the media remained positive to the increased diversity, which was seen more as a resource than as a problem. Any incident seen as an act of racism was strongly condemned. A policy of integration rather than assimilation was developed. Children of foreign-born parents received some teaching in their mother tongue. In 1976 non-citizen immigrants who had been living in the country for at least three years were given the right to vote in local elections.

In the post-war era Swedish culture changed in many respects: the new prosperity and welfare society, better communications and new media opened up the world to the Swedes and led, for instance, to changed leisure and food habits. Much of this may be called Americanisation, but there has also been a change towards a more Continental lifestyle. It may be difficult to point to specific immigrant influences among these changes, but most likely the new domestic heterogeneity fits in with and reinforces some of the more Continental habits. It should be noticed, however, that immigrant groups have not developed into ethnic minorities with demands on autonomy, and that the immigrant population in residential areas, in which its relative size are well above the average, is usually heterogeneous in origin. In suburban communities, in the metropolitan area with large numbers of immigrants, typically thirty to fifty nations were represented, and some teaching was given in up to twenty mother tongues.

In summary, the ethnically homogeneous population of the first post-war years developed into an increasing ethnic heterogeneity with first Nordic and mostly European labour-force immigration, and then refugees (and their relatives) from many corners of the world. However, the effects of this course of events largely made themselves felt after the period covered by the present study. In the cohort, members born abroad or having at least one foreign-born parent made 8% of the cohort, but of these 42% were Finns, and 25% were Scandinavians, leaving less than 3% non-Nordic, and these were mostly European members. There were very few non-white members. Note that no arrivals in the metropolitan area after 1963 were included in the cohort. This means that increasingly the project cohort became ethnically unrepresentative of the actual cohort of 1953 in the area. That is, at least from the time they reached young adulthood, the members lived in a society that contained more immigrants, often a different kind of immigrants than before. One may conjecture that the immigrants coming in later than the cohort members might somewhat change the ethnic handicap of the latter. Anyhow, with only very few non-white cohort members, there was no racial factor *within the cohort*. The delinquency and crime rates of the small non-Nordic category was only marginally higher than the cohort averages and generally not higher than the rates of the Nordic immigrants (Martens, 1994). Thus, there was no strong ethnic factor in cohort delinquency and crime.

Economic differences and social policy

The first post-war decades were times of progress, expansions, and high expectations. The standard of living increased rapidly. A few figures may illustrate the strong growth in the standard of living in 1953–83. The number of telephones per 1,000 persons was 264 in 1953 and 890 in 1983. Corresponding American figures were 311 and 760, respectively, whereas the British figures were 120 and 524, respectively. Infant mortality was already low in 1953 and fell from 19 per 1,000 live births that year to 7.0 per 1,000 live births in 1983, while the American figure fell from 28 to 10.5, respectively, and the British figure from 28 to 11.4 (in England and Wales).

The already rather limited range of income differences became further compressed until the mid-1980s, at which time it appears to have begun to expand somewhat. The reductions in differentials of disposable income occurred mostly in the low-income tail of the distribution. The proportion of destitute people was greatly reduced by new pensions and new forms of assistance. When Gini coefficients were calculated for the so-called Luxembourg Income Study data for nine Western countries around 1980 and adjusted for composition and size of family, Sweden earned the lowest value for disposable income inequality, 0.194. Norway came closest with 0.231; Switzerland (0.319) and USA (0.312) came out the highest (Fritzell, 1991, Table 6.1).

The welfare society, which had been started in the 1930s, was further developed.[2] Unemployment was kept low in the thirty-year period covered by Project Metropolitan, with rates varying around 2 per cent of the labour force. Only in 1982–84 did they exceed 3 per cent. At times the low rates also meant heightened prices. This was especially the case in the ten years from 1973 to 1983, when the cost-of-living index (excluding direct taxes and social benefits) increased some 160 per cent. During the total thirty-year period of 1953–83, the index increased almost fivefold.

Social policy in a wide sense together with related policy areas affecting the welfare of the population, expanded greatly in the first post-war decades. Social policy may help a household to manage on its own in two ways. One way is by moving at least a minimum version of a service or policy measure wholly or partially out of the market system so as to make the household less dependent on the economic resources of the targeted individuals. Thus, basic amounts of health care, care of the disabled, childcare, sick-leave and unemployment compensations, pensions and old-age care, housing, elementary and secondary education etc. may be made more or less independent on the wealth and income of the eligible persons. The second way is by simply reducing differences in economic resources by transfers, making market mechanisms less important in the services that are still distributed according to market processes.

In their classification of welfare societies, Korpi and Palme (1998) distinguish five ideal-typical models according to eligibility criteria and benefit principles. Sweden is placed in the 'Encompassing' type, historically the latest type to emerge. With Norway and Finland in the same category, it becomes something of a specialty of the Nordic countries. Its eligibility criteria are citizenship and labour-force participation, and its benefit principles are flat rate and earnings related. United States, United Kingdom and Canada (and Denmark) belong to the 'Basic Security' type, historically the second latest to emerge, with eligibility according to citizenship or residence and flat rate as benefit principle.

Both income differences and total benefit expenditures as a percentage of the Gross Domestic Product (GDP) vary between countries within the same model types, but the encompassing welfare states tend to have the lowest inequality rates and the highest benefit expenditure per GDP, whereas the Basic Security countries come third, after 'Corporatist' countries, such as France and Germany (Korpi and Palme, 1989, Tables 1–3; Diagram 1).

Let us take social expenditure in a wide sense.[3]

- In 1953, they cost 10.2% of the national income or 520 SEK (US $100) per person;
- In 1963 the cost was 14.0% of the national income or 1,450 SEK (US $280) per head;
- In 1973 it amounted to 21.4% of the GDP at market prices or 5,760 SEK(US $1,250),
- In 1983 it had grown to 32.8% of the GDP or 27,700 SEK (US $3,450), perhaps approaching the ceiling of what is possible for a system of social expenditure.

As to health care, the welfare system came almost as close as one can get to providing equal access to high quality medical treatment for all, regardless of their economic resources. Compulsory earnings-related insurance for sick-leave compensations was introduced in 1955. Hospital care, including deliveries, became free, out-patient treatment cost a nominal fee (from 1970), and private doctors' fees were strongly subsidised. Prescriptions were also subsidised with a ceiling on how much the patient paid. However, over the years the fees paid to the doctor or for medicine by the patient increased, and in-patient hospital care did not remain completely free of charge, although deliveries have. In 1974 sickness pay was increased to 90 per cent of gross earnings up to an income-related ceiling and made taxable. A general dental insurance started in the same year.

From 1948 there was a general non-taxable child allowance until the age of sixteen instead of tax reductions. For school children it was extended to nineteen. In 1948 the annual general allowance was 290 SEK (some US $80), paid directly to the mother. Over the years Riksdagen has adjusted its size. In 1986 it had risen to 4,800 SEK (US $700) per year and child, and from 1983 there were additions for three or more children. If one of the parents had custody of the child, and the other parent was negligent in paying maintenance allowance, the allowance was advanced by the social agencies. All pupils in primary and secondary school were served free meals, paid by the municipality.

In 1971 the taxation system changed its tax assessment unit from the family to the individual, so that even married spouses were assessed separately. Thus, a couple's second income would be less heavily taxed in the progressive income-tax system. Beginning in the early 1970s subsidised municipal day-care centres were created, and as of 1974 nine months paid leave for childcare following childbirth or adoption was available for parents to share. Fathers were encouraged to take their part of the leave. A parent staying at home to care for a sick child was entitled to sick-leave compensation. This became somewhat more popular with fathers than the other child-caring possibilities. Generally, from the mid-1960s both public authorities and ordinary people began to take gender equality seriously, in child rearing and in other fields (Rosenfeld and Kalleberg, 1990).

From 1938 there was at least two weeks of paid vacation for all employees. In 1951 this was extended to three weeks and later to five weeks. Unemployment insurance remained linked to union membership, and 1974 brought both protective regulations against dismissal and cash benefits to uninsured employees losing their jobs. Generally, this legislation strengthened the position of the unions, which already were very strong. In the mid-1980s 85 per cent of the employees, aged eighteen to sixty-four, including lower middle-class employees and professionals, were union members. The percentage was about the same among men and women. The working week in industry was still forty-eight hours in 1958 but was shortened by degrees, first to forty-five, then to forty-two and a half and finally to forty hours in 1973.

There had been old-age pension insurance since 1913, but not until 1946 were pensions brought to levels that at the time were considered sufficient for a meagre subsistence in most cases. However, in 1959 all political parties agreed that old-age pensions were often insufficient. After the period's fiercest political fight, in which different pension schemes stood against one another, a new pension scheme with an earnings-related supplementary pension (ATP) went through at the *Riksdag* with the slightest possible margin.

All pension systems applied also to persons below pension age who were unable to support themselves due to illness or handicap. Widows received a pension. Legislation in 1976 offered partial pensions from age sixty and lowered the age of retirement from sixty-seven to sixty-five as well as offering better chances of disability pensions. Municipal poor relief was regulated by acts in 1957 and 1982.

Just as this section describes and as the following will elaborate further, not only did Swedish society and the cohort show an unusually low ethnic heterogeneity in the early post-war decades, they also had an unusually low socio-economic heterogeneity. However, whereas the ethnic heterogeneity increased during the period studied, the socio-economic heterogeneity tended, if anything, to decrease further. Compared with an equally prosperous cohort, the one with less socio-economic variation has fewer and less deprived members. Thus, generally, life situations would be less distant from the average life situation. This, one may conjecture, *ceteris paribus*, should lead to less delinquency and crime: and less disorganised residential districts (disorganisation theory). There should also be less strain, because of better legitimate means to reach legitimate goals (strain theory); better internal controls and stronger bonds to conventional society, because of a more efficient socialisation process (control theory); and less of a breeding ground in a more average life situation for subculture values (subculture theory). Presuming then that delinquency and crime are relatively weakly connected to ethnic and socio-economic factors, this should strengthen the relative position of other, at least partly unrelated factors. Thus, for instance, psychiatric factors may come out more clearly than in a more heterogeneous cohort.

Furthermore, let power be 'the probability of one actor within a social relationship being in a position to carry out his own will despite resistance' (Weber, 1978, p. 53). Then, ethnic-racial and socio-economic homogeneity means that the span between the most powerless and the most powerful is less than in a heterogeneous society. Thus, another conjectured effect of the homogeneity would be that the bias against the powerless suspects and in favour of the powerful ones in the justice system would be less in the cohort than in a more heterogeneous one.

DWELLINGS AND NEIGHBOURHOODS

Dwelling and neighbourhood conditions are elements in the quality of life, and differences in the conditions are important components of inequality. Besides, the urban spatial structure has an impact on delinquency and crime rates, as well as on differential risks of detection and arrests.

Housing

In the 1930s housing conditions gave reasons for deep concern. Especially in urban areas most dwelling units were small. Urban working-class families often lived in one-room-and-kitchen apartments, yet still paid high rents. During the war construction work on new residential buildings was cut down, whereas the urban population increased. This triggered a housing shortage, and aggravated rather than eased the housing situation in the big cities. Even in 1945 48 per cent of children in big and medium-sized cities lived in overcrowded conditions, where overcrowding was defined as more than two persons per room, kitchen excluded. In Stockholm City, 78 per cent of the dwellings were one-room-and-kitchen or smaller units. Only 54 per cent of the dwellings had central heating and private bath.

Extensive actions were taken and conditions were radically improved. Social engineering was applied as in no other sector. Housing allowances to various categories, state loans and interest subsidies to new housing, and tax credits to mortgages on owner-occupied housing were introduced. New statutes on urban planning strengthened the position of the municipalities and made planning, construction and housing even more their responsibility (Dahlberg and Ödmann, 1969). An ambitious policy aimed at improving the housing situation by providing new, larger, well-equipped and moderately priced dwelling units. It tended to release a blocked housing demand, making the housing shortage in big cities and many other urban places more or less permanent. Finally, an extraordinary effort overcame the shortage (Söderqvist, 1999).

In 1965 *The Riksdag* pronounced that in ten years one million dwelling units should be built. For some years construction of new housing reached the highest level per capita in Europe (Dahlberg and Ödmann, 1969, p. 158). The building industry underwent a boom, and the objective was fulfilled with good measure. In the forty years from 1945 to 1985 the number of dwellings increased by 85% in Sweden. As 32% of the dwellings in the old stock were demolished, in fact 115% of new and larger dwellings, or 291 dwelling units per 1,000 population, were added to the stock. These changes meant that the average household size decreased from the not-very-high figure of 3.17 persons to the very low figure of 2.16. In 1985, 92% of all dwellings were fully equipped, that is, had hot and cold running water, drains, WC, central heating, bathroom, kitchen range and refrigerator. Overcrowding according to the old definition was practically extinct, so overcrowding was redefined as more than two persons per room, kitchen and one room excluded. According to this definition, 3.7% of the population and 5.7% of the children lived in crowded conditions. It may be added that in 1985 there were 162 leisure houses per 1,000 households.

Stockholm

Stockholm is situated where Lake Mälaren with its many islands opens into the archipelago of the Baltic Sea. The oldest part of the city, the Old Town, now part of the Central Business District (CBD), is an island with Lake Mälaren on the west side and the Baltic on the east side. North and south of the Old Town there is the rest of the Central City, with the CBD mostly to the north. The Central City is clearly defined by lakes and streams or open spaces, on the other sides of which suburbs extend, within and beyond the city borders. In 1940 the Central City had 458,700 inhabitants, in 1950 it had 427,000. The steady decline continued over the period depicted here and was almost totally due to decreasing dwelling density, even if the downtown area was completely rebuilt and much expanded.

Most residential neighbourhoods in the Central City consisted of blocks of multifamily four-to-six-storey buildings, usually with shops on the street level. Most residential houses had private owners. Buildings were placed along the streets round an enclosed yard, in which there were often buildings of somewhat lower social and housing standard. In the 1930s peripheral parts of the Central City were filled with neighbourhoods of open blocks of multifamily houses, often owned by non-profit organisations or by tenant-owner societies. The eastern parts, however, remained a vast park, the city's foremost leisure and entertainment area (at present also housing several museums and the university). In 1960 97 per cent of city central dwellings were in multifamily buildings.

In 1940 the city's suburban areas had no more than 131,800 inhabitants. With the exception of an industrial suburban city to the north-west and a few other neighbourhoods, the suburbs were low-density one-family areas. During the war this began to change, as new areas were built. In 1960, 82 per cent of the suburban dwellings within the city and 52 per cent of the dwellings in the suburban municipalities were in multifamily houses. In 1980 the latter figure had increased to 63 per cent.

With a little good will one can discern a metropolitan spatial structure of roughly the sector kind suggested by Hoyt (1939). However, as often is the case with European cities, there is no American-type correlation between high-quality residential neighbourhoods and distance from the CBD. Rather, most of the high-prestige neighbourhoods are in the Central City or in nearby suburbs.

When construction accelerated after the war, in Stockholm City urban planning was following ideas inspired by the British New Towns, but implemented here on a smaller scale (Popenoe, 1977). Construction was limited to a few areas at a time, and each area was built as a unit according to a common pattern adapted to the often hilly and woody landscape. Each unit was planned for about 5,000 to 15,000 initial inhabitants. In the middle there would be a small business district, which among other things would have a station in the metropolitan subway rail system, which was being built and extended to all new suburbs (it was underground only in the Central City but still was proudly named the *Tunnel banan*). Adjacent to the unit's business centre there would be some residential high-rise, that is eight-to-ten-storey houses. Beyond them, three-storey buildings were arranged by yards into neighbourhoods; further out, terrace houses (until this time rarely seen) completed the area. Between areas there would be green belts. Multifamily houses contained fully equipped one-, two-, and three-bedroom apartments and were almost equally divided between non-profit organisations, tenant-owner societies, and private owners. Each urban unit had primary schools with separate schools for the first three or six grades in the neighbourhoods. Units were grouped in clusters, and the central unit in each cluster had an extended business centre to serve the whole cluster of units. Among other things the extended centre would have a senior secondary school.

The City applied this planning policy in the 1950s and the early 1960s. In the 1960s and 1970s there was a trend towards denser neighbourhoods, centres and higher multi-storey buildings, in some cases with ten-storeyed houses or higher. Within the city borders land for these types of new, larger-scale suburbs was available almost only in the open areas to the north-west and south-west. However, several other neighbourhoods with high-density blocks were built in suburban municipalities during the costly programme.

During the protracted housing shortage the urban planning programme gave most young people entering the housing market a choice of just a few, rather similar areas to start in. This tended to increase segregation according to age, but to decrease segregation according to social class, which was fairly low already in the 1940s. Measured as a percentage of actual standard deviation of maximum standard deviation,[4] working-class segregation was 0.32 in 1948 in the suburban parts within the city and 0.24 in 1956. In the Central City the figures were 0.35 and 0.33 (Janson, 1987). In the 1970s, when the housing shortage was mostly over, working-class segregation ceased to decrease and possibly increased somewhat. As late as 1980, however, working-class segregation was 0.26 in the city's suburban parts and 0.25 in the suburban areas outside the city. In 1980, the foreign-born population in the metropolitan area had reached 13 per cent. In nine suburban districts of the high-density-block type, out of 227 metropolitan districts at least 30 per cent of the population were foreign-born. The ethnic segregation in these districts was 0.21.

There were no central or suburban slum districts. Note also that there was no place in urban-planning programmes for special neighbourhoods for low-income or welfare families. Furthermore, there were no American-style street-gangs and no gang wars (Klein, 1996, ch. 8). Youth gangs were small and temporary.

EDUCATION

Education went through almost uninterrupted reforms away from a continental elite-type system to a more egalitarian system. From 1950 elementary school with seven or eight years was gradually expanded into a nine-year comprehensive school, incorporating the four- or five-year junior secondary school, which in the old system had partially run alongside the primary school. From the mid-1960s senior secondary schools were changed to an integrated system. College and university reforms began in 1969 with open admissions from 1977. In the new system higher proportions of each cohort went on to secondary education and beyond, and the selection according to social class and gender was weaker than in the old system.[5]

In 1950 6,400 students passed senior secondary school; in 1968 the number was 35,400. The net enrollment of first-time college students was 3,600 in 1950 and 27,600 in 1968; or 241 per 100,000 heads in 1950 and 1,465 per 100,000 heads in 1968. One may say that the educational expansion changed the socio-economic meaning of higher education from a practically sufficient to an almost necessary condition for getting a non-manual occupation. However, the system provided ample opportunities for life-long education to compensate for missed chances or just for leisure.

Members of the Metropolitan cohort went through a nine-year comprehensive school with some gradual differentiation after sixth grade either to a track preparing for *gymnasium* (senior secondary school), with second and third foreign languages and more maths; or to general or vocational tracks. After passing the prep-track of comprehensive school, students could apply to and perhaps be accepted into three-year senior secondary school according to their grades. After completing *gymnasium* one might enter undergraduate studies, able males usually after their basic military training. The general track in upper comprehensive school might lead to a two-year secondary school (*fackskola*). After a few years the differentiation within comprehensive school was modified, and the two-year *fackskola* was integrated in senior secondary school (*gymnasie-skola*).

Three types of educational institutions targeting people above mandatory school-age supplemented the general educational system. By offering possibilities to take up studies again later, this might have some crime-preventive potential (cf Hagan, 1997). First, even in the second half of the nineteenth century, 'people's high schools' were created by special associations or foundations, often connected with popular movements, and later by some county councils. They soon received state support. Their main purpose was to provide a general citizen's education for adults. In 1948 there were seventy state-supported people's high schools.

Second, from 1898 adult education was available also in 'correspondence schools', in which both practical courses and courses from the formal school system were offered as sets of letters exchanged between student and teacher. After completing such a letter course in a school subject, the student might attempt, as a 'private study candidate', to pass the test on the subject at an ordinary school.

Third, while the new school system was developing, a municipality-run primary and secondary-level adult-education system was added. In 1983, courses in this system registered students numbering (with some double counting) about 1.3 times the average cohort between age 20 and age 45, whereas general leisure study-circles had participants amounting to 43 per cent of the adult population. Even in college adults, that is, people aged 25 and over, were a substantial proportion of the undergraduate students.

ALCOHOL AND DRUGS

In the post-war decades Sweden was a strong-liquor and beer country, even more so than now. Earlier the temperance movement was strong and was able to keep much of its political influence even after its membership began to dwindle in the 1930s and 1940s. Alcohol policy was restrictive (Bruun and Frånberg, 1985). From 1916 there was a rationing system for strong liquor. It was abandoned in 1955, but the retail monopoly for hard liquor, wine and the strongest kind of beer was kept, which meant that within the country these kinds of beverages could only legally be bought in special liquor stores. In order to discourage drinking, taxation was heavy. In order to encourage substitution of wine for hard liquor, the tax was calculated according to strength of alcohol. Total sales of 100 per cent alcohol per person (over the age of fifteen) were 4.92 litres in 1954 and had increased to 5.44 litres in 1964, when a marginally stronger type of beer was introduced. This 'middle-strength' beer became popular among youngsters and was abandoned in 1977, when total alcohol sales had increased to 7.70 litres. From then on sales decreased to 6.10 litres in 1983. Sales of 100 per cent alcohol per person (over the age of fifteen) went:

    from 3.59 litres of liquor in 1954 to 2.77 litres in 1983;
    from 0.39 litres of wine in 1954 to 1.63 litres in 1983; and
    from 1.36 litres of beer in 1954 to 1.70 litres in 1983.

Comparing alcohol sales in litres per person in Sweden, the US and Great Britain one finds, for what they may be worth, the following figures (see Table 3.1).

Being drunk in public places was decriminalised in 1977. However, after 1977 approximately the same number of persons as before were taken care of by the police according to a special ordinance and brought to the station or a hospital.

Table 3.1. *Sales of litres alcohol per person in Sweden,*
US, and Great Britain; in 1983

	Liquor 100%	Wine	Beer	Total 100%
Sweden	2.1	11.7	46.8	5.2
US	2.7	9.2	90.3	8.0
Great Britain	1.7	10.0	108.9	7.1

As late as the 1950s the use of drugs, mainly amphetamines, was primarily confined to certain bohemian groups. In the 1950s other kinds of central stimulants were introduced as well as the habit of injecting drugs. In the 1960s morphine and other opiates were used, with users recruited mostly from delinquent circles. In the later years of the 1960s, drug abuse increased rapidly, and from that time, as oral and intravenous use of central stimulants spread, in the first place to delinquent and problem cases among young Stockholmers, it was more generally regarded as a social problem (Olsson, 1994). The smoking of cannabis spread to young people even outside ordinary drug-using groups (Torstensson, 1987). Occasional and experimental drug use in the early 1970s has been estimated to be some 14 per cent of ninth-grade pupils and somewhat higher among military conscripts. Among the ninth-graders the drug-use figures was down to around 8 per cent by 1975 and to 5 per cent by 1983. In 1967 the hard core of abusers were estimated to be some 3,000 persons. It seemed to have stayed at approximately that number throughout the 1980s, whereas the abuse of hard drugs increased for a while outside the Stockholm area. Most drug abusers used more than one substance. Central stimulants were the most common form of narcotic substance, cannabis (hashish) the second most common. Intravenous drug abusers mostly used amphetamines, but the use of heroin increased from 1970. In 1979, 60 per cent of hard-core drug use and 80 per cent of daily intravenous drug use were found in the Stockholm, Gothenburg and Malmö areas. As the recruitment to the group of hard-core drug-abusers had slowed down since the 1960s, there were indications of 'a shift from younger to older age groups, and that there is today a fairly widespread abuse among adults, primarily of cannabis, which can neither be termed occasional nor hard-core'. In 1979, only 6 per cent of the heavy abusers were younger than twenty.[6]

Evidently our Metropolitan cohort happened to be one of the first Swedish cohorts to which drugs were available and tried out by some adolescents and young adults, some of whom developed an addiction.

CRIME AND JUSTICE

In evaluating the validity of the project's information on offenders and offences the Swedish crime situation and system of justice should be considered.

In 1950 the number of offences known to the police was only 27.7 per 1,000 inhabitants, but since then the number has risen steadily, although with minor fluctuations, to 81.1 in 1970 and 121.8 in 1985. (Ahlberg, 1992). Of reported offences against the Criminal Code, around 70 per cent were property offences. Homicides and assaults known to the police were 1.0 per 1,000 population in 1950, 2.4 in 1970, and 3.9 in 1985. Robberies were seldom heard of in the early 1950s but are now reported much more frequently (Andersson, 1994). Whereas the population increased 19 per cent from 1950 to 1985, the number of robberies known to the police increased 20 times, from 190 in 1950 to 3,851 in 1985, or from 0.03 per 1,000 heads in 1950, to 0.19 in 1970, and 0.46 in 1985. Organised crime remained insignificant for a short time, or, as a standard joke from the 1960s put it: 'everything is organised in Sweden except crime', although long-term prisoners eventually organised their trade union and were accorded an annual vacation.

As mentioned in the previous chapter, as soon as a suspect for a crime had been identified, the case was handed over to the public prosecutor's office and a prosecutor was assigned to take charge of further investigations. If the prosecutor believed it could be proved that an offence was committed by the identified suspect, the case was settled by a summary fine or by a court decision. If the perpetrator was under eighteen, or there were other reasons,[7] the prosecutor suspended prosecution. As mentioned earlier the age of criminal responsibility was fifteen.

In the Swedish system there could be no plea bargain, and no bail could be paid to keep a suspect out of jail. Furthermore, there were no grand juries. In criminal cases a lower court consisted of a judge and a panel of lay jurors. The judge, like the prosecutor, was an appointed career official, not politically appointed, with an appropriate law degree. The panel (*nämnd*) consisted of three to seven (exceptionally nine) lay jurors (*nämndemän*) appointed by the municipal council for six years (now three years) from a pool of jurors (after nominations by the political parties in the council). Jurors usually worked in teams under one or more judges for most of their term. The judge acted as chairperson during deliberations and instructed the lay court-members, who could overrule him or her, if they reached a consensus. The *nämnd* goes back to medieval law, at that time consisting of trusted members of the local community, but the effective post-war regulations were from 1948.

The system was *inquisitorial* rather than *adversarial*, and was not perceived as a competition by two parties but rather as a process to find out what actually happened. Proceedings were oral. They were much less regulated than in the Anglo-American system and had fewer restrictions on permissible evidence. Defendants were heard but not allowed to testify under oath. Defence lawyers played a decidedly less important role than in the US system. Defendants had the right to counsel, free of charge if they could not pay. There were no public defenders; instead the defendant could request any lawyer he wanted as counsel, or defendant and the court would agree on an experienced defence lawyer. Appointing the defender seldom turned out to be controversial, although after proceedings the court and the lawyer sometimes disagreed on the lawyer's fees.[8]

Criminal policy was liberal. The stated primary purpose of penal measures was rehabilitation of the offender ('individual prevention'). The only exceptions were the one-month prison policy (relaxed in later years) for drunken driving[9] and, later, sentencing large-scale drug pushers to heavy prison terms of several years. Both exceptions to the general policy had the purpose of deterrence ('general prevention', Andenaes, 1952). Otherwise, imprisonment was used sparingly and the terms tended to be short. In 1980 14,000 persons or 210 per 100,000 adults, were sentenced to prison. The average daily prison population was 4,600. Of the prisoners starting to serve time that year, 60 per cent were sentenced to one or two months and 11 per cent to one year or more. Almost three-quarters of those sentenced for drunk driving received prison sentences and constituted almost 40 per cent of those entering prison during the year. Prisoners serving terms longer than a few months were routinely paroled after two-thirds of their sentences. Leaves of absence and visits by family members were rather frequent, especially toward the end of the term. Only three prisons were high-security institutions. In 1980 11,200 youngsters aged between fifteen and seventeen were sentenced and 10,700 had their prosecutions suspended. A person below eighteen might be sentenced to prison only under very special circumstances. In 1980 this happened to thirty delinquents.

In Sweden, as in other countries during this period, treatment of the mentally ill moved dramatically away from protracted care in hospitals to out-patient care. In the twenty-year period from 1963 the number of mental hospitals dropped from thirty-five to sixteen, while the number of beds went down 35 per cent.

This leads us to one important message: the justice system operating on the cohort, as suggested in the previous chapter and outlined in the above section, is different from the American and British systems in several respects. On the whole, it has less room for a suspect's resources and power to influence the outcome of his case. Thus, it is suggested that recorded delinquency and crime would be somewhat less socially biased than in most American and British cohorts, even disregarding the low degree of socio-economic heterogeneity and the relative lack of racial and ethnic factors in the cohort.

THE COHORT

Finally, a summary sketch of the cohort was put together from our data sets. Eighty-two per cent of both boys and girls were born in the Stockholm area; at age seven 94% of the members lived in the area. As already mentioned those born abroad or having a foreign-born parent constituted 8%. Of them, Scandinavians were 25%, Finns 42% and others (almost all Europeans) 33%. Four per cent of the cohort members were born to teenage mothers, and 10% were born out of wedlock. At cohort age four, that is, in 1957, less than a third of the non-married mothers were still non-married. At age ten, 89% of the children were living with both parents, 9% with the mother alone, and 1% in other types of family.

At cohort age seven, 13% of the members already in the metropolitan area lived in the Central City, 53% in suburban areas within the city and 34% in the suburban municipalities. Eighteen per cent of the members lived in overcrowded dwellings, if over-crowding was defined as more than two persons per room, kitchen excluded; only some 2% lived in one bedroom or smaller dwellings. Although most dwellings were small, their level of equipment tended to be fairly high: 84% of the families had 'fully equipped' dwellings; most dwellings not fully equipped were so classified, because they lacked a refrigerator or bath.

Table 3.2 shows the parental families distributed according to social class in 1953 and 1963. In the pre-school period, that is, until the age of seven, almost 10% of the families became Child Welfare Committee (CWC) cases, and a good 6% of the children were at some time, mostly in their first year, in social care. Fifteen per cent of the families received social assistance at least once during this period. However, the average amount received was

Table 3.2. *Parental families distributed according to social class in 1953 and 1963*

Social class	1953	1963
Upper middle	13.4	17.1
Lower middle, employees	30.8	34.7
Lower middle, entrepreneurs	6.1	7.6
Skilled workers	27.3	21.9
Unskilled workers	18.6	16.0
Unclassified	3.8	2.7
Total	100.0	100.0

less than 1,700 SEK (about US $325) per year, presumably used to help out when clothing, a baby carriage, or other things were needed. When the children were of the early school age, 11% of the families received social assistance at least once, whereas 1% received some assistance each year. The average amount received was 2,050 SEK (around US $400). Less than 3% of the families became CWC cases in these years. However, 4% of the boys themselves became CWC cases due to their behaviour. Of teenagers, 22% of the boys and 8% of the girls became known to the CWC because of problem behaviour.

During the spring semester of 1966, the year the cohort members turned thirteen, we found 88% of the boys and 92% of the girls in sixth grade, whereas 10% of the boys and 5% of the girls were one year behind, and 2% of the boys and 3% of the girls were one year ahead. About the same number of boys and girls, 47 and 48%, respectively, said they thought they would apply for senior secondary school. The last three grades (seventh to ninth) comprise the upper section of the comprehensive school. The chances to go on to three-year senior secondary school directly from there were slim, if one did not take a preparatory track. This route was followed by 44% of the boys and 52% of the girls. Of the boys 41% actually entered senior secondary school and 35% completed it. The corresponding percentages were 38 and 30 for the girls. For the boys basic military training was ten months, fifteen months if the boy was selected to be trained to be a sergeant. At age thirty, 14% of the men and 10% of the women had got a basic college degree after at least three years of undergraduate *postgymnasium* studies. In addition, 13% of the male cohort and 15% of the female cohort had completed two-year college programmes or were admitted to university programmes longer than three years but had not yet completed them. Adding these students to the

Table 3.3. *Selection to secondary education in the cohort, by social class and gender*

	Social class				Gender	
	Middle	Upper middle	Working	Total	Girls	Boys
Planning to take prep track	91	85	71	80	85	76
Passing prep track	81	56	32	51	55	47
Entering senior secondary school	72	44	20	40	38	41
Passing senior secondary school	66	40	18	33	30	35
At least two years of college	54	27	13	26	25	27

category of college students would almost level out the gender percentages to 27 and 25, respectively (Table 3.3).

Table 3.4 shows the cohort's distribution according to marital status in 1980, at cohort age twenty-seven, for all members then still in Sweden. Several non-married members were cohabiting, taking the total percentage of cohabiting members up to 47% among the men and to 60% among the women. Only 10% of the men and 4% of the women lived with their parents.

Table 3.4. *Cohort members distributed according to marital status in 1980. By gender*

Marital status	Men	Women
Single	75.7	56.8
Married, not cohabiting	1.2	2.5
Married, cohabiting	21.0	35.7
Divorced	2.1	4.9
Widowed	–	0.1
Total	100.0	100.0

Note: Figures refer to members living in Sweden, 97 per cent of male members and 96.3 per cent of female members.

Table 3.5. *Cohort members distributed according to dwelling size in 1980. By gender*

Dwelling size	Men	Women
One room and kitchen or less	21	14
Two rooms and kitchen	24	19
Three rooms and kitchen	29	33
Four rooms and kitchen	11	16
Five rooms and kitchen	11	15
Missing value	4	3
Total	100	100

Note: See Table 3.4.

Of the men, 77% lived in multifamily houses and 22% in one- or two-family houses, usually (13%) detached one-family houses. For women corresponding figures were 72%, 27% and 16%. Most cohort members, 64% of the men and 59% of the women, were living in rented dwellings; 14% of either gender lived in tenant-owner's apartments, whereas 17% of the men and 23% of the women lived in owner-occupied houses. Well over half the cohort lived in houses built in the last fifteen years, and 93% of the men and 95% of the women lived in fully equipped dwellings. The distribution according to dwelling size is given in Table 3.5. Nine per cent of both men and women lived in crowded quarters.

Tables 3.6 and 3.7 show the distributions according to employment and social class, respectively, in 1980, that is around the age of twenty-seven. In 1983, at the end of the observed period, 72% of the male members and 36%

Table 3.6. *Cohort members distributed according to employment in 1980 (first week of October). By gender*

Employment (hour/week)	Men	Women
Employed 35+	81	52
16–34	6	24
1–15	2	3
Students	6	7
Others	5	14
Total	100	100

Note: See Table 3.4.

Table 3.7. *Cohort members distributed according to social class in 1980. By gender*

Social class	Men	Women
High-level employees, professionals	12	6
Middle-level employees	28	35
Entrepreneurs	5	2
Low-grade employees	4	13
Skilled workers	19	8
Unskilled workers	22	17
Students	8	8
Homemakers	—	9
Others	2	2
Total	100	100

Note: See Table 3.4. Note also that some 'students' were differently classified as to employment in Table 3.6.

of the female members had neither a child of their own, nor one of their partner's living in the household, whereas 25% of the males and 56% of the females had one or two children in the household (Table 3.8). Finally, at least once in the last two years 13% of the men and 14% of the women received some social assistance. In the last year 97% of the men and 96% of the women still in Sweden had an assessed income, the median value of which was 82,024 SEK for the men and 62,036 SEK for the women.[10]

Table 3.8. *Cohort members distributed according to number of children in the family in 1983. By gender*

Number of children	Men	Women
0	72	36
1	11	26
2	14	30
3	3	7
4+	—	1
Total	100	100

Note: The table refers to cohort members in Sweden in 1983, 96.2 per cent of the male members and 95.7 per cent of the female members.

POSTSCRIPT

When the project left the cohort members in 1985, they were around thirty-two years old. Since then some fundamental changes have fallen upon them and Swedish society generally. Immigration has continued, so that now around two million out of a population of some nine million are said to be first or second generation immigrants, which is a higher rate than in most other EU countries. Almost all recent non-Nordic arrivals are refugees or close relatives to earlier arrivals, often coming from the former Yugoslavia, the Middle East (Lebanon, Iraq), Africa (Ethiopia, Somalia), or south-west Asia (Iran). To most Swedes the fact that the state church is severing its ties to the state is less fateful than the fact that Muslims now have become a religious group of the same order of magnitude as Catholics and the non-conformist churches, as an indication of irrevocable change into a multicultural and ethnically heterogeneous society.

Another momentous change was more sudden, although with hindsight one might have seen it coming. In the early 1990s a rapidly growing national debt developed from a financial crisis into a general depression: from 1.6% unemployed in 1990 and 3.0% in 1991, the unemployment rose to 5.2% in 1992 and 8.2% in 1993, high above the rates in the post-war period.

A taxing and bewildering decade followed with local scandals, new priorities and reassessments. There were cuts made in the public sector and jobs were lost. There were new or increased fees and fares especially in the health services, lowered pensions and less social assistance. In the private sector cases of downsizing, outsourcing and emigration attracted attention. So did the booming export business – helped by an undervalued currency, the soaring share prices and dividends, and the ever increasing remuneration for the upper tiers of management. Then, in the last years of the old millennium, the depression seemed to be over, and good growth and budget surpluses expected for the next few years. However, although the unemployment rate went down somewhat, to 6.5 in 1998 and to 5.6 in 1999, it has not come near the low levels of the earlier post-war decades.

Furthermore, there seems to be slim chance of ever returning to the Swedish-model welfare state that overextended itself and led up to the overheated situation of the late 1980s. As a huge increase in the number of old people can be anticipated, a new and less generous pension policy has been put in place to start gradually for those born in 1938 or later. A widespread opinion has it that the post-war welfare policy made Sweden trail behind other countries from around 1970. Low inflation rather than low unemployment has become the prime task of economic policy.

However, since Sweden is part of the European Community and a global economy, her public sector is not much larger than other comparable countries. Thus, for the foreseeable future, at least the post-war decades up to the 1990s will remain, in some ways, the Swedish version of a welfare state. As emphasised in the first paragraph of this chapter, any empirical study is based on a given moment in time and space. A cohort of Stockholmers born in 1983 and living in Stockholm in 1993, say, would have a rather different composition and a rather different context, leading, presumably, to rather different outcomes.

NOTES

1. A more detailed distribution of foreign-born persons and non-citizens in Stockholm County runs as follows: Finland 6.4%, Scandinavia 1.1%; other European countries 4.8% (of which FRG 0.8%, Yugoslavia, Greece, Poland 0.6, and the Baltic states 0.6% each, UK and Hungary both 0.3%); North America 0.3%; South America 0.7% (of which Chile 0.4%); Soviet Union 0.1%; Turkey 0.8%; Middle East and North Africa 0.6%, Sub-Saharan countries 0.2%; others 0.6% (including adopted children, mostly from Korea). The metropolitan area had roughly the same percentages, as the somewhat lower rates outside the area were balanced by the concentration of (mostly) Turks in an independent industrial town. A clear majority of foreign citizens and foreign-born people lived outside districts that had at least twice the percentage of these categories.

   Generally, with regards to sources of information on Sweden and Stockholm: if other sources are not given, the information was taken from the annual *Statistical Abstract of Sweden, Statistical Abstract of Stockholm,* or other official statistics (*SOS*), or from the *Nationalencyklopedin* or other encyclopaedias. Especially on immigrants: SOS *Tema invandrare* (Theme Immigrants). Report 1984, p. 38; on immigrants in Stockholm County. Regionplankontoret *Invandrare i Stockholms län* (Immigrants in Stockholm County). Report 1984, p. 5, and Regionplanekontoret *Områdesdata 1983* (Data by District 1983). Report 1983: 1. Important policy decisions on immigration 1943–98 are listed in Lundh and Ohlsson, 1999, 173f.

2. For a history of the Swedish Welfare System, see Olson Hort, 1993 or Elmér *et al.,* 1998.

3. Including sickness insurance, public health care and hospitals, care of the mentally retarded, dental care, occupational injury insurance, unemployment insurance and benefits, retraining of unemployed persons, public works, retirement and early retirement pensions, national supplementary pensions (ATP), care of the disabled, assistance for the aged and the disabled, parent cash benefits, general child allowance, school meals, childcare (day nurseries and nursery schools etc.), individual and family social assistance, criminal care and administrative costs of these programmes.

4. Most readers probably feel more at home with Duncan's measure of dissimilarity (Duncan and Duncan, 1955), but the standard deviation measure (Jahn, Schmid and Schrag, 1947) was used on the old data and so was applied also on the

newer ones. In a sample of forty-four US cities in 1940 the standard deviation measure correlated 0.91 with a measure that effectively was dissimilarity, on race segregation. It gave an average segregation of 0.59, whereas the average dissimilarity was 0.53 (ibid, p. 301f).

5. For a discussion of inequality in the Swedish post-war educational system, see Erikson and Jonsson, 1996, chs 1 and 2).

6. All figures about drug abuse are taken from *Alkohol- och narkotikautvecklingen i Sverige*, 1995. The quote is from the same source, page 41.

7. Note that the Child Welfare Committee (after 1971 a section of the municipality's central social agency) to which the prosecutor may hand over a juvenile delinquent according to the Young Offenders Bill of 1964 (1944), is not concerned with the judicial aspects of the case but only with what would be best for the youngster (Janson and Torstensson, 1984).

8. On the whole, the Swedish law profession is less numerous and prominent than its US counterpart, with less litigation and much smaller damages meted out in Swedish courts.

9. This refers to the most serious case of drunken driving, driving while having more than 1.5 ml alcohol per litres blood. The severe sentence policy clearly turned drunken driving into a deviance.

10. According to the extreme exchange rate in 1983 the median assessed incomes were only US $10,250 and US $7,750, respectively.

CHAPTER 4

CRIMINALITY

We first proceeded with an epidemiological investigation comparing convictions for criminal offences[1] among subjects in the five groups. Three groups of subjects had been admitted to a psychiatric ward by age 30: (1) those with diagnoses of major mental disorders; (2) those with alcohol and/or drug related disorders; (3) those with other disorders. A fourth group of subjects were mentally retarded, and the fifth group is composed of all those cohort members who had never been admitted to a psychiatric ward nor to a special stream in school for retarded children.

PREVALENCE OF CRIMINALITY AMONG THE PROJECT METROPOLITAN SUBJECTS

Table 4.1 presents the percentages and numbers of subjects in each group that had been convicted of at least one crime by age thirty. Among the men with no mental disorder or retardation, 31.7% were registered for a crime. In comparison, 50% of those with a major mental disorder, 92.9% of those with a diagnosis of substance abuse/dependence, 37.5% of those with other mental disorders, and 56.7% of the mentally retarded men[2] were registered for at least one crime. The pattern is similar among the women. While 5.8% with no disorder were registered for at least one crime, 19.0% of those with a major mental disorder, 12.1% of those with other mental disorders, 70.7% of those with diagnoses of substance abuse/dependence, and 16.1% of the mentally retarded women[2] were registered for at least one crime. Both among men and women, more of the subjects who developed a major mental disorder than those who had not been admitted to a psychiatric hospital (and who were not mentally retarded) were convicted of at least one criminal offence by age thirty. While many more of the men than the women were convicted of offences, the difference in the percentages of subjects with

77

Table 4.1. *Per cent men and women in each group convicted for at least one offence*

	Men	Women
No hospitalisation,	31.7%	5.8%
no retardation (NMD)	(2475)	(389)
Major mental disorder (MMD)	50.0%	19.0%
	(41)	(15)
Other mental disorder (OMD)	37.5%	12.1%
	(24)	(15)
Substance use disorder (SA)	92.9%	70.7%
	(143)	(65)
Mental retardation (MR)	56.5%	15.3%
	(65)	(13)

	Men	Women
NMD × MMD	$X^2(1, N = 7029) = 12.50,$ $p = .004$	$X^2(1, N = 6738) = 23.94,$ $p = .00000$
NMD × OMD	$X^2(1, N = 7011) = 0.98,$ $p = .32$	$X^2(1, N = 6783) = 8.50,$ $p = .004$
NMD × SA	$X^2(1, N = 7101) = 254.79,$ $p = .00000$	$X^2(1, N = 6751) = 607.67,$ $p = .00000$
NMD × MR	$X^2(1, N = 7067) = 31.99,$ $p = .00000$	$X^2(1, N = 6746) = 13.37,$ $p = .00025$

major mental disorders and those with no disorder who offended is much greater for the women than it is for the men. In other words, the presence of a major mental disorder is associated with a greater increase in the risk of offending for women than for men. This can be expressed quantitatively using a statistic called the relative risk estimate. In using this statistic, the risk of offending among the non-disordered subjects is set at one. The risk of offending among men who developed a major mental disorder is 2.15 (1.39 to 3.33 at 95% confidence bounds) times greater than the risk among the non-disordered men. The risk among the women with major mental disorders is 3.78 (2.13 to 6.69 at 95% confidence bounds) times higher than that of the non-disordered women.

Several factors mitigated against finding a difference in the proportions of mentally disordered and non-disordered subjects who were convicted of crimes. First, as noted in Chapter 2, the cohort members sent to hospital by the court were not counted. All of them had a diagnosis of psychosis and if included in our major mental disorder group they increase the proportion of men with major mental disorders who offended by 6%. Second, men with psychoses had less opportunity than other subjects to commit crimes as they were hospitalised, on average, for 552 days. A third factor which also lessens the likelihood of finding higher rates of offending for those suffering from major mental disorders, is the way in which admissions were documented. Patients still in hospital at the time the data were collected were not included in the mentally disordered category. A fourth factor which lessens the likelihood of finding a difference in the proportions of mentally ill and non-mentally ill who offend is the age of the subjects. They were only thirty years old when criminal offences were documented. Both investigations of persons responsible for violent crimes and judged mentally disordered (Häfner and Böker, 1982; Hodgins, Webster, and Paquet, 1990; 1991; Hodgins, Webster, Paquet, and Zellerer, 1989; Pasewark, 1982; Walker and McCabe, 1973), and of inmates with major mental disorders (Hodgins and Côté, 1990), suggest that the mentally disordered commit crimes later in life than the non-mentally disordered. As well as not having passed through the risk period for criminal behaviour, the subjects in this cohort had not passed through the risk period for the major mental disorders (Robins *et al.*, 1984). Thus, the age of the subjects would be expected to lessen the probability of finding a difference in the proportions of the mentally disordered and the non-mentally disordered subjects who were convicted of a crime.

Finally, it has been suggested (Belfrage, 1998; Lidberg, Wiklund, and Jacobsson, 1988) that offenders who suffer from major mental disorders die at younger ages than other offenders and non-offenders. If this were true, it would lessen the likelihood of finding a greater proportion of the mentally ill than the non-mentally ill who offend. However, this was not the case in the present investigation. While rates of premature death were higher among both men (7.9%) and women (2.5%) with major mental disorders than among non-disordered men (1.6%) and women (0.7%), there was no increase in convictions among the deceased with a major mental disorder.

Number of convictions

The analyses which follow include only the subjects that have at least one conviction. Throughout, they are referred to as the offenders. The mean number of offences committed by offenders in each group is presented in Table 4.2. Among the non-hospitalised and non-retarded male offenders, the mean number of convictions was 8.2, among offenders with a major mental disorder it was 16.3, among substance abusers 36.7, among the offenders with other mental disorders it was 17.4, and 10.6 for the mentally retarded. Similarly, among the female offenders, those with no disorder and no handicap had a mean number of convictions of 4.1, those with a major disorder 4.6, those with other mental disorders 4.7, those with substance abuse 14.9, and the mentally retarded 13.8.

Table 4.2. *Mean number of offences*

	Men	Women
No hospitalisation,	8.2	4.1
no retardation (NMD)	(SD = 22.1)	(SD = 11.6)
Major mental disorder (MMD)	16.3	4.6
	(SD = 20.4)	(SD = 8.4)
Other mental disorder (OMD)	17.4	4.7
	(SD = 24.4)	(SD = 4.3)
Substance use disorder (SA)	36.7	14.9
	(SD = 46.0)	(SD = 24.5)
Mental retardation (MR)	10.6	13.8
	(SD = 17.1)	(SD = 17.8)

	Men	Women
NMD × MMD	t(2241) = 2.32, p = .02	t(402) = 0.15, p = .88
NMD × OMD	t(2224) = 2.02, p = .04	t(22.79) = 0.46, p = .65
NMD × SA	t(146.29) = 7.35, p = .000	t(68.85) = 3.48, p = .001
NMD × MR	t(70.47) = 1.10, p = .277	t(12.34) = 1.95, p = .074

In examining the average number of offences committed by the offenders in each group, note that the standard deviations (*SD*) are large. This
indicates that within each group some of the offenders were convicted of
many crimes while others were convicted of only one or a few crimes. Despite the large standard deviation, as a group, the mentally ill male offenders
have committed, on average, many more crimes than the non-disordered
male offenders. Why would the men suffering from major mental disorders
have accumulated so many more convictions than the non-mentally ill offenders? It may be the case that subjects with major mental disorders while
in the community commit more crimes than other types of offenders. If this
is true, it suggests that they are offending at a very high rate because they
spend time in hospital and are consequently in the community and at risk
to offend for less time than the non-disordered offenders. Alternatively, it
may be that they do not commit more crimes than other types of offenders, but that they are more likely to be detected, arrested, and prosecuted
for their acts. This possibility is discussed in greater detail in Chapter 5. A
third explanation for these findings relates to the classification of subjects
in the five groups. The non-disordered group should include the men in
the cohort who are usually thought to be the most likely to offend repeti-
tively, for example psychopaths, those with antisocial personality disorders

(ASPD) and rapists. It is possible, however, that some of these men who would be diagnosed as psychopaths or as having an antisocial personality disorder were not assigned to the non-disordered group but rather to the substance abuse group. It is well known that most men who meet diagnostic criteria for either psychopathy or ASPD also present alcohol and/or drug use disorders at an early age. Consequently, they may have been hospitalised and then by definition assigned to the substance abuse group. It is not possible to test this latter explanation as it is not known what proportion of offenders with substance abuse disorders were hospitalised before the age of thirty at this time in Stockholm. Regardless of whether the offenders who would be diagnosed as psychopaths or as having an antisocial personality disorder are classified in the non-disordered or substance abuse group, the male offenders with major mental disorders are very active and have committed, on average, many offences by age thirty. Even the women with major mental disorders have been convicted, on average, for as many offences as the non-disordered female offenders.

Types of offences
Offences were divided into seven categories. The category 'violent crimes' includes all offences involving the use or threat of physical violence (for example, assault, rape, robbery, unlawful threat, molestation). 'Theft' includes all forms of stealing other than robbery, as well as receiving stolen goods. 'Fraud' includes embezzlement, crimes related to debts, and crimes of falsification. The category of 'traffic crimes' does not include minor offences such as speeding. Drunken driving and driving without a licence are the most frequent offences in this category. The category 'other', is very heterogeneous, including offences such as defamation, sexual crimes other than rape, sexual coercion, perjury, gambling, bribery, absent without leave from the military, smuggling, and tax evasion.

As can be observed in Table 4.3, the various diagnoses are associated with all seven categories of crimes as indicated by significant across group chi-square comparisons. Two by two comparisons were conducted: the percentage of subjects with no mental disorder or retardation was compared to the percentage of subjects in each diagnostic group who were convicted of at least one crime in each category. These comparisons presented at the bottom of Table 4.3 demonstrate that, as compared to the men with no disorder and no retardation, male subjects with major mental disorders were registered for more crimes of every type except those related to driving. More of the men with other mental disorders committed fraud and vandalism. More of the men hospitalised for substance abuse, than the non-disordered

Table 4.3. *Per cent men in each group convicted by offence type*

Type of offence	No mental disorder or retardation	Major mental disorders	Other mental disorders	Substance abuse	Mentally retarded	All disorders
Violent offences	6.4%	24.4%^{A}	9.4%	53.2%^{I}	22.6%^{P}	X^2(1, N = 7362) = 526.19***
Theft	17.4%	35.4%^{B}	25.0%	79.2%^{J}	36.5%^{Q}	X^2(1, N = 7362) = 407.13***
Fraud	4.8%	15.8%^{C}	15.6%^{G}	57.8%^{K}	8.7%	X^2(1, N = 7362) = 758.93***
Vandalism	4.8%	14.6%^{D}	14.1%^{H}	42.2%^{L}	11.3%^{R}	X^2(1, N = 7362) = 411.90***
Traffic offences	14.5%	22.0%	20.3%	57.1%^{M}	30.4%^{S}	X^2(1, N = 7362) = 229.62***
Narcotic offences	3.2%	11.0%^{E}	3.1%	53.2%^{N}	4.3%	X^2(1, N = 7362) = 906.96***
Other	1.20%	26.8%^{F}	15.6%	57.1%^{O}	24.3%^{T}	X^2(1, N = 7362) = 292.05***

Statistically significant comparisons between each diagnostic group and the no mental disorder or retardation group

^{A}X^2(1, N = 7029) = 42.74** ^{F}X^2(1, N = 7029) = 16.70** ^{K}X^2(1, N = 7101) = 761.29** ^{P}X^2(1, N = 7062) = 48.07**

^{B}X^2(1, N = 7029) = 17.90** ^{G}X^2(1, N = 7011) = 16.61** ^{L}X^2(1, N = 7101) = 402.40** ^{Q}X^2(1, N = 7062) = 28.19**

^{C}X^2(1, N = 7029) = 21.41** ^{H}X^2(1, N = 7011) = 11.95** ^{M}X^2(1, N = 7101) = 210.70** ^{R}X^2(1, N = 7062) = 10.52*

^{D}X^2(1, N = 7029) = 17.10** ^{I}X^2(1, N = 7101) = 483.40** ^{N}X^2(1, N = 7101) = 910.86** ^{S}X^2(1, N = 7062) = 22.97**

^{E}X^2(1, N = 7029) = 15.07** ^{J}X^2(1, N = 7101) = 376.83** ^{O}X^2(1, N = 7101) = 272.11** ^{T}X^2(1, N = 7062) = 16.4**

*P = .01 corrected for Type 1 error by the Bonferroni's formula = .002

**P = .001 corrected for Type 1 error by Bonferroni's formula = .0001

***P = .00000

men, committed crimes of every type. More of the mentally retarded men committed violent offences, thefts, vandalism, traffic offences, and offences classified as 'other'.

In examining the types of offences committed by the men with major mental disorders, note that almost a quarter of the offenders had been convicted of at least one violent offence, more than a third for theft, and more than a quarter for offences classified as 'other'. These are the kinds of offences Belfrage (1998) has labelled as 'social drop-out criminality'. In fact, what distinguish the male offenders with major mental disorders are the proportions of subjects who commit violent and 'other' offences. The differences in the proportions of mentally ill and non-disordered men who committed crimes of violence and those classified as 'other' are greater than those for the other types of offences.

Among the men with major mental disorders, the risk of committing a violent crime was found to be greater than the risk of committing any offence. Men with major mental disorders were 4.74 (2.84 to 7.91 at 95% confidence bounds) times more likely to have been convicted of a violent offence than men with no mental disorder or retardation. The comparable relative risk estimate for men with other disorders is 1.52 (0.65 to 3.54 at 95% confidence bounds); 16.72 (12.01 to 23.28 at 95% confidence bounds) times for men with diagnoses of substance abuse/dependence; and 4.29 (2.74 to 6.71 at 95% confidence bounds) times for mentally retarded men.

As can be seen in Table 4.4, almost 14% of the women with major mental disorders were convicted for theft, 6% for violence, 4% for fraud, 1% for vandalism, traffic, and 'other' offences, and 0% for drug-related offences. While these percentages appear strikingly low after having reviewed those for men, in comparison to the women who had not been hospitalised and who were not mentally retarded, significantly more of the mentally ill women were prosecuted for violence and theft. The women with major mental disorders were 11.18 times (4.30 to 29.13 at 95% confidence bounds) more likely to have been convicted of a violent offence than women with no disorder or retardation. The comparable relative risk estimate for the women with other mental disorders is 2.71 (0.65 to 11.35 at 95% confidence bounds), 61.74 (35.46 to 107.52 at 95% confidence bounds) for women with diagnoses of substance abuse/dependence, and 10.34 (3.98 to 26.89 at 95% confidence bounds) for mentally retarded women.

Gender differences and similarities are notable in Tables 4.3 and 4.4. These tables emphasise again that many more men than women are convicted of crimes. This was found to be true for both the non-hospitalised, non-retarded group and for the group with major mental disorders. In

Table 4.4. *Per cent women in each group convicted by offence type*

Type of offence	No mental disorder or retardation	Major mental disorders	Other mental disorders	Substance abuse	Mentally retarded	All disorders
Violent offences	0.6%	6.3%^{A}	2.0%	27.2%^{C}	5.9%^{J}	X^2(1, N = 7039) = 631.67***
Theft	3.6%	13.9%^{B}	7.3%	53.3%^{D}	9.4%^{K}	X^2(1, N = 7039) = 550.55***
Fraud	1.3%	3.8%	4.0%	34.8%^{E}	13.52%^{L}	X^2(1, N = 7039) = 575.05***
Vandalism	0.2%	1.3%	0.0	18.5%^{F}	0.0	X^2(1, N = 7039) = 718.16***
Traffic offences	1.2%	1.3%	0.8%	10.9%^{G}	4.7%	X^2(1, N = 7039) = 69.50***
Narcotic offences	0.7%	0.0	1.6%	27.2%^{H}	3.5%	X^2(1, N = 7039) = 619.51***
Other	0.7%	1.3%	0.8%	27.2%^{I}	3.5%	X^2(1, N = 7039) = 600.84***

Statistically significant comparisons between each diagnostic group and the no mental disorder or retardation group

^{A}X^2(1, N = 6738) = 36.62*** ^{F}X^2(1, N = 6751) = 710.36*** ^{K}X^2(1, N = 6744) = 8.21*

^{B}X^2(1, N = 6738) = 23.66*** ^{G}X^2(1, N = 6751) = 63.59*** ^{L}X^2(1, N = 6744) = 13.52**

^{C}X^2(1, N = 6751) = 672.01*** ^{H}X^2(1, N = 6751) = 630.57***

^{D}X^2(1, N = 6751) = 552.55*** ^{I}X^2(1, N = 6751) = 611.60***

^{E}X^2(1, N = 6751) = 598.21*** ^{J}X^2(1, N = 6744) = 35.32***

*P = .05 corrected for Type 1 error by Bonferroni's formula = .007

**P = .001 corrected for Type 1 error by Bonferroni's formula = .0001

***P = .00000

noting this difference, it is important to remember that it may result in part from differences in the behaviours of men and women, but also from differences in the attitudes of the police, lawyers and judges to prosecuting and convicting men and women for criminal offences. A second gender difference relates to the types of crimes committed by the mentally ill subjects. While many men with major mental disorders were convicted of offences classified as 'other', this was not true for the women with the same disorders. The mentally ill men and women were similar in that both sexes were at greater risk of being convicted of a violent offence than of any other crime.

Age at first conviction

The patterns of the proportions of subjects within each diagnostic group who had been convicted of a criminal offence are relatively stable over time, both for the men and the women. In fact, chi squares calculated separately for gender, and on group differences for convictions before age fifteen, from ages fifteen to eighteen, eighteen to twenty-one, and twenty-one to thirty were all highly significant. In all age groups, the percentages of subjects with a major mental disorder, substance abuse, or mental retardation who had been convicted of a crime exceed those of the subjects with no mental disorder and no retardation. However, as indicated in Tables 4.5 and 4.6, these proportions are not always statistically significantly different from those of the non-disordered, non-retarded group, especially among the women. This is most likely due to the small number of subjects in each cell of the table.

As can be observed in Table 4.5, official criminal activity appears to begin at different ages for the different groups of male subjects. Among the men with no disorder and no retardation and those with an adult substance abuse diagnosis, the proportions of subjects beginning their criminal careers decrease with age. This pattern also describes the mentally-retarded subjects but the decrease only begins after age eighteen. By contrast, among the men who develop major mental disorders the proportions who begin their criminal career at each age are more erratic – 15.9% at less than fifteen years, 15.9% between the ages of fifteen and eighteen years, 6.1% between the ages of eighteen and twenty-one years, and 12.2% between the ages of twenty-one and thirty. The largest difference between the non-disordered and mentally ill men with regard to age at first offence, is evident after age twenty-one. Proportionately, twice as many mentally ill men as non-mentally ill men, begin offending as adults.

As can be observed in Table 4.6, the proportion of women with no disorder and no retardation who begin their criminal career remains relatively stable

Table 4.5. *Per cent men subjects in each group first convicted at different ages*

	No mental disorder	Major mental disorders	Other mental disorders	Substance abuse	Mentally retarded
Less than 15 years	10.8%	15.9%^{A}	9.4%^{E}	42.9%^{I}	18.3%
	(750)	(13)	(6)	(66)	(21)
15 to 18 years	8.3%	15.9%^{B}	10.9%^{F}	30.5%^{J}	20.9%
	(575)	(13)	(7)	(47)	(24)
18 to 21 years	6.2%	6.1%^{C}	14.1%^{G}	9.7%^{K}	7.0%
	(433)	(5)	(9)	(15)	(8)
21 to 30 years	6.4%	12.2%^{D}	3.1%^{H}	9.7%^{L}	10.4%
	(444)	(10)	(2)	(15)	(12)
Total number of offenders	32.3%	50%	37.5%	92.9%	56.5%
	(2243)	(41)	(24)	(143)	(65)
Total number of subjects	100.0%	100.0%	100.0%	100.0%	100.0%
	(6947)	(82)	(64)	(154)	(115)

The numbers of offenders are slightly smaller than those presented in the section on the prevalence of criminality. This is because sometimes the record indicated the offence but not the date of conviction.

^{A}NMD × MMD X^2(1, N = 7029) = 2.14 $\quad$ ^{G}NMD × OMD X^2(1, N = 5673) = 6.96*
^{B}NMD × MMD X^2(1, N = 6266) = 7.34* $\quad$ ^{H}NMD × OMD X^2(1, N = 5231) = 0.77
^{C}NMD × MMD X^2(1, N = 5678) = 0.12 $\quad$ ^{I}NMD × SA X^2(1, N = 7101) = 152.26**
^{D}NMD × MMD X^2(1, N = 5240) = 7.79* $\quad$ ^{J}NMD × SA X^2(1, N = 6285) = 189.50**
^{E}NMD × OMD X^2(1, N = 7011) = 0.13 $\quad$ ^{K}NMD × SA X^2(1, N = 5563) = 46.62**
^{F}NMD × OMD X^2(1, N = 6255) = 0.53 $\quad$ ^{L}NMD × SA X^2(1, N = 5215) = 77.81**
p = .05 corrected for Type 1 error by Bonferroni formula = .0125
*p < .05
**p < .00001

over time. Among the women who develop major mental disorders, there is a decrease in the proportion beginning their criminal career between the ages of fifteen and eighteen, with the proportions at other age periods being similar. Unlike the men, among the substance abusers the proportion of subjects beginning their criminal careers continues to increase up to age thirty.

To resume, while more than half of the men with major disorders were first registered for a crime before the age of eighteen, another 12 per cent of them were first registered after the age of twenty-one. This is double the percentage of non-disordered men who were first registered after age twenty-one. It suggests that there are two groups of offenders with major mental disorders: one group begins offending early before the symptoms of

Table 4.6. *Per cent women in each group first convicted at different ages*

	No mental disorder	Major mental disorders	Other mental disorders	Substance abuse	Mentally retarded
Less than 15 years	1.7%	5.1%	2.4%	12.0%	3.5%
	(112)	(4)	(3)	(11)	(3)
15 to 18 years	1.1%	2.5%	1.6%	17.4%	2.4%
	(78)	(2)	(2)	(16)	(2)
18 to 21 years	1.0%	5.1%	2.4%	18.5%	5.9%
	(69)	(4)	(3)	(17)	(5)
21 to 30 years	1.9%	6.3%	5.6%	22.9%	3.5%
	(130)	(5)	(7)	(21)	(3)
Total number of offenders	5.8%	19.0%	12.1%	70.7%	15.3%
	(389)	(15)	(15)	(65)	(13)
Total number of subjects	100.0%	100.0%	100.0%	100.0%	100.0%
	(6659)	(79)	(124)	(92)	(85)

The numbers of offenders are slightly smaller than those presented in the section on the prevalence of criminality. This is because sometimes the record indicated the offence but not the date of conviction.

the mental disorder would be present, while the second begins offending only later when symptoms of the disorder are likely to be present. This hypothesis applies equally well to the women with major mental disorders, as can be observed in Table 4.6.

Duration of criminal activity

Criminality was examined during four time periods based on the subjects' ages: before age fifteen, between the ages of fifteen and eighteen, between the ages of eighteen to twenty-one, and from age twenty-one to thirty. While 12.0% of the non-disordered, non-retarded men were convicted during two or more of these time periods, 30.5% of those with major disorders, 20.3% of the men with other disorders, 76.6% of the substance abusers, and 33.9% of the mentally retarded were convicted in at least two different time periods. Given the small number of female subjects in each group, patterns of convictions over time are difficult to verify.

Resume

The data from this birth cohort, followed prospectively from pregnancy to age thirty, have demonstrated that among both men and women, the proportions of subjects with at least one criminal offence vary significantly by adult mental status. Men with a major mental disorder were twice as likely as men with no mental disorder or retardation to be registered for a criminal offence. Among women, the risk of criminality for those with a major mental disorder was almost four times higher than for women with no mental disorder or retardation. This was true despite the fact that some seriously ill subjects were not prosecuted for offences, that the mentally disordered subjects spent less time in the community at risk of offending than did the non-disordered subjects, and that the subjects were only thirty years of age when the data were collected.

On average, the men with major mental disorders had been convicted of more offences than the non-disordered, non-retarded men, but fewer than the men who had been admitted to hospital with alcohol and/or drug use disorders. The women with major mental disorders had committed, on average, as many offences as the non-disordered women but fewer than the women with substance use disorders.

The risks of violent offending, for both males and females with major mental disorders, were even higher than for offending in general. Men with major mental disorders were almost five times more likely than non-disordered men to be convicted of a violent offence. Women with major mental disorders were eleven times more likely to be convicted of a violent offence than the non-disordered, non-retarded women. While many men with major mental disorders committed offences classified as 'other' in the present project, this was not true of the mentally ill women. Both mentally ill men and women offenders committed offences of all types, but the mentally ill male offenders were more diversified in their offending than the mentally ill females.

The criminal behaviour of subjects who eventually developed major disorders often appeared in early adolescence, well before the mental disorder would have been diagnosed. Another rather large group of subjects with major mental disorders began offending after age twenty-one. This age pattern at first conviction differentiated the men and women who developed major mental disorders from the men and women with no disorder.

GENERALISATION OF THESE RESULTS

Can we generalise from the results of this study to other places and times? The specific crime rates are not generalisable to other jurisdictions. The between group comparisons are probably only generalisable to other countries with mental health systems, criminal justice systems, and social welfare systems similar to those in Sweden. To illustrate, the present results, as will be seen in a subsequent section of this chapter, are similar to results from other birth cohort studies conducted in Scandinavia (Hodgins, Mednick, Brennan, Schulsinger, and Engberg, 1996; Ortmann, 1981; Tiihonen, Isohani, Räsänen, Koiranen, and Moring, 1997), and to those from an Australian population cohort (Wallace, Mullen, Burgess, Palmer, Ruschena, and Brown, 1998). But consider extrapolating these results to a society with different health and social systems, like the United States. Presume that in the US there is more crime and substance abuse than in Sweden, but similar prevalence rates for the major mental disorders. Follow-up studies of mentally disordered persons would be expected to show that disproportionately more of the disordered than non-disordered subjects living in the same neighbourhood commit crimes and violence. US offenders would be expected to include greater proportions of subjects with major mental disorders than the general US population. This is exactly what most studies have reported. However, given the high rate of crime and of crime by substance abusers in the US, the crimes of those with major disorders may seem insignificant in comparison (see for example, Monahan and Arnold, 1996). Since the prevalence rates of the major mental disorders are similar in most Western industrialised countries, the lower the overall crime rate in these societies the greater the proportion of offences that are committed by the mentally ill. This seems to be especially true for homicide.

The within group rates from the present investigation may be generalisable. In other words, the differences in the relative risks for crime and for violence documented for subjects with major mental disorders and those with no disorders may be generalisable to other societies with similar mental health policies and practices. The external validity of these findings may depend on the similarity of the ratio of crimes leading to prosecution compared to crimes committed, and to the similarity of the attitudes of the police and prosecutors towards the mentally disordered. Given what we have learned about the effect of mental health policy and services on the likelihood of criminal behaviour among persons with major mental disorders, the results of the present investigation may not be generalisable to other periods of time when these policies and services differed.

CONSISTENCY

Are the findings on the criminality of persons with mental disorders from the Project Metropolitan consistent with findings from other similar investigations? Yes.

BIRTH COHORT STUDIES

One study of a Danish birth cohort was completed before the present study, and three other investigations of birth cohorts subsequently. They used methodologies very similar to that of the present study: the cohorts were defined to include all the individuals born in a designated geographical area during a specific time period; hospitalisation on a psychiatric ward was used as an indicator of mental disorder; and all hospitalisations and convictions for criminal offences were documented from national registers.

Men born in Copenhagen in 1953, followed to 1975

Ortmann (1981) examined the criminal records of a birth cohort composed of 11,540 men born in Copenhagen in 1953 and still alive in Denmark in 1975. Data on admissions to psychiatric wards were collected from the central Danish psychiatric register in 1978 when the subjects were twenty-five years old. Data on offences were collected from the central police register in 1976 when the subjects were twenty-three years old. While 34.8% of the men with no disorder had been registered for at least one offence, 43.5% of those admitted with a major disorder, 83.2% of those admitted with abuse and/or dependence, and 50.9% of those with other diagnoses had been registered for an offence. Significantly more of those with psychiatric admissions had been convicted for every type of offence. While there were not many subjects within each diagnostic group, Ortmann's results suggested that the rates of conviction for criminal offences varied considerably by diagnosis.

Men and women born in Denmark in 1944 to 1947, followed to 1990

The cohort was composed of all persons born in Denmark in the years 1944 through 1947. After excluding those who died and who emigrated before 1990, 158,799 female and 165,602 male subjects remained in the analyses (Hodgins *et al.*, 1996). In 1990, when they were between forty-three and forty-six years old, the psychiatric register was screened to identify all of the subjects' admissions to psychiatric wards, dates of admission and discharge, and discharge diagnoses. At the same time, the national police register was screened to identify all arrests and convictions. Once the information from the psychiatric and criminal registers had been computerised, a third party named by the Minister of Justice merged the two tapes and de-identified the information.

As had been done in the Project Metropolitan, the first step in the data analysis was to divide the subjects into diagnostic groups, seven of whom

Table 4.7. *Danish cohort: Per cent men registered for at least one crime (n = 165,602)*

	Ages 12–15 – 30–33	Ages 30–33 – 43–46
No hospitalisation (n = 155, 580)	8.3%	6.1%
Major mental disorder (n = 3130)	19.1%	23.0%
Mental retardation (n = 297)	46.8%	42.4%
Organic disorder (n = 101)	27.7%	31.7%
Antisocial personality disorder (n = 3069)	34.7%	32.4%
Drug use disorder (n = 208)	45.2%	46.2%
Alcohol use disorder (n = 1731)	29.1%	35.8%
Other disorder (n = 1486)	20.6%	16.7%

had been admitted to a psychiatric ward at least once and one group who had never been admitted. The national police data-recording procedure changed in Denmark in 1978 when a computerised system was instituted. In order to ensure that the results were valid, all analyses were conducted separately for the manual criminal register and for the computerised register.

As can be seen by examining Tables 4.7 and 4.8, both men and women who had been hospitalised in psychiatry were more likely than individuals never admitted to a psychiatric ward to have been convicted of a criminal offence by age forty-three. While the percentages of subjects who had been convicted of a crime are much lower in the Danish cohort than in the Swedish Project Metropolitan, as can be seen in Table 4.9 the increases in the risk of criminality among the mentally disordered as compared to the non-disordered are similar. This is noted by comparing the relative risk estimates which take account of the differences in the base rates of crime in the two cohorts by setting the risk among the non-hospitalised group at one. As presented in Table 4.9, the risks of criminality among the subjects with a

Table 4.8. *Danish cohort: Per cent women registered for at least one crime (n = 158,799)*

	Ages 12–15 – 30–33	Ages 30–33 – 43–46
No hospitalisation (n = 147, 367)	1.3%	2.1%
Major mental disorder (n = 3900)	4.4%	9.5%
Mental retardation (n = 318)	13.5%	11.6%
Organic disorder (n = 73)	4.1%	9.6%
Antisocial personality disorder (n = 3553)	7.0%	13.6%
Drug use disorder (n = 249)	8.8%	23.7%
Alcohol use disorder (n = 568)	6.7%	18.7%
Other disorder (n = 2771)	4.0%	7.8%

major mental disorder are similar in the two cohorts. In the Swedish cohort, the risk of violence is greater than that for any type of criminality among both men and women with major mental disorders. In the Danish cohort this is true only of the women. Until age thirty, the differences in the proportions of mentally ill and non-disordered women who are convicted of crimes are greater than those of the mentally ill and non-disordered men. However, in the Danish cohort after ages thirty to thirty-three, the difference between the proportions of mentally ill and non-disordered men who offend increases, and is almost of the same magnitude as the difference between the mentally ill and non-disordered women. Generally, however, our conclusion drawn from the Swedish project that a major mental disorder increases the risks of criminality and of violence among women more so than among men is supported by the findings from the cohort.

As we had observed in the Swedish Project Metropolitan, in the Danish cohort the male offenders who developed major mental disorders were convicted, on average, of more offences than the non-disordered male offenders. The finding for the women was also the same as in the Swedish project:

Table 4.9. *Relative risk estimates for crime and violence*

	Swedish Project Metropolitan		Danish Project			
			Men		Women	
	Men	Women	to age 30–33	to age 43–46	to age 30–33	to age 43–46
Any crime						
No hospitalisation	1	1	1	1	1	1
Major mental disorder	2.15	3.78	2.29	3.74	3.37	4.50
	(1.39–3.33)	(2.13–6.69)	(2.13–2.49)	(3.49–3.99)	(2.89–3.93)	(4.06–4.99)
Violent crime						
No hospitalisation	1	1	1	1	1	1
Major mental disorder	4.74	11.18	2.42	4.48	5.86	8.66
	(2.84–7.91)	(4.30–29.13)	(2.06–2.84)	(3.91–5.14)	(3.57–9.62)	(6.04–12.43)

the mentally ill female offenders committed, on average, as many offences as the non-disordered female offenders. The types of offences committed by the males and females with major mental disorders in the Danish cohort are also similar to what we observed in the Swedish cohort. More of the mentally ill men than the non-disordered men were convicted of all types of offences; while more of the mentally ill women, as compared to the non-disordered women, were convicted of all types of offences except those related to drugs. Among the mentally ill subjects in the Danish cohort, the ages at which the subjects were convicted of their first offence are also similar to what we observed in the Swedish cohort. Among the mentally ill male offenders in the Danish cohort, 38.6% were convicted for their first offence between the ages of fifteen and twenty years, 27.0% between the ages of twenty-one and thirty, 24.0% from ages thirty-one to forty, and 10.4% from ages forty to forty-three. Among the mentally ill women, the comparable figures were 15.2%, 17.5%, 43.3%, and 24.0%. As in the Swedish cohort, there are early- and late-starters among the mentally ill offenders, with a greater proportion of early-starters among the men, and a greater proportion of late-starters among the women. It is also interesting to note that 34% of the male and 67% of the female mentally ill offenders were first convicted after the age of thirty. Consequently, in the Swedish Project Metropolitan the estimates of the prevalence of criminality among persons with major mental disorders are low.

As in the Swedish cohort, the subjects in the Danish cohort who developed a major mental disorder were at increased risk for premature death as compared to those never admitted to a psychiatric ward (Hodgins, 1998). In the results presented here for the Danish cohort as for the other cohorts, the cohort members who were deceased at the end of the follow-up period were excluded. In other analyses, the criminality of those who died before the end of the follow-up period and those who were living was compared. No differences between the deceased and the living were found except among the women with major mental disorders after age thirty, for whom the risk of criminality for the dead exceeded that for the living.

Specific disorders and crime
The Danish cohort was large enough to allow calculation of rates of criminality by specific diagnoses. Among the males, 11.3% of those with schizophrenia and 5.2% of those with affective psychoses were arrested for at least one violent crime. Among the females, 2.0% of those with schizophrenia and 0.5% of those with affective psychoses were arrested for at least one violent crime. Thus, the risk of a male cohort member with schizophrenia

being arrested for a violent offence was 4.6 times that for a male cohort member never admitted to a psychiatric ward by his early 40s. For men with affective psychoses the likelihood of an arrest for violence was twice that for the non-disordered cohort members. Among the female cohort members, the presence of schizophrenia increased the risk of an arrest for violence 23.2 times, and an affective psychoses 3.9 times (Brennan, Mednick, and Hodgins, 2000).

Men and women born in two Finnish provinces in 1966 and followed to 1993

The cohort is composed of all 12,058 persons born in two northern provinces of Finland in 1966 (Tiihonen *et al.*, 1997). The seventy-five mentally retarded subjects were excluded as were the deceased and those who had emigrated. In 1993, when the subjects were twenty-seven years old data were collected from the Hospital Discharge Register. The criminal data cover only the period from age fifteen to twenty-five. In order to compare these findings to those from other projects the DSM-III-R diagnoses of schizophrenia, schizoaffective disorder, schizophreniform disorder, affective psychoses, and paranoid and other psychoses (but not organic psychoses) were grouped together as major mental disorders. Among the men with major mental disorders, 21.9% had been convicted of an offence and 13.7% of a violent offence compared to 7.9% and 2.3% of the males who had never been admitted to a psychiatric ward. None of the women with major mental disorders had been convicted of an offence as compared to 9.8% of the non-disordered females.

A POPULATION COHORT

Men and women in Victoria, Australia in 1993 to 1995

The cohort included all adults in the state of Victoria, Australia in 1993 to 1995 (Wallace *et al.*, 1998). The psychiatric register which includes almost all in-patient and out-patient contacts for mental health care was screened as were official criminal records. As in the earlier studies conducted elsewhere, both men and women with major mental disorders were found to be at increased risk for criminality. Among the men, those with schizophrenia were 3.2 times more likely than those with no disorder to have a criminal record, 4.4 times more likely to have a conviction for a violent crime, and 10.1 times more likely to have been convicted of homicide. Men with affective psychosis were 3.4 times more likely to have a record of offending, 4.1 times more likely to have been convicted of a violent crime, and 5 times more likely to have been convicted of homicide. Women with schizophrenia were 4.2 times more likely to have a conviction and 4.3 times more likely to have a conviction for a violent crime than were women with no mental disorder. The comparable figures for women with affective psychosis are 3.3 and 3.4.

Conclusion

The results of the other three investigations of birth cohorts and one study of a population cohort all concur with those from the Swedish Project Metropolitan in showing that greater proportions of persons who develop major mental disorders in adulthood than persons of the same gender and age without these disorders commit crimes and crimes of violence. As well, the large Danish study (Hodgins *et al.*, 1996) demonstrated, as does the present investigation that, on average, the mentally ill offenders commit many crimes and many different types of crimes. The Danish study which followed subjects through their mid-forties, documented that 34 per cent of the mentally ill male offenders and 67 per cent of the mentally ill female offenders committed their first offence after age thirty. These findings suggest that the estimates from the present investigation are low, because data collection ended when subjects were thirty years of age.

It is important to note that the association observed in the birth cohort studies between the major mental disorders and criminality is not the result of an association between socioeconomic status and criminality. Despite the fact that Sweden was a social democratic society when the cohort members were growing up, there is a relation between low socioeconomic status of the family of origin and having an adult criminal record. However, this relation is evident only among non-disordered subjects and not among either the men nor the women with major mental disorders.[3] The absence of a relation between socioeconomic status and criminality among the mentally ill was also found in the Danish and Finnish cohort studies.

Three important aspects of these investigations are often misunderstood or ignored. The first concerns the difference between the increased *risk* of offending that has been documented for persons who develop major mental disorders and the proportions of them who offend. The increases in the risk of any type of offending and of violent offending associated with the presence of a major mental disorder which have been observed in these five investigations are very similar, but the proportions of subjects, both disordered and non-disordered, who offend, vary quite considerably. This is because the calculation of *risk* takes account of the crime rate in the general population. In other words, *risk* is calculated by comparing the proportions of offenders among those who develop a major mental disorder as compared to those who do not. The findings that the *risks* of offending among persons who develop major mental disorders are similar in different countries but that the proportions of them who offendvary, are intriguing for they suggest that factors which influence criminality generally also influence criminality among those who develop major mental disorders.

The second aspect of the birth cohort studies that is often not taken into account in interpreting the results is the fact that all crimes are counted, even those which occurred before the onset of the major mental disorder.

The third aspect of these investigations that is often overlooked when interpreting the findings concerns the use of hospitalisation to index the presence of a mental disorder. The presence of a disorder was identified through the psychiatric register of hospitalisations in all but the Australian study, which identified persons who received either in-patient or out-patient care. While the major mental disorders were very likely to lead to hospitalisation in the countries where these studies were conducted, personality disorders, alcohol- and drug-related disorders were not. Further, among persons with these latter disorders, the differences between those who are and are not hospitalised are unknown and could be related to the commission of crimes. Consequently, the psychiatric registers may adequately index the presence of a major mental disorder but not other disorders, and therefore may be useful only for studying the association between criminality and the major disorders.

In interpreting the results of these birth cohort studies, a number of methodological considerations need to be taken into account.

1. The presence of a major mental disorder is identified when the subject is hospitalised. The proportions of persons with these disorders who are not hospitalised are unknown. As we and others have argued elsewhere (see for example, Hodgins *et al.*, 1996), it is reasonable to assume that in the countries where these studies have been conducted these proportions are low. Given the characteristics of the health and social service systems it would be unlikely that a person with a major mental disorder would not be hospitalised, at least once, by age forty. However, we do not know how this bias introduced by using hospitalisation to index the presence of a major mental disorder influences the results. Some studies suggest that persons with a major mental disorder who are antisocial are more likely to be hospitalised than those who are less troublesome (Monahan and Steadman, 1983), while other studies suggest that mentally ill patients who are antisocial are less likely to be hospitalised (Taylor and Gunn, 1984).

2. All of these studies used clinical diagnoses made at the time of discharge from the hospital. However, there are studies comparing the diagnoses of major mental disorders in the psychiatric registers in Denmark (Munk-Jorgensen, Kastrup, and Mortensen, 1993), Sweden (Lindqvist and Allebeck, 1990), and Finland (Tiihonen *et al.*, 1997) to diagnoses made for research purposes demonstrating very good correspondence. Further, the agreement between clinical and research diagnoses of simply the presence or absence of a major mental disorder is usually quite substantial (Hodgins, 1995b).

3. Finally, unselected birth cohorts are biased in time and place. Consequently, the increased risk of criminality among persons with major mental disorders may be characteristic only of those born since the mid-1940s.

FOLLOW-UP STUDIES OF PATIENTS DISCHARGED FROM PSYCHIATRIC WARDS

Since the investigations of the birth cohorts have shown that proportionately more of the persons who develop major mental disorders than those with no disorder commit crimes, it would be expected that an excess of criminality would also be observed among samples of patients. This is what has been reported.

Lindqvist and Allebeck (1990) followed all in-patients in Stockholm county with a diagnosis of schizophrenia, who were born between 1920 and 1959 and discharged in 1971. Patients were re-diagnosed by an independent clinician, using DSM-III criteria, and 85 per cent (644) met the criteria for schizophrenia. These 644 patients were then followed for 14 years. The relative risk of a criminal offence among these schizophrenics as compared to the general Swedish population was 1.2 for the men and 2.2 for the women. However, the schizophrenics '. . . committed four times as many violent offences as the general population' (pp. 346–7). This finding is important considering the fact that subjects who had committed a homicide were excluded from this sample because they were hospitalised outside of Stockholm County.

In a carefully designed investigation, Link and his co-workers (Link, Andrew, and Cullen, 1992) examined the criminality of psychiatric patients compared to subjects who lived in the same neighbourhood of New York but who had never received any mental health treatment. Four groups were followed: 1. patients who received psychiatric treatment for the first time in the year preceding the study; 2. patients who were in treatment during the previous year and once before; 3. former patients who received no treatment in the previous year; 4. and a community sample with no history of psychiatric treatment.

Among the patients, 34% had received a diagnosis of major depression, 19% schizophrenia, 10% another psychotic disorder and 37% another mental disorder. While 6.7% of the community cohorts had been arrested and 6.0% of the first contact patients, 12.1% of the repeat treatment patients and 11.7% of the former patients had been arrested. The arrests of the patients were more likely than the arrests of the subjects in the community sample to have been for felonies and for violent behaviour.

A follow-up study conducted in Finland examined all 281 males released from a forensic hospital. Seventy per cent had a history of at least one violent offence. During the first year in the community after discharge, the patients were 300 times more likely than the males in the general population to commit a homicide. During the follow-up period that averaged 7.8 years, the increased risk of committing a homicide for the discharged male patients was 53 times that for the general Finnish male population (Tiihonen, Hakola, Eronen, Vartiainen, and Ryynänen, 1996). While the odds ratios reflect the greatly increased risk of violent crime among patients with a history of violence, it is important to note that the numbers of homicide offenders are low (ninety-seven before, seven during follow-up).

Belfrage (1998) followed for ten years all patients with a major mental disorder who were discharged from psychiatric wards in Stockholm in 1986. Forty-two per cent of the men and 14% of the women were convicted of a crime during the decade studied. Among the patients aged seventeen to thirty years old (similar in disorder and age to those in the present investigation), 43% of the men and 24% of the women were convicted of at least one offence. Among those thirty-one to forty years old, 52% of the men and 16% of the women were convicted of a criminal offence. This high proportion of mentally ill subjects who commit crimes after the age of thirty is similar to what has been observed in the large Danish cohort (Hodgins *et al.*, 1996).

In the Australian state of Victoria, the criminality of persons admitted to an in-patient ward for schizophrenia for the first time in 1975 and in 1985 was compared. While the 1975 sample included persons treated at a time when there were still large psychiatric hospitals in Victoria, the 1985 sample was treated in a deinstitutionalised mental health care system. For each person with schizophrenia, a randomly selected control subject was matched for age, sex, and place of residence. Among the men in the 1975 sample, 21.6% of those with schizophrenia had at least one conviction for a criminal offence, as compared to 6.5% of the non-disordered comparison group. Among the men in the 1985 sample, 26.3% of those with schizophrenia had a criminal record as compared to 8.6% of the non-disordered. Similarly, the proportions of men with schizophrenia who had been convicted of a violent offence exceeded those among the non-disordered men in the 1975 sample (4.3% versus 0.7%) and in the 1985 sample (4.8% versus 0.9%).

Unlike the results of other studies, no excess of criminality was observed among the women with schizophrenia. In the 1975 sample, 2.4% of those with schizophrenia as compared with 1.5% of the non-disordered had a criminal record. In the 1985 sample, the comparable figures were 5.7% and 2.8%. Given the size of the samples of women with schizophrenia (1975 n = 205; 1985 n = 246), these results are not surprising and they do not contradict those of previous investigations in which the numbers of subjects are much greater (Mullen, Burgess, Wallace, Palmer, and Ruschena, 2000).

Conclusion

Recent investigations of samples of persons with major mental disorders who are discharged from in-patient psychiatric wards consistently find that proportionately more of the discharged patients than other persons living in the same community are convicted of criminal offences. Other investigations, for example Wessely and colleagues (1994) working in England, Modestin and Ammann (1995) in Switzerland have examined all patients within a geographically defined catchment area receiving in-patient and out-patient care and have produced similar findings. It is important to note, however, that our conclusion is based on the results of investigations conducted since the late 1960s. This issue is addressed in Chapter 5.

These conclusions about the association between the major mental disorders and criminality and/or violence drawn from studies of patients living in the community, need to be tempered by consideration of the methodological characteristics of these investigations.

1. By their design, such studies include samples which are biased by the admission and discharge practices of the hospitals and clinics from which the patients have been recruited. This may result in important differences across studies in the characteristics of the subjects. For example, one hospital may have a policy and/or practices which limit admissions of psychotic patients with a history of criminality, while another because of its location or mandate may admit this type of patient almost exclusively. Thus depending on where subjects are recruited, the proportions likely to commit crimes vary. Some studies (see for example, Wesseley, Castle,

Douglas, and Taylor, 1994) have limited the effect of this design problem by including both in-patients and out-patients from a geographically
defined catchment area, thereby reducing sampling bias.

2. Most of these studies use diagnoses which have been made for clinical
purposes and which may not always correspond to diagnoses made using
more stringent research protocols and criteria.

3. There is often a significant loss of subjects by the end of the follow-up
period which seriously affects the calculation of recidivism rates. Subject
loss may be directly related to criminality (subjects are incarcerated and
not found for follow-up) or indirectly related (the most antisocial refuse
to complete the follow-up).

4. The length of the follow-up periods varies from one study to another
making comparisons difficult because generally the longer the follow-up
the greater the proportion of subjects who offend.

5. Many of these studies do not measure the intensity, adequacy, and appro-
priateness of the treatment received by the patients while they are in the
community and its relation to the observed criminality.

INVESTIGATIONS OF THE MENTAL HEALTH
OF CONVICTED OFFENDERS

If proportionately more of those who suffer from major mental disorders
than of those who do not commit crimes, then the prevalence rates for these
disorders would be expected to be higher among convicted offenders than
in the general population. This has been found to be true in studies of
offenders in North America, but not in the United Kingdom.

Recent studies of representative samples of US prison inmates (Collins
and Schlenger, 1983; Daniel, Robins, Reid, and Wilfley, 1988; Hyde and
Seiter, 1987; Neighbors, Williams, Gunnings, Lipscomb, Broman, and
Lepkowski, 1987; Robins and Regier, 1991) and Canadian penitentiary inmates (Hodgins and Côté, 1990; Motiuk and Poporino, 1991) have revealed
higher prevalence rates of mental disorders, and particularly of the major
disorders, within these facilities than in the general population. In the study
of Canadian penitentiary inmates (Hodgins and Côté, 1990), the major
mental disorder was present, in most cases, before the incarceration. However, it was not identified during the trial by the court or subsequently in
the penitentiary. These five investigations all employed the same diagnostic
criteria, and standardised, reliable and valid diagnostic instruments. These
same instruments have been used to examine the prevalence of mental
disorders in the general population. Consequently, comparisons between

the prevalence of disorders among inmates and in the general population, controlling for gender and age, can be made with some confidence.

Findings from similar types of studies among incarcerated offenders in England and Scotland have found few cases of major mental disorders (Cooke, 1994; Gunn, Maden, and Swinton, 1992). This may well be due to a difference in laws and practices, particularly programmes to divert the mentally ill from the criminal justice system into the mental health system (for a description of such programmes see Blumenthal and Wessely, 1992). However, Cooke's (1992) follow-up study of 120 persons diverted to a forensic hospital in lieu of prosecution indicated that within 31 months, 25 per cent of them had been convicted of another offence. An alternative explanation is that persons suffering from major mental disorders in the United Kingdom are receiving adequate treatment which is preventing crime. Other information suggests that this might not be true (Hodgins, 1994c).

Conclusion

Investigations in North America document an over-representation of persons suffering from major mental disorders among incarcerated offenders as compared to the general population. This is consistent with the findings from the birth cohort studies and from the studies of patients living in the community indicating that mentally ill persons are at higher risk of conviction for criminal offences than are non-mentally ill persons. In England and Scotland, it appears as if mentally ill persons who commit crimes are often diverted to the health system in lieu of prosecution and possible incarceration.

In drawing conclusions about the association between the major mental disorders and criminality from diagnostic studies of offenders, the following methodological characteristics of the investigations need to be considered.

1. These samples are often biased and not representative of offender populations principally because the characteristics of those who agree to participate in the study differ from the characteristics of those who refuse to complete the diagnostic interview.
2. The accuracy and completeness of the information provided by the offenders depends, at least to some extent, on their belief that the information provided to the researchers will remain confidential (Hodgins and Côté, 1990).
3. The instrument used to make diagnoses affects the results obtained. Most of these studies have used the Diagnostic Interview Schedule (DIS),

which has been shown to underestimate the prevalence of the major mental disorders (Hodgins, 1995b).

4. The time interval between arrest and the diagnostic interview may affect the accuracy of the diagnoses. This is important because in the hours and days following arrest subjects may be reacting emotionally to their predicament and may be under the influence of alcohol and/or drugs.

5. Certain sub-types of mentally disordered offenders may be more likely to be arrested than other sub-types and than offenders without such disorders. Similarly, policies and practices vary from country to country, but also from one time period to another, such that the likelihood that a person with a major mental disorder who commits a crime will be deferred to the health system or sentenced to incarceration varies.

Studies of major mental disorder among homicide offenders

In addition to these studies showing that major mental disorders are more prevalent among incarcerated offenders in North America than in the general population, six investigations suggest that the prevalence of the major disorders is even higher among homicide offenders. These studies differ from most investigations of homicide offenders, which include only compilations of the cases for which psychiatric and psychological assessments have been conducted at the request of the court. These latter samples are biased and represent only a small proportion of homicide offenders. In contrast, there are five studies from Scandinavia where the diagnoses of all persons accused of homicide are established by several mental health professionals after intensive in-patient evaluations and consultations with family members, colleagues from work, and others who knew the accused well. These diagnoses are thought to represent the diagnoses present at the time of the offence. A study of all homicide offenders in Copenhagen over a twenty-five-year period revealed that 20% of the men and 44% of the women were diagnosed psychotic (Gottlieb, Gabrielsen and Kramp, 1987). A similar investigation was conducted in Northern Sweden between 1970 and 1981 (Lindqvist, 1986). Thirty-four of the sixty-four (53%) individuals who were convicted of committing a homicide, were found to suffer from a major mental disorder. A recent analysis of homicides in Stockholm over the past forty years has found that 18% of all the homicides were committed by persons with major mental disorders (Wikström, 1996). Eronen, Tiihonen and Hakola (1996) have studied all the 1,423 homicide offenders in Finland over a twelve-year period. Schizophrenia with no secondary diagnosis of an alcohol use disorder was found to have increased the risk of homicide 6.4 times among men and 5.3 times among women. Schizophrenia with a secondary diagnosis of alcohol increased the risk of homicide by 16.6 times in men and 84.6 times in women. In Iceland, 28% of the fifty-two individuals who committed a homicide between 1900 and 1979 were found to be psychotic, almost all received a diagnosis of schizophrenia (Petursson and Gudjonsson, 1981). The sixth study, conducted in Canada, examined a representative sample of incarcerated homicide offenders and found that 35% met DSM-III lifetime criteria for a major mental disorder (Côté and Hodgins, 1992).

Schizophrenia and homicide

As suggested by the Finnish study described above, there is evidence that persons with schizophrenia are at increased risk of committing homicide. As noted in Chapter 1, this disorder affects less than 1% of men and women. Those affected have been found to be responsible for disproportionate numbers of murders, in different countries and at different periods of time: Iceland 1900 to 1979, 14.9% (Petursson and Gudjonsson, 1981); Copenhagen 1959 to 1983, 8.0% (Gottlieb *et al.*, 1987); Northern-Sweden 1970 to 1980, 28.4% (Lindqvist, 1989); Contra Costa county, California 1978 to 1980, 9.9% (Wilcox, 1985); Greater London and the Home Counties 1979 to 1980, 11% (Taylor and Gunn, 1984; Taylor, 1995), and Finland 1984 to 1991, 6.1% (Eronen, personal communication, 1999), and Hessen, Germany 1992 to 1996, 10% (Erb, Hodgins, Freese, Müller-Isberner, and Jöckel, 2001).

CONCLUSION

Results from the present investigation show that proportionately more of the men and women who developed major mental disorders, than those of normal intelligence who were never admitted to a psychiatric ward, were convicted of non-violent and violent crimes. Further, the men and women with major mental disorders who offended committed, on average, many crimes of various types. The differences in the prevalence rates between the mentally ill and non-retarded non-disordered subjects were greater for violent than for non-violent crime. Further, the increase in the risk of offending associated with the major mental disorders was greater for women than for men.

The results of the present investigation are consistent with findings from three other investigations of Scandinavian birth cohorts, one Australian population cohort, recent follow-up studies of persons with major mental disorders living in the community, and North American studies of mental disorder among incarcerated offenders. The largest of the birth cohort studies (Hodgins *et al.*, 1996) indicated that many persons with major mental disorders commit their first crime after the age of thirty. Consequently, it may be that the differences between the mentally ill and non-disordered groups observed in the present investigation in which the subjects were tracked only to age thirty are low estimates of the real differences between persons with and without mental illness. The consistency in the findings from different types of investigations conducted in different places by different research teams greatly increases confidence in our conclusion that persons who develop major mental disorders are at increased risk, as compared to non-disordered persons, for criminality and violence. Each individual investigation has methodological limitations. For example, the present investigation, like the other birth cohort studies, counted only individuals admitted to psychiatric wards as having major mental disorders. Some of the follow-up studies of patients discharged to the community counted only crimes committed in one state or province of a country, others included only convictions with a sentence of three months or longer, while others excluded patients transferred out of a catchment area for treatment in specialised forensic hospitals. The studies of large samples of convicted offenders used lay interviewers and a diagnostic instrument (Diagnostic Interview Schedule) which has been shown to underestimate major mental disorders (see Hodgins, 1995). While some of these methodological limitations would increase the likelihood of finding an association between the major mental disorders and crime, other limitations would have the opposite effect. Consequently, similar findings from investigations which vary in design, subject selection criteria, and measures suggest that the observed phenomenon is real.

However, in concluding this chapter, it is important to emphasise that the present investigation and all the other studies reviewed examined samples that were biased in one way or another. Even large birth cohorts are samples in time and place and in these ways, each is biased. The subjects examined in the birth cohort studies, in the investigations of patients living in the community, and in correctional facilities were for the most part born since the late 1940s or early 1950s. There may be something different about these persons as compared to previous generations of individuals who suffered from the same disorders. This idea will be further discussed in Chapters 5 and 6. In addition, this was the first generation of mentally ill persons in this century to live outside of institutions and to be treated almost exclusively with anti-psychotic medications.

NOTES

1. We are really interested in studying the behaviours of persons with major mental disorders. However, direct continual observation of an adult's behaviour is almost impossible and far too expensive to be feasible. Consequently, we, like many other researchers, use official criminal records as indicators of these behaviours. Depending on where and when a study is conducted, the number and types of antisocial and aggressive behaviours which are labelled criminal vary. This difference between what a subject has actually done and what is officially labelled as a crime has two important consequences for understanding research in this area. One, because of changes in society, in policies and practices of policing and the courts, comparisons of the proportions of mentally ill persons who are convicted of crimes in different countries or in different time periods are problematic. To overcome this problem, researchers compare criminality among the mentally ill and non-mentally ill in the same society at the same time period. In a second step, in order to compare findings from different countries or time periods, statistics which estimate the difference in the risk of crime for the mentally ill as compared to the non-mentally ill are used. Thus, the fact that the proportions of illegal behaviours which lead to criminal prosecution vary from one society to another, and even within societies from one time period to another can be overcome. However, the second problem is less easily solved. The likelihood that an antisocial or aggressive act is labelled criminal may not be equivalent for the mentally ill and the non-mentally ill. In other words, the proportion of antisocial or aggressive behaviours of a mentally ill person that are prosecuted in criminal court may be higher or lower than the proportion of such behaviours of a non-mentally ill person that are prosecuted. This problem will be further discussed in Chapter 5.

   Of course, other researchers are interested in the functioning of the criminal justice system and why and how mentally disordered offenders are processed in this system. Many investigations are undertaken, for example, to describe how the courts assess mental disorders among those accused of committing crimes, how judges use expert testimony from mental health professionals, how the presence of a mental disorder influences the court's decision and sentencing. However, we are principally interested in what mentally ill people do and why.

2. Mentally retarded men and women were almost three times more likely to be registered for a criminal offence than men and women with no disorder or retardation. The risks of violent offending among the mentally retarded males and females were even more elevated than those for offending generally. These findings are more fully described and explored in Crocker and Hodgins (1997).

3. Socioeconomic status was indexed by father's occupation, or in the case of a single mother, mother's occupation, measured at the time of birth and when the subject was ten years old. An indicator of poverty was the number of years the subject's family received social assistance. Among both the men and women with no disorder and no mental retardation, there are highly statistically significant relations between socioeconomic status of the family of origin and criminality of the subject. These relations are evident for measures at the time of subjects' births (men, $X^2(4, N = 6710) = 129.27, p = .0000$) (women, $X^2(4, N = 6456) = 25.79, p = .00003$), and when they were ten years old (men, $X^2(4, N = 6743) = 139.24,$

$p = .00004$); (women, $X^2(4, N = 6509) = 25.46$, $p = .0004$). Also, among the subjects with no disorder or handicap, significantly more of the offenders, as compared to the non-offenders, were raised in families who received social welfare payments (men, $X^2(1, N = 6947) = 135.09$, $p = .0000$; women, $X^2(1, N = 6659) = 40.72$, $p = .0000$).

However, among the men with major mental disorders, there is no relation between socioeconomic status and criminality. Among the women with major mental disorders who offended, 50 per cent were born into upper-middle class families. A positive significant relation was obtained between the socioeconomic status of their families of origin (measured when they were born) and a record of criminality in adulthood ($X^2(4, N = 77) = 14.32$, $p = .006$). When the subjects were aged ten, 43% of their families were upper middle class and another 43% lower middle class ($X^2(4, N = 78) = 9.10$, $p = .06$). Approximately equal proportions of the families of those with and without a criminal record received welfare payments.

CHAPTER 5

EXPLANATIONS OF THE CRIMINALITY
OF THE MENTALLY ILL

HYPOTHESES

This chapter critically reviews explanations of the criminality and violence perpetrated by persons suffering from major mental disorders. Three principal hypotheses are examined.

Hypothesis 1: facilitated arrest and conviction

Persons suffering from major mental disorders are not more likely to commit crimes than persons without these disorders. However, they are more likely to be detected by the police and successfully prosecuted. Consequently, studies find that greater proportions of persons with major disorders than persons without these disorders are convicted of crimes. It is further hypothesised that facilitated detection and successful prosecution of persons with major mental disorders also explains why offenders with these disorders accumulate, on average, more convictions than do offenders without these disorders.

Hypothesis 2: inadequate and inappropriate treatment

The implementation of the policy of deinstitutionalisation in the mental health field has led to a situation in which many persons with major mental disorders receive no treatment or inadequate and/or inappropriate treatment. This lack of care is associated with the commission of illegal acts.

(2a) It is further hypothesised that because of this lack of adequate and appropriate treatment, persons with major mental disorders become symptomatic while living in the community. The development of psychotic symptoms generally but especially threat-control-override (TCO) symptoms[1] is associated with aggressive behaviour.

(2b) The lack of adequate and appropriate treatment has also created a context in which many persons with major mental disorders are using and abusing alcohol and drugs. Substance abuse is associated with criminal activity.

Hypothesis 3: two sub-groups of persons who develop major mental disorders

There are two types of offenders with major mental disorders. The explanations of the criminality of these two groups differ. The early-starters display a stable pattern of antisocial behaviour from childhood or early adolescence. This pattern of antisocial behaviour includes the abuse of alcohol and then drugs beginning at a young age. Adult criminality is simply a continuation of this pattern of antisocial behaviour. The late-starter by contrast, shows no antisocial or criminal behaviour until the symptoms of the major mental disorder become apparent. Proximal factors such as psychotic and/or TCO symptoms and intoxication play a role in the offending of the late-starters.

HYPOTHESIS 1: FACILITATED ARREST AND CONVICTION

Whether or not an illegal behaviour leads to prosecution depends on a number of factors. For example, more severe crimes, those causing significant injury to another person or extensive, and costly property damage, are more likely to lead to prosecution than are minor offences. Attitudes of police to a particular crime may also affect the likelihood that it leads to arrest. For example, until recently, in many jurisdictions, assault by a husband of his wife was not considered by many police officers as a reason for arrest or prosecution even though assault was clearly prohibited by law. In another example, police in certain jurisdictions may more readily arrest certain types of persons – a young, poor, black male as opposed to a well dressed, middle-aged white woman, even if both have behaved in a similar way. In addition, the rate of resolution of crimes varies from region to region even within the same country, from country to country, and from one time period to another.

It has been suggested that the findings indicating that greater proportions of mentally ill than non-mentally ill persons are convicted of crimes are due to the fact that for the same behaviour a mentally ill person is more likely to be arrested and prosecuted than is a non-disordered person. This has been referred to as the criminalisation of the mentally ill. In 1983, in a thorough and detailed review of US studies on this question, Teplin concluded that there was 'only tentative support for the speculation that the mentally ill have been criminalized.' (p. 64). The following year, she published a report of a study of police in Chicago. Research assistants were trained to identify acute symptoms of major mental disorders. They accompanied police officers from two precincts for 2,200 hours of working time over a 14-month period in 1980 to 1981. Arrest was found to be a relatively rare event, occurring in only 12.4% of the police-citizen encounters that were observed. Of the suspects, 5.9% were considered to be mentally ill. While 46.7% of the mentally ill suspects were arrested, this was true of only 27.9% of the non-disordered suspects. The higher arrest rate for the mentally ill held true for every type of crime except interpersonal conflict.

This study demonstrates that in Chicago in 1980 to 1981 police were more likely to arrest a mentally ill than a non-mentally ill suspect. Why did they do this? One explanation is that the police discriminated against the mentally ill. Teplin reported that 30% of the suspects were identified by the research assistants as being mentally ill. Of those, the police recognised only 15% as being mentally ill. They arrested 40% of the suspects they thought were mentally ill and 53% of those that they did not identify as being mentally ill. These results, while based on a small number of cases, suggest that the police officers did not discriminate against the mentally ill suspects. Teplin offered another explanation of the increased arrest rate of the mentally ill based on an observation that the likelihood of arrest was increased if suspects were belligerent, verbally abusive and/or disrespectful towards the police officers. Acutely symptomatic mentally ill suspects she argued, may have behaved disrespectfully towards police officers and thereby increased the likelihood that they would have been arrested. A third explanation of the higher arrest rate of the mentally ill emerges from the finding that police arrested them in many cases, only when a hospital refused admission. Arrest was a back-up procedure.

More easily detected?

There is an alternative or simply an additional explanation for these findings. The mentally ill may have been more often arrested than the non-mentally ill for the same offence because they are more easily detected. Robertson (1988), working in England, interviewed ninety-one mentally ill and seventy-six non-disordered men who were awaiting trial. Eighty-six per cent of the mentally ill men were arrested on the day of the offence, three-quarters of them at the scene of the crime. There was a witness present at 63% of the crimes committed by the mentally ill, as compared to 28%

of the crimes committed by the non-mentally ill offenders. Further, 23% of the mentally ill men reported their offence to the police, as compared to 12% of the non-mentally ill men. These findings suggest that the rate of resolution of crimes committed by the mentally ill may be higher than that of crimes committed by suspects who do not suffer from a mental illness.

The results of two US investigations, however, contradict those of Robertson. In Albany County, New York, Steadman and Felson (1984), from 1979 to 1980, interviewed a representative sample of the general population, all patients discharged from state hospitals who had resided in the community for at least one year, and all inmates released from correctional facilities who had been living in the community for at least six months. The former patients reported having committed more serious acts of aggression than did the general population sample, and more such acts involving weapons. The former patients were not more likely to be arrested for a similar incident than were the general population subjects. Further, it appeared that they were less likely than the general population subjects to be arrested for offences involving weapons. In a study conducted in New York City from 1979 to 1982, former patients and residents with no history of psychiatric treatment of a high crime neighbourhood were interviewed (Link, Andrews, and Cullen, 1992). These authors suggested that the higher arrest rate of the former patients was due to a higher rate of violent behaviour.

More aggressive behaviour

A stratified random sample of 4,914 Israeli-born Jews completed the same instrument used in the New York City study described above, the Psychiatric Epidemiology Research Interview (PERI). All of those who presented a mental disorder plus an 18% sample of those who did not (2,741) completed another diagnostic interview using the Schedule for Schizophrenia and Affective Disorders (SADs). Violent behaviour was indexed using self-reports of aggressive behaviour and weapon use during the five years preceding the interview. Among the men, 26% of those with major mental disorders reported fighting and 12.0% using weapons, as compared to 12.1% and 1.8% of the non-disordered. Among the women, 24.0% of those with major mental disorders reported fighting and 4.0% using weapons, as compared to 3.4% and 0.2% of the non-disordered (Stueve and Link, 1997).

A US study recruited subjects being discharged from hospitals in three cities and a non-disordered comparison group recruited in one of the cities.

These samples appear to differ from those included in other studies in ways which may affect the results. The refusal rates were high, 20.7% depression, 32.1% bipolar disorder, and 43.7% schizophrenia, as was subject loss during follow-up, 49.5% for all the patients for a one-year period. The average length of the hospitalisation at entry into the study was nine days, and not exceeding twenty-one days. Persons with major mental disorders constituted less than 70% of the sample, depression (including dysthymia) 40.3%, bipolar (including cyclothymia) 13.3%, and schizophrenia (including schizotypal personality disorder) 17.2%. Violent behaviours were reported by subjects, identified from records, and reported by collaterals. Almost twice as many subjects with major mental disorders (11.5%) as the non-disordered (4.6%) were found to have behaved violently (Steadman, Mulvey, Monahan, Robbins, Appelbaum, Grisso, Roth, and Silver, 1998).

Conclusion

There are not many studies that compare the likelihood of arrest and of prosecution of mentally ill and non-mentally ill persons who have engaged in similar behaviours. Our understanding of the literature suggests the following. A number of investigations have found that a sub-group of persons suffering from major mental disorders more often engage in antisocial and aggressive behaviour than do non-disordered subjects of the same gender, age, and socioeconomic status. The proportions of these antisocial and/or aggressive behaviours which lead to arrest and prosecution vary as a function of the intensity and quality of policing, the ease with which the police can have a mentally ill suspect admitted to hospital (and thereby divert him/her from the criminal justice system), and the severity of the offence. It may be, however, that mentally ill offenders are more easily detected than other offenders because they stay at the scene of the crime and/or turn themselves in to police. Thus, the higher rate of criminality among persons with major mental disorders than among non-mentally ill persons of the same gender and age is partially explained by: 1. the greater proportion of mentally ill than non-mentally ill who engage in antisocial and/or aggressive behaviours; 2. the tendency of the mentally ill to stay at the scene of a crime that they have committed or to turn themselves in to the police; and 3. the inability of police in many jurisdictions to have mentally ill suspects admitted to hospital.

HYPOTHESIS 2: INADEQUATE
AND INAPPROPRIATE TREATMENT

The policy of deinstitutionalisation

Another factor which contributes to the criminality of persons with major mental disorders is the type and intensity of mental health care that they receive. Since the 1960s, policies and services for the mentally ill have changed dramatically. Similar changes in policies and practices have been made in most of the industrialised Western countries. However, descriptions of how this massive re-orientation of mental health care occurred and its consequences for the persons involved are difficult to find. We review here how these changes were implemented in the US and the findings from studies which documented an increase in the criminality of the mentally ill as fewer and fewer were institutionalised for long periods.

Deinstitutionalisation in the US

The policy of deinstitutionalisation was implemented in the US in two phases: from 1955 to 1965, there was a 15% reduction in the number of state psychiatric hospital patients, and from 1965 to 1980 a further reduction of 71%. The first phase involved discharging patients who had spent many years in institutions and treating newly admitted patients for only short periods of time. During this phase, patients could be easily readmitted and the asylums essentially provided back-up services for the new community treatment programmes. During the second phase, however, the asylums stopped readmitting former patients and admitting new patients. Morrissey and Goldman (1986) state that the demarcation between these two phases can be located in the late 1960s. The policy of deinstitutionalisation was defined and implemented in similar ways in countries with universally accessible national health care systems (see for example, Barnes and Toews, 1983).

A number of other events were occurring at the same time, and they may have had an impact on the criminality and violence of the mentally disordered. The community treatment programmes were understandably more interested in treating new patients rather than those who had spent years in the asylums. It is clear, however, that the problem with the new community treatment programmes was more profound than simply their interest in young patients, as opposed to those who had spent many years in the old asylums. In retrospect, we can see that the empirical data on which the community treatment programmes rested were inadequate. The movement towards community care appears not to have been based on empirical data demonstrating the superiority of this form of treatment over that provided by the asylums (for reviews see, Hodgins and Gaston, 1987a and b). Rather, the movement was bolstered by the belief that the new antipsychotic medications would cure, or at least, eliminate the symptoms of the major mental disorders, and by the descriptions of the deplorable conditions discovered in many asylums and the deterioration in life skills among patients institutionalised for lengthy periods. Further, we now know, that the newly organised community programmes were overwhelmed by the number of patients requiring care, that some proportion of persons with major mental disorders refused care, that services were not diversified to meet the needs of different types of patients, and that staff were not trained to diagnose or to treat patients with substance abuse co-morbid with a major disorder.

Not surprisingly, given the ethos of the time, several cases were taken to court in the US, in an effort to obtain discharges for patients held in institutions for the criminally insane. J. Baxstrom was serving a sentence in a New York State prison. During his prison stay, he had been transferred to a state hospital. When he had served his sentence, he was further detained in the hospital on a civil commitment warrant. In 1966, he convinced the US Supreme Court to discharge him and 966 other persons with similar status to civil hospitals where they were to be assessed and discharged to the community if they did not meet the criteria for civil commitment. In 1971, the Dixon case led to a similar reassessment of 586 patients from an institution for the criminally insane in Pennsylvania. As a result of the assessments, approximately half of the Baxstrom patients (Steadman and Coccoza, 1974), and 65% of the Dixon patients were discharged (Thornberry and Jacoby, 1979). In other words, even after long periods of hospitalisation (and supposedly treatment), large proportions of these patients who had a history of criminality were considered a danger to society and consequently held in hospitals under civil commitment warrants. Of those who were discharged, 20.4% of the Baxstrom patients and 23.7% of the Dixon patients committed a crime within four years. The authors noted that these recidivism rates were comparable to those for non-mentally ill criminal offenders.

In retrospect, it is surprising, that at the time these studies were published, the conclusions added to the growing concern that mentally ill persons were being abused by mental health professionals and being unnecessarily and unfairly confined to institutions with deplorable conditions that provided little care. These findings were used by those attempting to reduce the authority of mental health professionals to involuntarily hospitalise patients using civil or criminal legislation (for example, Abramson, 1972). At the same time, legislation which accorded patients rights, and including the right to refuse treatment, became more and more prevalent.

Looking back, the data from the studies of the Baxstrom and the Dixon cases can be interpreted differently. Alternatively to the interpretation of the authors, it could be noted that after lengthy hospital stays in which clinicians had more than adequate time to observe these individuals, and after careful assessments conducted under the scrutiny of the courts, one-fifth of those who were discharged committed new offences. The data from the follow-up studies of the Baxstrom and Dixon cohorts could have been interpreted as indicating that even among carefully assessed and older subjects who suffered from major mental disorders, criminal activity is relatively common. In hindsight, it can be noted that other findings were also available as the policy of deinstitutionalisation was being implemented to indicate that significant numbers of individuals who suffered from major mental disorders were committing crimes.

Guze (1976) examined 223 male and 66 female parolees in the US state of Missouri. The male offenders were paroled in 1959 and 1960, and the female parolees were studied in 1969. Approximately 2 per cent were found to suffer from schizophrenia or bipolar disorder. Guze stated that his findings were similar to those obtained in previous studies. He described two studies of mental disorder among samples of prisoners. In 1918, Glueck examined an unbiased sample of 608 prisoners admitted to a California prison. Twelve per cent were found to be psychotic, and one half of them were diagnosed as schizophrenic. In another US study, Thompson (1937) examined 1,380 repeat offenders. Less than 1 per cent (0.6 per cent) were found to be psychotic.

Guze noted that the low rates of mentally disordered persons in the prisons did not necessarily mean that persons with these disorders were not committing crimes. During that period in Missouri, mentally disordered persons suspected of crimes were not necessarily prosecuted and/or sentenced to prison. He stated that two alternatives were possible: 1. mentally ill persons suspected of having committed a crime could have been diverted directly to a psychiatric hospital without any criminal charges; or 2. mentally ill persons suspected of having committed a crime could have been formally accused and then remanded for a pre-trial psychiatric examination.

In an attempt to assess the relation between mental disorder and crime, he evaluated the prevalence of criminality among patients with major mental disorders in a general psychiatric hospital in 1967 to 1969, and the prevalence of major mental disorders among persons accused of crimes and remanded for a pre-trial psychiatric evaluation from 1973 to 1974. Among the general psychiatric patients, 4 per cent of the men and 1 per cent of the women had a criminal record. Among those remanded for a pre-trial psychiatric evaluation, 32 per cent were diagnosed as suffering from schizophrenia or bipolar disorder. Guze concluded that the risk of offending was not increased among persons with major mental disorders.

Why are the rates obtained in earlier studies so much lower than the rates obtained in more recent studies of unbiased samples of incarcerated offenders and among samples of general psychiatric patients? The policy of deinstitutionalisation was only beginning to be implemented in the US at the time Guze recruited his subjects. Consequently, the large majority of persons with major mental disorders would have still been in asylums. Further, as noted, these asylums had the legal authority to rehospitalise discharged patients at the request of the community, family members, or others who complained of antisocial behaviour or violence by the patient. Patients had no, or very few, rights under the law to contest the decisions of the medical staff of psychiatric hospitals.

By the early 1970s, psychiatrists who worked in jails were reporting increases in the numbers of arrestees with serious mental disorders (see for example, Allodi, Robertson, and Kedward, 1974). While the clinicians responsible for jail mental health services continued to insist that there was an increase in the numbers of arrestees who suffered from major mental disorders, academic researchers pointed out possible biases in these perceptions. It was noted that counting cases referred for treatment did not provide robust data documenting an increase in arrest rates of mentally disordered persons. Further, it was noted that police have discretionary powers and could divert mentally ill persons to hospitals rather than officially charge them with a criminal offence. At the time, many jurisdictions did not have adequate data to examine whether there was an increase in the numbers of persons being found unfit to stand trial and not guilty by reason of insanity (see for example, Hodgins and Webster, 1985).

Studies of criminality among the mentally ill before and after deinstitutionalisation. There are few data available that document criminality among patients with major mental disorders over time. One exception is a study from the twin registry at the Maudsley Hospital in London. While the sample is not large (n = 490), is biased (all twins, one of whom was treated for a major mental disorder), the findings clearly demonstrate that from 1948 through 1988 the proportion of patients with a criminal record increased. In the decade 1948 to 1958 only, 5 to 10% of the patients had a criminal record, as compared to 15 to 20% in the decade 1979–88 (Coid, Lewis, and Reveley, 1993).

In what has turned out to be a prophetic study, Grunberg, Klinger, and Grumet examined homicide offenders in Albany County, New York, comparing two time periods: 1963–69, when institutional care was available, and 1970–75 after the new community mental health centre opened. Even in this short period of time, they observed an increase in the proportion of homicides committed by mentally disordered (principally schizophrenic) subjects. In their paper they refer to a Finnish psychiatrist (Virkkunen) who also was noting the disproportionate amount of violence perpetrated by persons suffering from schizophrenia.

In 1979, Rabkin published a detailed review of studies of criminality among patients discharged from psychiatric wards. She concluded: 'Since 1965, eight American studies including nine samples were designed to contribute further empirical evidence to the question of the dangerousness of discharged mental patients. Each study found that arrest or conviction rates of former mental patients equalled or exceeded those of the general population in at least some crime categories when patients were considered as a homogeneous group' (p. 13). However, she noted that before 1965, data indicated that discharged patients committed fewer crimes than the general population. British authors (Mullen, Taylor, and Wessely, 1993) came to a similar conclusion with respect to violence.

A US study also documented a similar change. Criminal records of men admitted to psychiatric hospitals in six states were examined. It was found that 38.2% of those admitted in 1968 had a record of arrest as compared to 55.6% of those admitted to hospital in 1978. Further, the proportions of patients with two or more arrests increased substantially in the decade 1968 to 1978, as did the proportions of patients who had previously served a term of imprisonment, as did the proportions of patients who had been arrested for a violent offence (Steadman, Monahan, Duffee, Hartstone, and Robbins, 1984).

Häfner and Böker (1982) examined the 533 persons who had been recognised by a court in the Federal Republic of Germany as having committed or attempted a homicide and as being mentally ill from January 1955 to December 1964. Häfner and Böker estimated the risk of violence among persons diagnosed with schizophrenia to be 0.05% and 0.006% among persons with affective psychoses. They inferred from these numbers '. . . that there is no support for the assumption that any form of mental illness or mental defect is associated with an excessive tendency to violent crime' (p. 285). However, the logic underlying this inference is slightly erroneous. Their data are limited to cases identified by the courts as being both mentally ill and as having committed a violent offence. The number of mentally ill persons who killed during the decade 1955 to 1964 in Germany is low (533 persons out of a population of 42.6 million). Why did Häfner and Böker observe so little violent criminality among the mentally ill when there is evidence from many investigations demonstrating that some significant proportion of mentally ill persons behave violently?

In an attempt to address this question, a similar sample (all persons with schizophrenia who had killed or tried to kill) was examined in the German state of Hessen, for a five-year period 1992 to 1996 (Erb *et al.*, 2001). In this recent period, 10% of all the homicide offenders, were found to suffer from schizophrenia, as compared to 8.2% in the period, almost three decades earlier that was examined by Häfner and Böker. In the period 1992 to 1996, persons with schizophrenia were 16.56 times more likely than persons without this disorder to commit a homicide, as compared to an increased risk of 12.68 in the older period. While there is an increase over the three decades, it is relatively small.

Why do the results of Häfner and Böker's study differ from the results of the present study and more recent investigations reviewed in Chapters 4 and 5? The studies reviewed in Chapter 4 examined the prevalence rates of criminal prosecution among persons who have been hospitalised because of a major mental disorder. In other words, they counted the number of individuals in a given population who have both a record of hospitalisation for a major mental disorder and a record of having committed a crime. Häfner and Böker studied only those persons whom the court identified as being both mentally ill and as having committed a violent crime. Their study then is comparable to studies from other countries of patients found not guilty by reason of insanity, or of mentally ill patients sentenced to psychiatric treatment as a result of a violent offence. At this same time in other countries, for example, Canada (Hodgins and Webster, 1992), US (Monahan and Steadman, 1983), Denmark (Kramp and Gabrielsen, 1994), and Sweden (Holmberg, 1994), the numbers of accused recognised as mentally ill were also low. As we noted in Chapter 4, in the Project Metropolitan , few of the subjects who had both a record of hospitalisation for a major mental disorder and a record of violent crime were recognised by the courts as mentally ill. As described in Chapter 5, during the past three decades in many of the industrialised Western countries, the number of mentally ill persons found not guilty by reason of insanity or sentenced to psychiatric treatment has increased. In Germany as elsewhere, there has been an increase in the number of persons accused of crimes who are remanded for a psychiatric evaluation and in the number of offenders who are sentenced to psychiatric treatment (hospital orders) (Leygraf, 1988; Nedopil, 1996).

At the time that Häfner and Böker conducted their study, few patients with major mental disorders were discharged from psychiatric hospitals. If they were, there was usually a way for them to be rehospitalised quickly and against their will if necessary if they caused any trouble in the community. Consequently, few patients lived in the community and few were at risk to offend. The comparison sample examined by Häfner and Böker was recruited from Landeck hospital. This hospital had 1,692 beds for a catchment area of 1,300,000 or 1.32 beds for every 1,000 persons. Today, in Germany as elsewhere, the number of beds per habitant is much lower. For example, in 1996, in the neighbouring state of Hessen, the general psychiatric hospital in Haina has 170 beds for a catchment area which includes 330,000 persons, or 0.52 beds per 1,000 persons. Yet, no differences were found between the recent cohort and that studied by Häfner and Böker thirty years earlier as to the proportions of the offenders with schizophrenia who had been hospitalised before the homicide (Erb et al., 2001).

As larger proportions of the mentally ill live in the community today than did thirty years ago, larger proportions abuse alcohol and/or drugs. In the Häfner and Böker cohort, 8% of the patients with schizophrenia met DSM-II-R criteria for alcohol abuse as compared to more than a third in the recent German cohort. In the Project Metropolitan in which the lifetime data were collected in 1983, of those with a major mental disorder who committed a violent offence, 33% of the men and 10% of the women had a secondary diagnosis of alcohol abuse and/or dependence. In more recent studies, rates are even higher (see for example, Helzer and Pryzbeck, 1988). As noted in Chapter 5, the prevalence rates of secondary alcohol and drug use disorders among individuals with major mental disorders vary by region and by time period. For example, in the US study described above in which patients being discharged from hospital were recruited in three cities, 50% received a diagnosis of substance abuse and/or dependencies (Steadman et al., 1998). Less substance abuse among the mentally ill is associated with less criminality and violence. Further, Häfner and Böker reported that 10% of the male schizophrenics were intoxicated at the time of the index offence, while this was found to be true of one-third of the more recent German cohort of homicide offenders with schizophrenia. Thus the proportion of homicide offenders with schizophrenia who were intoxicated at the time of the offence seems to be increasing.

The study described in Chapter 4 and conducted in Victoria, Australia, compared the criminal activities of samples of patients with schizophrenia first admitted to hospital in 1975 (when care for mental illness was provided primarily by large institutions) and 1985 (when care had been deinstitutionalised) to those of matched comparison groups. While the proportions of patients with any conviction (21 per cent and 26.3 per cent) increased over the decade being studied, the relative risk ratios did not 4.1 and 3.4. As explained in Chapter 4, this statistic calculates the risk of criminality among persons with schizophrenia as compared to that of persons with no disorder. Thus, if the proportions of persons with no disorder and with schizophrenia who commit crimes increase at similar rates, the risk ratios will remain the same. As in previous investigations, the results of this one suggest again that the criminality of those with major mental disorders is influenced, at least to some extent, by the same factors which influence criminality among those without these disorders (Mullen *et al.*, 2000).

Deinstitutionalisation in Sweden

In Sweden in 1961, Inghe published a study of individuals who had been referred for pre-trial assessment prior to a criminal trial in 1935. He reported that while the 'psychically abnormal' (mental disorder and mentally retarded) represented only 4 per cent of the accused, they committed $40.6 \pm 4.1\%$ of the serious violent offences. Further, he noted that 'psychical abnormalities were more common among female than male offenders'. (p. 455) As in the US, these findings were disregarded and a policy of deinstitutionalising the mentally disordered was implemented in a similar manner to what was done in other countries. However, the changes were made somewhat later. Between 1960 and 1995, the number of psychiatric beds was reduced by 80% (SOU, 1992). This reduction in beds would have directly affected the subjects with major mental disorders in the Project Metropolitan. For example, in Stockholm County from 1973 to 1978, when the cohort members were aged twenty to twenty five, 13% of the psychiatric beds were closed (Ågren, 1996). For comparison, in England and Wales during the same period there was a 16% reduction in the number of beds (Reed, 1995).

Not only was there a reduction in the number of in-patient beds available, there was also a reduction in the number of patients hospitalised involuntarily (Munk-Jørgensen, Lehtinen, Helgason, Dalgard, and Westrin, 1995). As noted in Chapter 4, the few studies of criminality of subjects with major mental disorders conducted at the same time as the Project Metropolitan indicated increased criminality and violence among subjects with major mental disorders as compared to the non-disordered. For example, a follow-up study of 644 patients with schizophrenia discharged from hospitals in Stockholm in 1971 and followed for 14 years, found increased rates of non-violent and violent criminality among the female schizophrenics as compared the general female population, and increased rates of violent crime among the male schizophrenics as compared to the general male population (Lindqvist and Allebeck, 1990). The study of all homicides in Northern Sweden from 1970 to 1981 found that 53% of the offenders suffered from a major mental disorder (Lindqvist, 1986). Further, from 1950 to 1992, there was a 195% increase the number of prison sentences and a 30% decrease in the number of sentences to psychiatric care. From 1974 to 1983, when the cohort members were age twenty-one to thirty, the proportion of offenders sentenced to prison increased dramatically, while the proportion sentenced to psychiatric care decreased (from Belfrage, 1993, cited in Holmberg, 1994).

Conclusion

There is evidence from the US that as soon as the policy of deinstitution-alisation of the mentally ill was implemented, persons with these disorders were being arrested for crimes, and particularly for crimes of violence. Civil commitment legislation and patient rights were strengthened during this time making it more difficult than it had previously been to involuntarily hospitalise individuals. The adequacy of care and the compliance of patients with the new forms of treatment were quickly called into question. No one seemed to listen. During this period, some patients received no community care, while others received little; probably there was less after-care than in the past, and than today. For example, we examined a cohort composed of all the persons found not guilty by reason of insanity in Québec between 1973 and 1975 (Hodgins and Hébert, 1984; Hodgins, Hébert, and Baraldi, 1985). Almost half of these patients received no follow-up care after discharge. Today, this rarely occurs (Hodgins, Toupin, Fiset and Moisan, 1996).

The principal difference in the era prior and subsequent to the implementation of the policy of deinstitutionalisation, was the intensity and quality of supervision of persons suffering from major mental disorders.[2] Before de-institutionalisation, individuals with these disorders were feared by the community and most spent their adult lives within asylums (for a description, see Hodgins and Lalonde, 1999). Even if they were discharged, which was unlikely, they could be readily rehospitalised, even against their wishes. From what we can understand of the period, often the family or police or community at large, demanded readmission as a result of difficulties experienced with the patient. Today, with much more stringent rules for involuntary commitment and substantial patient rights to refuse treatment, it is very difficult in most jurisdictions to hospitalise a patient against his/her wishes. When involuntary hospitalisation is used, the court-ordered hospital stay usually lasts only a few days or weeks. The limited number of available psychiatric beds and policies dictating short hospital stays further limit the use of hospitals to treat persons with major mental disorders. Many of these persons refuse out-patient treatment altogether, accept parts of it, or accept it sporadically. This lack of supervision and care of the severely disordered was examined empirically, and its impact on serious violence noted immediately.

Inadequate and/or inappropriate treatment

The increase in criminality and violence among persons suffering from major mental disorders which has been documented since the policy of deinstitutionalisation has been implemented, may result, at least in part, from inadequate and/or inappropriate treatment. J. Swanson and colleagues (Swanson, Borum, Swartz, and Monahan, 1996; Swanson, Holzer, Ganju, and Jono, 1990) have been analysing data from the Epidemiological Catchment Area Project (ECA) conducted in the US in order to examine the relation between violence and treatment among persons with major mental disorders. The ECA was an epidemiological investigation of approximately 20,000 subjects thought to be representative of the US population which was carried out in the early 1980s. All information on violence came from the subjects' self-reports. These data showed that individuals who met diagnostic criteria for schizophrenia or a major affective disorder were four times more likely than non-disordered individuals to have behaved violently in the preceding year (Swanson et al., 1990). These data were combined with data collected prospectively over a two and a half year period on a sample of persons with major mental disorders discharged from psychiatric wards in North Carolina (Estroff, Zimmer, Lachicotte, and Benoit, 1994). Analyses of the combined samples indicated that the absence of contact with a community mental health provider was associated with an increased risk of violence, even when sociodemographic and clinical factors were controlled, but that treatment had no effect on violence among subjects with secondary diagnoses of alcohol and drug use disorders. However, using only data from the ECA, it was found that persons who used mental health services were more likely to report behaving violently than were persons with the same kinds of disorders and symptoms who received no treatment (Swanson, Borum, Swartz, and Monahan, 1996).

These contradictory findings emerge from studies of community samples. In certain settings persons with major mental disorders and a co-morbid antisocial personality disorder and/or a history of alcohol and drug abuse, are most likely to commit crimes, may be less likely to be hospitalised or attend out-patient clinics than are patients with major mental disorders who do not behave violently. In other settings, such patients may be more likely than mentally ill patients with no history of aggressive or disruptive behaviour to be in treatment. Whether or not mentally ill persons with co-morbid substance abuse and/or a history of criminality or aggressive behaviour are receiving treatment at any point in time probably depends on a number of factors including the proportions of such persons who are incarcerated, the availability of mental health professionals to treat multi-problem mentally ill patients, the ease of obtaining involuntary treatment orders, and the availability of specialised programmes for patients with multiple problems. Despite the difficulty in knowing how to interpret these findings about treatment from the ECA and North Carolina data, other studies indicate that criminality can be prevented even among the most high risk patients. As was noted in Chapter 1, evaluations of specialised after-care programmes for patients with a history of criminality and violence demonstrate positive crime prevention effects. Such studies have been conducted in Canada (Hodgins, Lapalme, and Toupin, 1999; Wilson, Tien, and Eaves, 1995), Germany (Müller-Isberner, 1996), and the USA (for reviews see Heilbrun and Peters, 2000). One study of a non-specialised community programme has also shown a positive crime prevention effect (Wessely *et al.*, 1994). Taken together, these studies suggest that specialised forensic community programmes succeed in keeping crime and violence to a minimum even among high risk patients.

Conclusion

Many studies have documented increased criminality among persons with major mental disorders since the implementation of the policy of deinstitutionalising care. It is tempting to interpret the results of these investigations as showing that a lack of treatment is associated with criminality in this population. However, the findings are not so clear-cut. The evaluations of the specialised forensic after-care programmes strongly suggest that criminality can be prevented even among patients at high risk to recidivate. The evaluated programmes were obligatory, included intensive supervision, medications for the symptoms of the major mental disorder, monitoring of alcohol and drug use, treatment for substance abuse, as well as other components. It appears to have been the combination of all of these components which had the effect of preventing crime. In light of these findings, the results of studies of the impact of deinstitutionalisation on criminality among persons with major mental disorders could be interpreted as suggesting that inadequate and/or inappropriate care for these persons leads to situations in which they behave illegally. However, other changes occurred during the period when care for the mentally ill was being deinstitutionalised. These changes included the introduction and massive use of antipsychotic, antidepressant and mood stabilising medications and in many jurisdictions, according the mentally ill the right to refuse treatment except when they present an immediate danger to themselves or others. These changes may also contribute to increasing the risk of criminality.

Consider the Finnish example. Prior to 1978 in Finland it was possible to conditionally discharge into the community patients who had been sentenced to psychiatric treatment following commission of a crime and to obtain a court order to require them to attend out-patient treatment. Tuovinen (1973) followed for an average of 9.3 years, the patients admitted in 1955 to 1959 who were discharged into the community with obligatory after-care. None of them committed a new violent crime. Hakola (1979) followed for an average of 4.1 years, a sample of patients sentenced to psychiatric treatment in 1970–71. All were required to attend after-care. As in the previous study, no patient committed a violent offence during the follow-up period. After the law had been changed, Vartiainen and Hakola (1992) followed for an average of 8.2 years a sample of patients sentenced to psychiatric treatment. They were not obliged to use after-care services after discharge from in-patient care. During the follow-up period, they committed seven homicides and nine aggravated assaults. In a similar follow-up study of male patients sentenced to psychiatric treatment and discharged to the community with no obligation to attend to after-care, the risk of homicide during the first year in the community was estimated to be 300 times that of the general Finnish male population, and 53 times greater during the subsequent 7.8 years of follow-up (Eronen, Hakola, and Tiihonen, 1996). As Bloom and colleagues argued (Bloom, Williams, and Bigelow, 1991), and these data from Finland so clearly demonstrate, among high-risk patients the legal requirement to use specialised forensic after-care services is necessary to prevent recidivism. Consequently, changes to laws or criteria for compulsory out-patient or in-patient treatment made during the period when mental health services were being moved to the community, have contributed to creating a context in which the proportions of mentally ill persons who commit crimes have increased.

Finally, in attempting to understand the present situation, it is important to remember that almost all the available scientific evidence on the criminality of persons with major mental disorders, comes from studies of persons born after the mid-1940s. Is it possible that these persons are more likely to be antisocial than persons born prior to this time? Findings from the ECA project in the US did in fact document an increase during this century in the prevalence of persons who displayed a stable pattern of antisocial behaviour (Robins and Regier, 1991). If this increase is real and has occurred elsewhere, it is possible that among mentally ill persons today, there are more who are antisocial than there were in the past.

HYPOTHESIS 2A: PSYCHOTIC AND TCO SYMPTOMS[1]

Consider again findings from the study which combined data from the ECA and from the patients discharged to the community in North Carolina. A curvilinear relationship was identified between the number of psychotic and agitated symptoms and past violent behaviour: more than one-quarter of the subjects with none of these symptoms, just less than half of those with one symptom, almost 70% of those with two symptoms, and 45 per cent of those with three or more of these symptoms reported violence. Among these symptoms, most notably the perception of being threatened and of losing internal cognitive controls (commonly referred to as threat-control/override or TCO symptoms) were found to be associated with violent behaviour. To resume, while one-quarter of the patients with no psychotic-agitated symptoms reported behaving violently, much greater proportions of those with one, two, or three of these symptoms reported violence (Swanson et al., 1996).

Using data from the ECA project on 10,066 subjects, Swanson and his colleagues (1996) have shown that the presence of delusions increases the risk of violence 2.6 times, and the combination of delusions and hallucinations increases the risk 4.1 times. While 16.1% of the subjects who reported one or more TCO symptoms reported having behaved violently during the past years, this was true of only 6.1 per cent of those reporting any other psychotic symptom. Similarly, 56% of those with current TCO symptoms reported behaving violently since age eighteen, as compared to only 29% of those reporting non-TCO delusions or hallucinations. These authors used logistic regression models to identify the variables that predicted violence. The risk of having behaved violently during the past year was increased 6.4 times by having an alcohol or drug use disorder, 2.4 times by being in treatment, 1.7 times by being male, and 0.9 times by having a low level of education. By contrast, the factors which were found to increase the risk of violence since age eighteen differed. This risk was increased 5.1 times by the presence of an alcohol or drug use disorder, 2.9 times by the presence of TCO symptoms, 2.1 times by being male, 1.8 times by non-TCO psychotic symptoms, 1.7 times by being in treatment, 1.7 times by the presence of a major mental disorder, and 0.9 times by being young.

These findings replicate those obtained by Link and Stueve (1994). Their study comparing the aggressive behaviour of mentally disordered persons and their non-disordered neighbours in New York City was described in Chapter 4. They found a significant increase in the proportions of patients who reported hitting, fighting and using weapons when TCO symptoms were present and to a lesser extent when other psychotic symptoms were present. However, looking just at the patients in this study, it becomes clear that most of them had few or no psychotic or TCO symptoms. For example, in the analyses on fighting, 191 patients were included. Of those 191, 76% had few or no symptoms (psychotic or TCO), 3% had high psychotic but low TCO symptoms, 9% had high TCO but low psychotic symptoms, and 12% had both high psychotic and high TCO symptoms. Among these 191 patients, 45 reported hitting during the past year. Of these forty-five who had hit, twenty-two had low symptoms, one had high psychotic and low TCO symptoms, ten had high TCO and low psychotic symptoms, and twelve had both high psychotic and high TCO symptoms. These data indicate that most patients who reported hitting had low levels of both psychotic and TCO symptoms. This was also true for reports of fighting during the last five years. Forty-nine patients reported fighting: twenty-seven with low symptoms, three with high psychotic and low TCO symptoms, six with high TCO and low psychotic symptoms, and thirty with high psychotic and high TCO symptoms. The same pattern emerges for weapon use. Nineteen patients reported using weapons during the past five years: twelve had low levels of symptoms, one had high psychotic symptoms and low TCO symptoms, two had high TCO and low psychotic symptoms, and four had high TCO and psychotic symptoms. For fighting and weapon use, as for hitting, the majority of the patients who reported these behaviours had low levels of symptoms. While most patients living in the community did not have psychotic or TCO symptoms, this does not negate the fact, however, that the presence of such symptoms alone or in combination with other psychotic symptoms increased the risk of fighting, hitting and weapon use.[3]

The results of the three studies reviewed indicate that the presence of TCO symptoms in particular, but also of other psychotic symptoms increases the risk of violent behaviour.[4] These results echo much clinical lore and are similar to findings from older studies that demonstrated an association between paranoid symptoms and violent behaviour (Blackburn, 1968; Gibbens and Robertson, 1983). The results of the studies reviewed suggest that treatment with antipsychotic medications that reduces these symptoms may reduce the risk of violent behaviour. The presence of these symptoms in addition to substance abuse further increases the risk of violent behaviour. Persons with a major mental disorder and these other risk factors may be less likely than other persons with similar disorders, but no additional risk factors to seek treatment voluntarily. They are also much less likely than other persons with the same disorders to agree to participate in research. Consequently, findings about paranoid symptoms and suspiciousness must be interpreted cautiously.

However, the US study previously reported that recruited discharged patients in three cities found no (Appelbaum, Robbins & Monahan, 2000) relation between TCO symptoms and violence in the months that followed. In contrast to previous studies, this one used prospectively collected data and interviewers' judgements of the presence of delusions rather than self-reports of symptoms. Self-reported TCO symptoms were associated with violent behaviour, but also with four subscales of the Novaco Anger Scale and three subscales of the Barrat Impulsiveness Scale. The authors suggest that a generally suspicious attitude towards others combined with anger and impulsiveness are associated with violent behaviour.

As noted earlier, it is difficult to interpret contradictory findings from studies which have examined samples of patients. The characteristics of the samples examined in the different studies may differ in ways which affect the results. This is because the population of persons with major mental disorders who offend is very heterogeneous, being composed of sub-groups who are at differential risk of offending. Consequently, one sample in one study may include many patients at high risk of offending, while another sample includes few such patients. As long as samples include only those who sought treatment and who sign informed consent forms to participate in the study, samples will be biased. Not knowing anything about those who are not seen in treatment and/or who refuse to participate in studies, seriously limits understanding of the biases of the samples that are studied.

HYPOTHESIS 2B: THE USE OF ALCOHOL AND DRUGS

Co-morbid diagnoses of alcohol and drug use disorders

One of the consequences of treating persons afflicted with major mental disorders in the community, rather than institutionalising them for life, has been an increase in their use and abuse of alcohol and drugs. The prevalence of alcohol and drug use disorders among persons with major mental disorders varies from region to region and from one time period to another, but is generally higher than among non-disordered persons of the same gender and age living in the same place and at the same time. For example, in the ECA study, it was found that the risk of alcohol abuse and/or dependence was four times higher among persons with schizophrenia, five times higher among persons with bipolar disorder, and not elevated among persons with major depression as compared to persons with no disorder. The prevalence of drug abuse and/or dependence was found to be six times higher among subjects with schizophrenia, and four times higher among subjects with major depression and among those with bipolar disorder, as compared to subjects with no disorder (Helzer and Przybeck, 1988).

In the present investigation it was found that 32.9% of the men and 10.0% of the women with major disorders had additional diagnoses of alcohol and/or drug use disorders. The prevalence is very high given that these were file diagnoses made during a period when little or no attention was paid by clinicians to co-occurring disorders. Even experienced clinicians using structured diagnostic interview protocols underestimate alcohol and drug use disorders among individuals suffering from major mental disorders (Bryant, Rounsaville, Spitzer, and Williams, 1992).

Substance use disorders increase the risk of criminality and violence among subjects with major mental disorders. This has been found in a number of investigations. In the Danish birth cohort study described in Chapter 4, the proportions of subjects arrested for a violent crime were higher for those with than for those without secondary diagnoses of substance abuse and/or dependence. Among the males with schizophrenia, 23.2% of those with substance abuse, as compared to 7.1% of those without, had at least one arrest for violence. Similarly among the women with schizophrenia, 7.0% of those with and 1.9% of those without substance abuse had been arrested for violence. Similarly, among the men with affective psychoses, 11.8% of those with co-morbid diagnoses of an alcohol and/or drug use disorder and 3.2% of those without had been arrested for violence. Among women with affective psychoses the comparable figures are 1.6% and 0.3% (Brennan et al., 2000). Similarly, in the Australian cohort study, co-morbid substance use further increased the risks of offending, violent offending and homicide. Among the men, the risk of offending of those with schizophrenia and substance abuse was 12.4 as compared to men with no disorders and for those with only schizophrenia the risk was increased 1.9 times. The risk ratios for these two groups for violent offending were 18.8 and 2.4, and for homicide 28.8 and 7.1. Among men with affective psychosis and co-morbid substance use, the risk of offending was increased 13.5 times, whereas for persons with no disorders and for those with only an affective psychosis the risk was increased 2.6 times. The risk ratios for these two groups for violent offending were 19.0 and 2.9, and for homicide 17.5 and 4.4 (Wallace *et al.*, 1998).

In follow-up studies of patients discharged from psychiatric wards to the community, it has also been shown that the presence of co-morbid substance abuse increases the likelihood of criminality (see for example, Cohen, 1980; Giovanni and Gurel, 1967; Lindqvist and Allebeck, 1989; Mesnikoff and Lauterbach, 1975; Mullen *et al.*, 2000; Rappeport and Lassen, 1966; Steadman *et al.*, 1998). In studies of convicted offenders with major mental disorders (Abram and Teplin, 1991; Hodgins and Côté, 1990), and in studies of homicide offenders with major mental disorders, substance abuse was again found to increase the already elevated risk of offending among those with major mental disorders (Côté and Hodgins, 1992; Eronen, 1995; Eronen, Tiihonen, and Hakola, 1996; Gottlieb, Gabrielsen, and Kramp, 1987; Lindqvist, 1986).

However, it is important to note that not all persons with major mental disorders who commit crimes have a co-morbid alcohol or drug use disorder. There is even some hint in the available data that the association of alcohol and drug use disorders with criminality and violence is less among the mentally ill than among those with no major disorders (Lindqvist, 1986; for a further discussion, see Beaudoin, Hodgins, and Lavoie, 1993). Rather, these co-morbid disorders increase the risk of criminality and violence, which is already increased by the major mental disorder. This point is well illustrated by the Finnish study described in Chapter 4 that examined 1,423 homicide offenders. Schizophrenia, without a secondary diagnosis of an alcohol use disorder, was found to have increased the risk of homicide 6.4 times among men and 5.3 times among women. Schizophrenia plus alcoholism increased the risk of homicide by 16.6 among men, and 84.8 times among women (Eronen *et al.*, 1996). The additional increase in the risk of offending among persons with major mental disorders that is associated with co-morbid substance abuse, as seen with the Danish birth cohort and the Australian population cohort, no doubt varies from place to place and also from one time period to another.

In the present investigation, 51.2% of the male offenders with a major mental disorder (not of the men with a major mental disorder), and 60.0% of the female offenders with a major mental disorder (not of the female subjects with a major mental disorder), had secondary diagnoses of alcohol and/or drug use disorders. The finding that about half of the offenders with major disorders did not have additional diagnoses of alcohol or drug use disorders concurs with results from the studies of unbiased samples of homicide offenders. In these investigations (Gottlieb *et al.*,

1987; Lindqvist, 1986), despite intensive, in-patient assessments, about half of those with major disorders did not receive additional diagnoses of alcohol or drug use disorders.

Intoxication at the time of an offence

However, in order to further understanding of offending among persons suffering from major mental disorders, it is important to distinguish between a diagnosis of alcohol or drug abuse or dependence and intoxication at the time of the offence. Not surprisingly, few studies have succeeded in documenting intoxication during an offence. Several obstacles to obtaining such information are common. Often, an offender is not arrested until long after having committed the crime. Consequently, no objective measure of intoxication is possible. In some jurisdictions, it has proven impossible for researchers to obtain objective measures of intoxication even for those accused who were arrested at the scene of the crime. Further, self-reports of intoxication at the time of the offence taken from persons accused of crimes before their trials are of questionable validity. In some jurisdictions it may be in the interest of the accused to say that he/she was intoxicated at the time of the offence, even if this was not the case. Given that many offenders have a history of antisocial behaviour which includes lying and manipulating, great prudence must be exercise in using statements that they provide to the courts as scientific data.

Not only is it difficult to obtain valid measures of intoxication at the time of an offence, it may be easier to obtain such information from offenders with major mental disorders than from other offenders. This is true for two reasons. First, as noted previously the mentally ill are more often arrested at the scene of the crime than are other offenders, and consequently intoxication can be measured (whether by breathalyser, blood or urine samples, police reports, or self-reports). Second, mentally ill persons accused of crimes often readily describe what has occurred. Given this situation, it is difficult at the present time to compare the prevalence of intoxication among offenders with and without major mental disorders.

One of the few investigations that distinguished diagnoses of abuse and dependence from intoxication is the study of all homicides in Northern Sweden over an eleven-year period. It was reported that among the offenders who received a diagnosis of a major mental disorder, 38% had a history of substance abuse and of them, 85% were intoxicated at the time of the murder. Among those with major mental disorders and no history of substance abuse, 33% were intoxicated at the time of the murder (Lindqvist, 1986). In a Canadian study, two groups of convicted male homicide offenders, twenty-six who suffered from schizophrenia and fifteen with no major mental disorder were compared. While one-third of those with schizophrenia were reported to have been intoxicated at the time of the homicide, two-thirds of the non-disordered offenders were intoxicated when they killed (Beaudoin *et al.*, 1993). In the study of homicides by persons with schizophrenia in Hessen, Germany, a third had been drinking at the time of the offence (Erb *et al.*, 2001).

Investigations examining aggressive and/or violent behaviour which did not necessarily lead to criminal convictions, have, for the most part, observed an elevation of risk associated with the use of alcohol and/or drugs. For example, in the ECA study, the risk of violence among persons with a major mental disorder, as compared to non-disordered persons, rose from four among subjects with only a major disorder, to 17 among subjects with a major disorder plus an alcohol or drug use disorder (Swanson 1993; Swanson *et al.*, 1990). In the Israeli study, among the men with major mental disorders and no substance abuse, 20.7% reported fighting and 4.4% using weapons, as compared to 25.1% and 8.7% of those with schizophrenia and substance but no antisocial personality disorder (Stueve and Link, 1997). In the recent US study of patients being discharged from hospitals in three cities, among those with schizophrenia, substance abuse at admission was not found to be related to violent behavior in the twenty weeks after discharge. Bivariate correlations indicated only that a psychiatric file history of drug abuse (0.17) and the reported use of alcohol (0.18) were related to violent behavior (Monahan, 1999). This result, which differs from findings from so many studies, may be due to characteristics of the sample – all were former in-patients, all consented to participate in the research, and there was a high rate of refusals to participate (Steadman *et al.*, 1998).

Substance abuse in childhood and adolescence

As many studies have confirmed, among persons with a major mental disorder, substance abuse in adulthood increases the risk of criminality and violence, as does intoxication. Surprisingly, substance abuse in childhood appears to be an even more powerful risk factor. Table 5.1 presents relative risk estimates for any crime and for violent crime, among the male subjects who developed a major mental disorder, taking account of substance abuse and the life period when it occurred. As can be observed, substance abuse during childhood increases the risk of crime and of violent crime even more than does substance abuse in adulthood. It is important to note that not all of the offenders with major mental disorders were substance abusers. Abuse was more common among the men with major mental disorders who

Table 5.1. *Risk of crime and violence by men with major mental disorders*

	Relative risk estimates for crime	95% confidence bounds	Relative risk estimates for violent crime	95% confidence bounds
Major mental disorder (n = 82)	2.15	(1.39–3.33)	4.74	(2.84–7.91)
Major mental disorder, no substance abuse in childhood or adulthood (n = 47)	1.11	(0.61–2.04)	2.15	(0.91–5.09)
Major mental disorder plus childhood substance abuse (n = 18)	10.77	(3.12–37.25)	23.07	(8.90–59.80)
Major mental disorder plus adult substance abuse (n = 27)	6.16	(2.60–14.58)	8.64	(3.93–18.97)
Major mental disorder plus substance abuse in childhood and/or adulthood (n = 35)	5.39	(2.58–11.24)	9.79	(4.94–19.38)

began their criminal activity before age eighteen. Of those men with major disorders who offended before the age of eighteen, 69.2% were identified as abusing alcohol and/or drugs as children, and 53.8% as adults. Of those who began offending after age eighteen, 20% were identified as abusers before the age of eighteen and 40% after age eighteen.

Table 5.2 presents the raw data on the women with major mental disorders. There are simply too few to permit calculation of statistics. Six of the eight women with a diagnosis of major mental disorders and substance abuse/dependence in adulthood were registered for a crime, and three of eight for at least one violent crime. In contrast, only seven of the 66 disordered women without substance abuse in childhood or adulthood were registered for a crime and two of them for a violent crime. To resume, among the men with major mental disorders who had been identified as having substance abuse problems as children, 83.3% were convicted of a crime and 40% for a violent crime by age thirty. Similarly, among the women with major

Table 5.2. *Crime and violence by women with major mental disorders*

	Crime	Violent crime
Major mental disorder	15/79	5/79
Major mental disorder, no substance abuse in childhood or adulthood	7/66	2/66
Major mental disorder plus childhood substance abuse	4/7	1/7
Major mental disorder plus adult substance abuse	6/8	3/8
Major mental disorder plus substance abuse in adulthood or childhood	8/13	3/13

mental disorders who had abused drugs and/or alcohol as children 57.1% were convicted of a crime and 23.1% of a violent crime.

Not only did substance abuse in childhood significantly increase the risk of criminality and violence among persons who developed major mental disorders, they were more likely to have had such problems in childhood than were the cohort members who remained free of mental illness. Among the males who developed a major mental disorder, 22% had been identified for substance abuse as children as compared to 7.1% of the non-disordered non-retarded men, and 50% of those who were admitted to a psychiatric ward with a primary diagnosis related to alcohol or drug problems. Similarly, among the mentally ill females, 8.9% had been identified in childhood for substance abuse as compared to 2% of the non-disordered non-retarded women, and 34% of the women admitted to hospital because of substance abuse. These data, together with findings on co-morbid alcohol and drug use disorders in adulthood, suggest that individuals who will develop major mental disorders, as compared to those who do not develop a major mental disorder, are at greater risk to abuse alcohol and drugs both as children and as adults.

Conclusion
The prevalence of alcohol and drug use disorders was found to be higher among the mentally ill males and females than among the non-disordered males and females both in childhood and adolescence before the symptoms of the major disorder became apparent and in adulthood when the major mental disorder was diagnosed. The presence of substance

Table 5.3. *Per cent men with and without substance abuse who offended*

		Major mental disorders	No major mental disorders
Males			
Childhood or adolescent	present	83.3%	78.3%
substance abuse	absent	40.6%	29.1%
Adult substance abuse	present	74.1%	92.9%
	absent	38.2%	31.7%
Females			
Childhood or adolescent	present	57.1%	58.2%
substance abuse	absent	15.3%	5.2%
Adult substance abuse	present	75.0%	70.7%
	absent	12.7%	5.8%

abuse increases the risk of criminality among the mentally ill as among the non-mentally ill. Substance abuse in childhood or early adolescence is more strongly associated with criminality than is substance abuse in adulthood.

Table 5.3 presents comparisons of criminality among the mentally ill and non-mentally ill taking account of substance abuse problems early or later in life. In order to better estimate the prevalence of alcohol and drug use disorders among the cohort members, the subjects who had been admitted to hospital with a primary diagnosis of an alcohol and/or drug use disorder were added to the 'no major mental disorder' group. While in Tables 5.1 and 5.2 the comparison group includes all the non-mentally retarded cohort members who had never been admitted to a psychiatric ward, in Table 5.3 the comparison group includes all of these latter subjects plus those admitted to a psychiatric ward because of an alcohol or drug problem. As reported in Chapter 4, most of the men and women admitted to hospital with a primary diagnosis of an alcohol and/or drug problem had been convicted of at least one crime. Consequently, the comparisons presented in Table 5.3 differ from those in Tables 5.1 and 5.2 and further clarify the links between alcohol and drug disorders co-morbid with major mental disorders and criminality.

As can be seen in Table 5.3, among the males who had abused alcohol and/or drugs in childhood or adolescence, the proportions of those with and without mental illness who were convicted of a criminal offence are similar. However, among the men who had no childhood or adolescent history of substance abuse, more of those who developed a major disorder than those who developed no disorder or substance use disorder had a criminal record. The same pattern is evident among the females, where among those with no history of childhood or adolescent substance abuse, more of those who developed a major mental disorder than those who developed no disorder or a substance use disorder had a criminal record. Among both the males and females, a diagnosis of an alcohol and/or drug use disorder whether or not it is co-morbid with a major mental disorder is associated with criminality. Note that the proportion of mentally ill women with co-morbid diagnoses of substance abuse who have been convicted of a crime is as great as the proportion of women with primary diagnoses of substance abuse who have been convicted of a crime. Among the men with no diagnoses of alcohol or drug use disorders, the proportions of those with and without a major disorder who had been convicted of a crime were similar. Not so among the females, where the proportion of mentally ill women with non-co-morbid alcohol or drug problems who were convicted of a crime was twice that of the women with no alcohol or drug problems. Again, these figures demonstrate that the presence of a major disorder without a co-morbid alcohol or drug use disorder, increases the risk of criminality to a greater extent among women than among men.

Together, existing data suggest a relation between substance abuse, and possibly intoxication, and crime, violent crime, and homicide among subjects with major mental disorders. Data from the present investigation indicate that abuse in childhood increases the risk to a greater degree than does abuse or dependence in adulthood. Further, co-morbid alcohol and/or drug use disorders increase the risk of criminality more among women than men with major mental disorders. In addition, the data are very clear in demonstrating that many subjects with major mental disorders and no history of substance abuse and no intoxication commit crimes, violent crimes, and homicide and other crimes. It is important to note that the association which has been identified between substance use or abuse and criminality is not specific to subjects with major mental disorders. As can be seen in Tables 4.7 and 4.8 of Chapter 4, significant proportions of subjects with primary diagnoses of alcoholism and drug dependence commit crimes and violent crimes. Given that the prevalence of alcohol and drug use disorders is higher among persons with major mental disorders than among persons of the same gender and age without these disorders, and that alcohol and drug use disorders increase the risk of crime, violent crime, and homicide, substance abuse is an important part of the explanation of the criminality of the mentally ill. This conclusion is also supported by the studies of specialised forensic after-care programmes which have successfully pre-vented recidivism among high-risk patients. These programmes which are compulsory carefully monitor and control alcohol and drug use. Unfortu-nately, as pointed out by Swanson and his colleagues (1996), among those with major mental disorders, those who abuse alcohol and/or drugs are the least likely to comply with treatment programmes.

HYPOTHESIS 3: TWO TYPES OF OFFENDERS WITH MAJOR MENTAL DISORDERS: EARLY AND LATE-STARTERS[5]

No doubt many factors contribute to the criminality of persons with major mental disorders. Some of these factors, as discussed, relate to the context or environment in which mentally disordered persons now live, while oth-ers relate to their behaviours. Consider first the environmental factors. As Teplin (1984) showed, police may discriminate against the mentally ill by arresting a mentally ill suspect for an act that would not lead to the ar-rest of a non-mentally ill suspect. This, she has suggested, is due to the increased likelihood that a mentally ill suspect will behave in a disrespect-ful manner towards the police officer. The importance of this factor in explaining the crime rate among the mentally ill, varies, no doubt, from jurisdiction to jurisdiction and from one time period to another. A second environmental factor which contributes to explaining the criminality of the mentally ill is the type and intensity of treatment services and particularly of out-patient treatment services provided to persons with major mental disorders. Since the policy of deinstitutionalisation has been implemented in the mental health field, many persons with major mental disorders live in the community and receive little or no treatment that directly targets the multiple difficulties that they experience. Further, obtaining and main-taining treatment is their responsibility, and they have a right to refuse treatment even when actively psychotic. Finally, another consequence of providing care for the mentally ill in the community is easier access to al-cohol and drugs. The ease of access varies to some extent, depending on the region where these persons live, the supervision they receive, and their income.

While the criminality of persons with major mental disorders is partially explained by factors related to the environments in which they live, it is also explained by patterns of behaviour more common among them than among persons who do not suffer from these disorders. As one study (Robertson, 1988) and much clinical lore suggest, the mentally ill who commit crimes may be more easily detected by police and convicted than are non-mentally ill persons. The increased risk of detection is the result of the fact that the mentally ill offender will often commit a crime in front of a witness, stay at the scene of the crime until the police arrive, and/or confess to the police. A second individual factor related to the criminality of the mentally ill is alcohol and drug abuse. For reasons not yet understood, both men and women who will develop major mental disorders in adulthood are more likely than individuals who do not develop mental illness to abuse or to become dependent on alcohol or other drugs, both as children and as adults. Substance abuse in childhood or early adolescence increases the risk of criminality and violence to a greater extent than does substance abuse in adulthood. Further, substance abuse in childhood or early adolescence increases the risk of criminality and violence to a greater extent among persons who develop major mental disorders than among those who do not develop these disorders. It is important to remember in concluding that while psychotic symptoms, particularly TCO symptoms, and substance abuse increase the risk of illegal behaviour among persons who will or who have developed a major mental disorder, the studies reviewed, as well as the results of the present project, indicate that the vulnerability to the major mental disorder or the disorder in-and-of-itself does increase the risk of illegal behaviour.

Another individual factor which contributes to explaining the higher rates of criminality among the mentally ill than among the non-mentally ill, is the increased proportion of mentally ill persons who show a stable pattern of antisocial behaviour from childhood or early adolescence. The diagnosis of antisocial personality disorder (ASPD) defined according to the DSM-II and DSM-III-R requires evidence of a stable pattern of antisocial behaviour before the age of fifteen. This diagnosis, consequently, identifies individuals who have displayed a stable pattern of antisocial behaviour across the life-span. We have found that ASPD is more prevalent among persons with schizophrenia than among age and sex matched non-disordered persons. Among schizophrenics not identified because of criminal or violent behaviour, the prevalence of ASPD is several times the rate of 3.9% to 4.9% found for men in the general population (Robins *et al.*, 1984). For example, in a sample of thirty male and thirty female schizophrenics treated in out-patient clinics of general hospitals, we have found that the prevalence of ASPD was 23% among the men and 16.7% among the women (Léveillée, 1994). Among schizophrenics accused or convicted of crimes, not surprisingly the prevalence of ASPD is even higher. For example, in a study of persons accused of crimes who were being evaluated for competency, 37% of the schizophrenics received a diagnosis of ASPD (Hart, 1987).

In our study of incarcerated offenders, 62% of the schizophrenics received a DSM-III diagnosis of ASPD (Côté and Hodgins, 1990). Of the seventy-four men with schizophrenia recruited from a forensic hospital and a general psychiatric hospital, twenty (27%) received a secondary diagnosis of ASPD. This is five times the highest prevalence rate reported for men in the general population (Hodgins, Toupin, and Côté, 1996). This evidence strongly suggests that the proportion of persons who show stable patterns of antisocial behaviour across the lifetime is greater among the mentally ill than the non-mentally ill.

This hypothesis of the existence among persons who develop schizophrenia and major affective disorders[6] of sub-groups who present a pattern of antisocial behaviour from a young age is consistent with etiological research on these disorders. This is important, because most of these data were collected before data were available indicating that there is a relation between the major mental disorders and criminality and because they were documented by scientists, who for the most part, were unaware of research on crime and mental disorder. Prospective longitudinal studies of children of parents with schizophrenia have identified a sub-group, larger among the males than the females, that show disruptive, aggressive behaviour from a young age (Asnarow, 1988; Olin, John, and Mednick, 1995). Further, a prospective longitudinal study of a Dutch general population sample found, like so many other studies, that aggressive behaviour in childhood was associated with aggressive behaviour in adulthood, but equally strongly predictive of thought disorder in adulthood (Ferdinand and Verlust, 1995). A similar US study, found that antisocial behaviour in childhood was associated with the development of cluster A personality disorders (Bernstein, Cohen, Skodol, Bezirganian, and Brooke, 1996).

Similarly, recent epidemiological investigations of community samples of children have documented relatively high rates of affective disorder co-morbid with conduct disorder (see for example, Angold and Costello, 1993). A prospective longitudinal study of children of parents with major affective disorders and investigations of children with affective disorders have also documented significant co-morbidity with conduct disorder, both among children with major depression and bipolar disorder (Carlson and Weintraub, 1993; Geller, Cooper, Watts, Cosby, and Fox, 1992; Harrington, Rutter, and Fombonne, 1996; Kovacs and Pollock, 1995). The prevalence of childhood conduct disorder is higher among adults with major depression than among the general population (Rowe, Sullivan, Mulder, and Joyce, 1996). In a longitudinal prospective study, we have found that the sons and daughters of parents with bipolar disorder, as compared to children of parents with no mental disorder, were three and a half times more likely to present an externalising disorder before age twelve. Most also presented internalising disorders. These findings are important as previous work has shown that one-in-two of the children of parents with bipolar disorder are likely to develop a major affective disorder in adulthood (Hodgins, 1994). Children with depression and conduct disorder have been found to differ from those with only depression by the absence of anxiety symptoms and the presence of impulsivity, delinquency and having witnessed violence at home (Meller and Borchardt, 1996). Such boys have been described as disruptive and socially withdrawn (Kerr, Tremblay, Pagani, and Vitaro, 1997).

We (Hodgins, Côté, and Toupin, 1998; Hodgins, Toupin, and Côté, 1996) have proposed a parsimonious hypothesis which takes account of both contextual and individual factors in an effort to explain the relation between the major mental disorders and criminality. We interpret recent findings as suggesting that there are two types of persons who develop major mental disorders and who commit crimes. The 'early starters' display a stable pattern of antisocial behaviour from a young age and through adulthood.[6] As noted by Robins and McEvoy (1990) antisocial children are exposed to alcohol and drugs earlier than other children, and many become substance abusers and criminals. The 'late-starters' begin offending in adulthood as the symptoms of the major mental disorder emerge. Both psychotic and TCO symptoms and intoxication may play a role in the illegal behaviours of the 'late-starters'. This hypothesis is more fully explored in Chapter 6.

NOTES

1. Threat/control-override (TCO) symptoms have been defined as:
   • feeling that your mind is dominated by forces beyond your control
   • feeling that thoughts were put into your head that are not your own
   • feeling that there were people who wish to do you harm
                          Source: Link and Stueve, 1994, p. 144
2. The implementation of a policy of deinstitutionalisation which was applied to services for the mentally retarded as well as to those provided for the mentally disordered, may also partially explain the high rates of criminality that we documented in Chapter 4 among the mentally retarded (for further discussion, see Crocker and Hodgins, 1997).
3. We are grateful to Bruce Link who provided us with the data to make these calculations.
4. Sample bias affects the association between symptoms and illegal behaviours. For example, Virkkunen (1974) working in Finland where all persons accused of a violent offence undergo an intensive psychiatric pre-trial evaluation, found that only 37% of the violent behaviours of schizophrenic subjects occurred when

the perpetrators had delusions or hallucinations. By contrast, in England, Taylor (1985) examined a sample of accused remanded for a pre-trial psychiatric evaluation and found that only 9 of 121 had no positive symptoms at the time of the index offence. Whereas Virkkunen's sample included all persons accused of violent crimes, out of whom he selected the schizophrenics, the latter study included men accused of criminal offences whom the court thought might be mentally ill or had been mentally ill at the time of the offence. Consequently, it is not surprising that in this sample an association was found between the presence of positive symptoms and violent behaviour.

5. This hypothesis has been developed over several years in collaborative studies with Gilles Côté and Jean Toupin (Hodgins, Côté, and Toupin, 1998; Hodgins, Toupin, and Côté, 1996).

6. The idea that personality traits or disorders rather than the major mental disorder are primarily associated with criminality is not new. It has often been suggested especially with respect to schizophrenia (see for example, Blackburn, 1968; Kallman, 1938).

CHAPTER 6

EARLY AND LATE-STARTERS

As was noted in Chapter 4, some of the offenders who developed major mental disorders began offending in early adolescence and as was presented in Chapter 5, some of them had been identified even before that by the child welfare agency for substance abuse. Others who also developed a major mental disorder did not begin offending until adulthood. Among the offenders, the early-starters were defined as those who were convicted of their first offence before the age of eighteen[1], and the late-starters as those who were convicted of their first offence at or after the age of eighteen.

PREVALENCE OF EARLY AND LATE-START OFFENDERS

The prevalence of the early and late-start offenders is presented in Table 6.1. The increased prevalence of offenders among both the males and females with major mental disorders as compared to the non-disordered subjects is reflected in greater proportions of both early and late-starters. However, there is a significant gender difference, both among the disordered and the non-disordered. Among the males, the proportions of early-start offenders are greater than the proportions of late-start offenders. The reverse is true among the females.

COMPARISONS OF OFFENDING OF THE EARLY AND LATE-START OFFENDERS

Males

Table 6.2 presents comparisons of the proportions of early and late-start male offenders convicted of non-violent and violent offences. Consider first

Table 6.1. *Prevalence of early and late-start offenders among subjects with major mental disorders and the non-disordered*

	Major mental disorder		Non-disordered	
	Early-starter	Late-starter	Early-starter	Late-starter
Males	31.7%	18.3%	19.1%	12.6%
Females	7.6%	11.4%	2.9%	4.7%

the men with major mental disorders. Half of the early-starters as compared to 13% of the late-starters had been convicted of eleven or more non-violent offences. By contrast, the proportions of early and late-starter males with major mental disorders convicted for zero, one, or two or more violent offences are similar. This finding among the mentally ill men, that the early-starters and late-starters differ with respect to the pattern of convictions for non-violent offences but not for violent offences, is also true for the non-disordered men. However, among the non-disordered men the differences between the early and late-starters are much less dramatic than those identified among the mentally ill men.

Females
Table 6.3 presents comparisons of the proportions of early and late-start female offenders convicted of different types and numbers of offences.

Table 6.2. *Comparisons of criminal activities of male offenders*

	Major mental disorder		Non-disordered	
	Early-starter	Late-starter	Early-starter	Late-starter
Non-violent offences				
0	3.8%	0	1.4%	4.7%
1	11.5%	40.0%	27.5%	51.5%
2–5	15.4%	33.3%	38.7%	33.5%
6–10	19.2%	13.3%	11.5%	5.6%
11 or more	50.0%	13.4%	20.8%	4.7%
Violent offences				
0	46.2%	60.0%	77.0%	84.3%
1	23.1%	13.3%	11.7%	11.2%
2+	30.7%	26.6%	11.3%	4.6%

Table 6.3. *Comparisons of criminal activities of female offenders*

	Major mental disorder		Non-disordered	
	Early-starter	Late-starter	Early-starter	Late-starter
Non-violent offences				
0	0	55.6%	4.7%	1.5%
1	50.0%	44.4%	47.4%	59.3%
2–5	16.7%	0	31.6%	28.1%
6 or more	33.4%	0	16.4%	11.0%
Violent offences				
0	66.7%	66.7%	86.8%	92.5%
1	16.7%	22.2%	7.9%	4.0%
2 or more	16.7%	11.1%	5.3%	3.5%

Consider first the women with major mental disorders. As can be observed, half of the early and all of the late-starters had none or only one conviction for a non-violent offence, while a third of the early-starters had more than six convictions. No differences were detected between the proportions of early and late-starters who had been convicted of none, one, or two or more violent offences. Few differences emerge in the patterns of convictions of early and late-start non-disordered female offenders.

COMPARISONS OF OFFENDING OF MENTALLY ILL AND NON-DISORDERED EARLY-STARTERS

Males
More of the mentally ill than the non-disordered early-starters had been convicted of eleven or more non-violent offences (50% versus 21%), and two or more violent offences (31% versus 11%).

Females
This same pattern was evident among the female offenders, where 33% of the mentally ill and only 16% of the non-disordered early-starters had been convicted of a non-violent offence and 33% of the mentally ill and only 13% of the non-disordered early-starters had been convicted of one or more violent offences.

COMPARISONS OF OFFENDING OF MENTALLY ILL
AND NON-DISORDERED LATE-STARTERS

Males

More of the mentally ill than the non-disordered late-starters had been convicted of six or more offences (27% versus 10%) and of at least one violent offence (40% versus 16%).

Females

Among the women the pattern of offending that emerges is different. While more than half (56%) of the mentally ill late-starters had never been convicted for a non-violent offence almost all (98.5%) of the non-disordered late-starters had. However, while a third of the female mentally ill late-starters had been convicted of a violent offence, this was true of only 8 per cent of the female non-disordered late-starters.

Conclusion

Four conclusions about offending patterns can be drawn from these analyses. First, among both male and female offenders with major mental disorders, early-starters differ from late-starters with respect to convictions for non-violent offences but not for violent offences. More precisely, larger proportions of early than late-starters have been convicted of numerous non-violent crimes. Second, mentally ill early-starters were more often convicted of criminal offences than were the non-disordered early-starters. Third, the offending patterns of male and female late-starters differ. Fourth, greater proportions of male and female mentally ill late-starters than non-disordered late-starters were convicted of violent offences.

The results of other studies concur with these findings from the Project Metropolitan, that early-starters commit more crimes than late-starters when time at risk is controlled. A Swedish cohort which included all the men with schizophrenia remanded for a pre-trial psychiatric examination for a violent offence in the years 1988 to 1995 was examined. Early-starters were defined as those with a conviction before age eighteen. The early-starters had been convicted of more non-violent and violent crimes than the late-starters controlling for time at risk (Tengström, Hodgins, and Kullgren, 2001). In the Israeli study described in Chapter 5, the subjects diagnosed with major mental disorders and antisocial personality disorder would be early-starters. Almost all of them (93.4%) reported fighting and 65.8% reported weapon use as compared to only 20.7% and 4.4% of those with the same primary disorder but no substance use or personality disorder (Stueve and Link, 1997).

ANTECEDENTS OF OFFENDING

In an effort to begin to understand the developmental trajectories of mentally ill early and late-start offenders, we examined a number of childhood factors. Given the lack of research on childhood factors associated with offending among the mentally ill, we turned to reports from other longitudinal studies of cohorts that had identified childhood characteristics which distinguish adult offenders from non-offenders. Most of these investigations have focused on the childhood characteristics of non-mentally ill early-starters (as was described in Chapter 1). Based on this literature review, we identified factors operative in childhood and adolescence that have previously been associated with adult offending. The objective of the analyses described below was to identify the developmental trajectories of early and late-starters, both those with and without major mental disorders. These analyses were conducted using only the data available on the male subjects. It was not possible to include the female cohort members because so few of them developed both a major mental disorder and offended.

Measures of childhood and adolescent factors

Pregnancy and birth complications. Pregnancy and birth complications were documented from medical files. These files were transcribed and coded in the early 1970s. For the present analyses, the subject was rated as having experienced prenatal complications if two or more of the following had been noted in the medical file: premature pelvic contractions, maternal illness, hospitalisation, or surgery, presence of Rhesus factor, length of pregnancy more than one standard deviation below or above the mean for the cohort, abnormal mode of presentation, neonatal asphyxia, ruptured membranes prior to the onset of labour, duration of labour one or more standard deviations longer or shorter than the average for the cohort, birth weight one of more standard deviations below the mean for males in the cohort[2].

Family problems. Family problems were rated for three time periods based on the subject's age: from birth to age six, from age seven to age twelve, and from age thirteen to age eighteen. If the parents had received social welfare payments for one year or more during a period and/or if the Child Welfare Committee had intervened in the family (therapy, supervision, placement of the child) because of the parents' behaviour, the subjects' family was rated as problematic.

Intellectual performance. Intelligence test scores were obtained using the Härnqvist Swedish Intelligence Test when the subjects were twelve years old. Intellectual performance was rated as poor if the standardised global test score was more than one standard deviation below the cohort mean.

School performance. The subjects' academic performance was recorded from their school files when they were twelve (grade 6) and fifteen years of age (grade 9). Performance was rated as poor if the average over-all mark fell more than one standard deviation below the mean for the males in the cohort.

Behaviour problems. Behaviour problems were documented for two time periods: age seven to age twelve and ages thirteen to seventeen. Behaviour problems were rated based on information extracted from the records of the Child Welfare Committee. For the period when the cohort members were seven to twelve years old, behaviour problems were rated as present if the Child Welfare Committee had intervened because of the child's behaviour or if any of the following behaviours were noted: disorderly conduct in the community, vandalism, theft. During the later period when cohort members were aged thirteen to eighteen, behaviour problems were rated as present if any intervention was required because of the subject's behaviour or if any of the following behaviours were reported: disorderly conduct, vandalism, assault, theft, substance abuse, traffic accidents due to alcohol and/or drug use, and other moving traffic violations.

Comparisons of childhood and adolescent characteristics of mentally ill and non-mentally ill early and late-start offenders and non-offenders

Table 6.4 presents comparisons of the childhood and adolescent characteristics of the early and late-start offenders and of the non-offenders, classified as mentally ill or not. As can be seen, thirteen comparisons between the mentally ill and non-ill subjects were made, first for the early-starters, then for the late-starters, and finally for the non-offenders. When making so many comparisons, it is inevitable that some will be statistically significant, not necessarily because the groups of subjects who are being compared are different as to the characteristic in question, but simply because of chance. To infer a group difference when none exists is referred to as a Type II error. In order to protect against making Type II errors (erroneously inferring that

Table 6.4. *Childhood and adolescent characteristics categorised according to subjects' mental status and criminal record*

	Major mental disorder (n = 81)	Non-disordered (n = 6933)	Between-group tests	
			X^2	p
Birth to 6 years old				
Obstetrical complications				
early-starter	28%	14%	1.22	ns
late-starter	14%	13%	0.36	ns
non-offender	13%	15%	0.41	ns
Family problems				
early-starter	38%	31%	0.55	ns
late-starter	29%	22%	0.32	ns
non-offender	22%	13%	2.29	ns
7 to 12 years old				
Family problems				
early-starter	33%	22%	1.95	ns
late-starter	21%	15%	0.47	ns
non-offender	21%	7%	9.59	.007
Poor intellectual performance				
early-starter	24%	23%	0.00	ns
late-starter	0%	19%	2.87	ns
non-offender	17%	11%	1.17	ns
Poor grades				
early-starter	42%	39%	0.09	ns
late-starter	36%	29%	0.28	ns
non-offender	11%	17%	0.86	ns
Behaviour problems				
early-starter	26%	11%	5.34	.034
late-starter	0%	4%	0.42	ns
non-offender	3%	1%	0.48	ns
13 to 18 years old				
Family problems				
early-starter	35%	22%	2.14	ns
late-starter	31%	14%	2.73	ns
non-offender	32%	8%	27.1	.000
Poor grades				
early-starter	63%	32%	8.09	.003
late-starter	23%	24%	0.00	ns
non-offender	11%	10%	0.01	ns

Table 6.4. (*cont.*)

	Major mental disorder (n = 81)	Non-disordered (n = 6933)	Between-group tests	
			X^2	p
Behaviour problems				
early-starter	74%	71%	0.15	ns
late-starter	23%	19%	0.27	ns
non-offender	22%	7%	13.42	.002

Note: Level of significance based on one-tailed probability test.

there is a difference when there is not), the level of statistical significance used to indicate a group difference was raised to .01 (99% confidence level).

Consider first the comparisons of the mentally ill and non-mentally ill early-start offenders. Using the adjusted level of statistical significance, it can be noted in Table 6.4, that these two groups of offenders differ on only one characteristic that was measured in childhood and adolescence: proportionately more of the mentally ill early-starters (63%) than the non-mentally ill early-starters (32%) obtained poor school grades in adolescence. Consider next the comparisons between the mentally ill and non-mentally ill late-start offenders. They did not differ as to any of the childhood and adolescent characteristics that were measured. Finally, look at the comparisons in the table between the mentally ill and non-mentally ill subjects who had no record of criminal activity by age thirty. These two groups differed on two characteristics. Proportionately more of those who grew up and developed a mental illness had been raised in families rated as having had problems from the time that they were aged seven to eighteen years old. In addition, by adolescence, proportionately more of them presented behaviour problems severe enough to require some kind of intervention by the Child Welfare Committee.

Comparisons of childhood and adolescent characteristics of offenders and non-offenders without mental illness

Among the non-mentally ill subjects, consider first the comparisons between the early-start offenders and the non-offenders. These comparisons are also presented in Table 6.4. Proportionately more of the early-start offenders than the non-offenders were raised in problem families in all three time periods, they performed poorly on the intelligence test at age twelve, they obtained low marks throughout all their years at school, and they presented behaviour problems consistently from age seven onwards.

Next, still considering the non-mentally ill men, look at the comparisons in Table 6.4 between the late-start offenders and the non-offenders. A general pattern emerges suggesting that the proportions of late-start offenders characterised by difficulties in childhood and/or adolescence were smaller than those observed among the early-start (non-mentally ill) offenders, but greater than those observed among the non-offenders without mental illness. This pattern is especially evident for family problems from birth to age twelve, for low scores on the intelligence test and low marks at school from age seven through eighteen. It is interesting to note that the proportions of non-mentally ill late-starters who presented behaviour problems in either time period never exceeded those observed among the non-mentally ill non-offenders.

Comparisons of childhood and adolescent characteristics of offenders and non-offenders with mental illness

Among the mentally ill males, few comparisons are statistically significant. This is not surprising given the small number of subjects with mental illness who offended. Proportionately more of the mentally ill early-start offenders than the mentally ill non-offenders obtained poor marks in school from age seven onwards, and presented behaviour problems during these two age periods.

DEVELOPMENTAL TRAJECTORIES

Statistical procedures

The combinations of childhood and adolescent characteristics that distinguished the different groups of offenders and non-offenders were identified using configural frequency analysis (Bergman and Magnusson, 1997; Bergman and El-Khouri, 1995; Krauth and Lienert, 1982). These analyses identify sub-groups of subjects with various combinations of childhood and adolescent characteristics, and then calculate whether the sub-group includes more or fewer subjects than would be expected by chance. Sub-groups which include more subjects than would be expected by chance are called Types and those with fewer subjects are called Anti-Types. Nine childhood and adolescent characteristics considered to be risk factors for adult criminality were included in the configural frequency analysis: during the period birth to six years, prenatal factors and family problems; during the period from seven to twelve years of age, family problems, poor intellectual performance, poor academic performance, and behaviour problems; and during adolescence, family problems, poor school performance, and behaviour problems. Once the sub-groups of subjects at each age period had been identified, the movements of subjects from one sub-group to another throughout the three age periods were tracked. Typical and atypical developmental pathways from one age period to another were identified by cross-sectional linkage using exact cellwise tests (Lienert and Bergman, 1985).

Like other multivariate analyses, configural frequency analysis requires complete data for all of the subjects. The proportions of mentally ill and non-mentally ill subjects who were missing data were similar: no missing data, 54% mentally ill and 63% non-mentally ill; one missing value, 24% mentally ill and 20% non-mentally ill; two missing values, 9% mentally ill and 5% non-mentally ill; and three or more missing values, 14% mentally ill and 12% non-mentally ill. These latter subjects with three or more missing values were excluded from the analyses. This procedure resulted in the loss of 11 (14%) of the subjects who developed major mental disorders in adulthood, and 819 (12%) of the non-mentally ill subjects. Of the remaining 6,193 subjects, 1,417 subjects had a missing value for 1 of the 9 variables and 363 subjects had 2 missing values. Rather than exclude these subjects, a value for this variable was assigned to each subject using an imputation procedure (Bergman and El-Khouri, 1992). For each subject with a missing value, a twin subject was identified who had the same values on all of the other variables included in the analysis. The twin's value was imputed to the subject for whom a value was missing. In the present analyses, a twin was defined by a Euclidean distance smaller than .05; this condition was respected for all subjects.

Patterns of risk factors at the three age periods were identified by submitting all possible combinations of risk factors to a Configural Frequency Analysis (CFA) using exact binomial tests. The resulting sub-groups of subjects are presented in Table 6.5.

Empirically derived risk groups
Early childhood. During the age period of pregnancy to six years, the results indicated that none of the four combinations of risk factors were observed more or less often than would be expected by chance. Given the large number of subjects with each combination of factors, four groups were created. Group I includes the subjects with no family problems (71.9%). Group II includes subjects who had experienced prenatal complications (but no family

problems) (10.7%). Group III includes those whose families had problems but who had not experienced prenatal complications (14.7%) and Group IV includes those characterised by both prenatal complications and problem families (2.6%).

Middle childhood. During the age period seven to twelve years, as can be noted in the table, six Types (combinations of factors that occurred more often than would be expected by chance) and four Anti-Types (combinations of factors that occurred less often than would be expected by chance) were identified. These results lead to the creation of ten sub-groups. Group I, the no risk group, includes the subjects whose families did not have problems, who obtained intelligence test scores within the normal range, whose academic performance was within the normal range, and who had not been identified by the Child Welfare Committee as having problems (65.7%). This group included more subjects than would be expected by chance, that is if subjects were distributed evenly amongst the ten groups. Therefore, this group is referred to as a Type. By contrast, Groups II, III, IV, and V were found to include fewer subjects than would be expected by chance and are consequently referred to as Anti-Types. These groups, II to V, include subjects characterised by only one risk factor (II family problems (5.1%), III low intelligence (4.7%), IV poor academic performance (10.2%), V behaviour problems (1.2%). Group VI includes subjects from problem families who either performed poorly on the intelligence test or on school examinations (0.9%). This latter group, VI, included approximately the numbers of subjects expected by chance. Group VII, a significant Type, includes subjects who performed poorly on both the intelligence test and school examinations (2.4%). Group VIII, also a significant Type, includes subjects who came from problem families, and who performed poorly on both the intelligence test and school examinations (6.5%). Group IX includes subjects with behaviour problems and one or two other risk factors. It includes no more or fewer subjects than would be expected by chance (1.6%). Group X includes subjects with behaviour problems, poor academic performance, and one or two other risk factors (0.3%). As can be noted in Table 6.5, this is a significant Type.

Adolescence. During the period from age thirteen to eighteen, as can be seen in Table 6.5, four Types and three Anti-Types were identified. From these results, eight groups were constituted. Group I includes subjects whose

Table 6.5. *Groups of subjects based on typical and atypical individual patterns of risk at the three age periods*

Birth to 6 years

Groups by age periods	Prenatal complications	Family problems	Observed	Expected	
			Frequencies		
I. No risk	no	no	4454	4434.55	ns
II. Prenatal complications	yes	no	664	683.45	ns
III. Family problems	no	yes	912	931.45	ns
IV. Prenatal complications and family problems	yes	yes	163	143.55	ns

7 to 12 years

Groups by age periods	Family problems	Poor intellectual performance	Poor grades	Behaviour problems	Observed	Expected	
I. No risk	no	no	no	no	4071	3574.21	T***
II. Family problems	yes	no	no	no	315	430.69	AT***
III. Poor intellectual performance	no	yes	no	no	290	607.74	AT***
IV. Poor grades	no	no	yes	no	629	1003.88	AT***
V. Behaviour problems	no	no	no	yes	72	113.74	AT**
VI. Family problems and poor intellectual performance or poor grades	yes	yes	no	no	55	73.23	ns
	yes	no	yes	no	146	120.97	ns
VII. Poor intellectual performance and poor grades	no	yes	yes	no	400	170.70	T***

	Family problems	Poor grades	Behaviour problems		n		
VIII. Family problems, poor intellectual performance and poor grades	yes	yes	yes	no	96	20.57	T***
IX. Behaviour problems and one or two other risk factors	yes	no	no	yes	18	13.71	ns
	no	yes	no	yes	7	19.34	ns
	yes	yes	no	yes	7	2.33	ns
	no	no	yes	yes	29	31.91	ns
X. Behaviour problems, poor grades and one or two other risk factors	yes	no	yes	yes	13	3.85	T**
	no	yes	yes	yes	29	5.43	T***
	yes	yes	yes	yes	16	0.65	T***

13 to 18 years

	Family problems	Poor grades	Behaviour problems		n		
I. No risk	no	no	no		4006	3644.58	T***
II. Family problems	yes	no	no		309	453.26	AT***
III. Poor grades	no	yes	no		535	754.35	AT***
IV. Behaviour problems	no	no	yes		641	918.88	AT***
V. Family problems and poor grades	yes	yes	no		96	93.81	ns
VI. Family problems and behaviour problems	yes	no	yes		175	114.28	T***
VII. Poor grades and behaviour problems	no	yes	yes		326	190.19	T***
VIII. Family problems, poor grades and behaviour problems	yes	yes	yes		105	23.65	T***

Note: T: Types, AT: Anti-Types. p* $\le$ .05, p** $\le$ .01, p*** $\le$ .001.
Level of significance based on exact cellwise test and binomial probability after Bonferroni correction for the number of tests performed.

families did not have problems serious enough to warrant intervention, who obtained marks at school within normal limits, and who had not been identified by the Child Welfare Committee as presenting behaviour problems (64.7%). As in the period seven to twelve years, this no-risk group includes more subjects than would be expected by chance. Groups II, III, and IV include subjects with one or other of the risk factors (5.0%, 8.6%, 10.4%). Each includes fewer subjects than would be expected by chance. Groups V and VI include subjects from problem families; those in Group V performed poorly at school (1.6%) and those in Group VI had behaviour problems (2.8%). While Group V included only the approximate number of subjects expected by chance, Group VI included more. Group VII includes subjects who did poorly on examinations at school and who also had behaviour problems (5.3%). Group VIII includes subjects who in addition to family problems and poor academic performance, also presented behaviour problems (1.7%). Both Groups VII and VIII included more subjects than expected by chance.

Development

Developmental trajectories were identified by examining the movement of the subjects, from one sub-group to another, as they grew up. Subjects' membership in the sub-groups was tracked through the three age periods and to one of six possible adult outcomes: (1) no mental illness and no criminality; (2) mental illness and no criminality; (3) no mental illness and early-start criminality; (4) mental illness and early-start criminality; (5) no mental illness and late-start criminality; and (6) mental illness and late-start criminality.

From early to middle childhood. The developmental pathways from the period of birth to six years to the period seven to twelve years that reached statistical significance are represented in Figure 6.1. Almost three-quarters (74%) of the subjects who did not experience prenatal complications and who were raised in non-problem families during their first six years, continued to be free of risk factors in middle childhood. Conversely, subjects raised in families with problems in the first six years of their lives, both those who had experienced prenatal complications and those who had not, are under-represented in the no-risk group and over-represented in groups characterised by risk factors in middle childhood. Less than one-third (31%) of the children whose families had problems during their early years presented no risk factors in middle childhood. The other two-thirds, as can be seen in

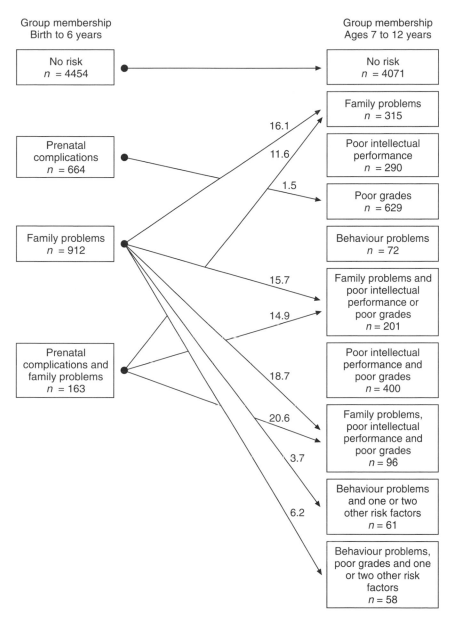

Figure 6.1 Developmental pathways from the first six years of life to middle child-hood. The numbers on the arrows indicate how many times more likely it is for these subjects, as compared to those from the no-risk group, to follow this pathway.

the figure, were at least 15 times more likely than the subjects with no risk to continue experiencing family problems in middle childhood, and as well, to perform poorly on both the intelligence test and school examinations. Subjects who had experienced both family problems in the first six years and prenatal complications were 20 times more likely than those without these problems to continue to have problem families in middle childhood and to perform poorly on the intelligence test and on school examinations.

Very few of the children who presented behaviour problems severe enough to warrant an intervention in middle childhood had experienced prenatal complications and/or family problems during their first six years. In fact, 60% of the subjects who manifested behaviour problems (only) in middle childhood had no risk factors in the early period. Those who manifested behaviour problems accompanied by other risk factors were more likely to have had families with problems in early childhood, but 40 to 48% of them had no risk factors.

Problems measured from conception to six years, did not always lead to problems in middle childhood. Among those who experienced only prenatal complications, 68% presented no risk in middle childhood. However, being raised during the first six years in a family with problems severe enough to warrant intervention greatly reduced the likelihood of having no risk in middle childhood. In fact, only 31% of the subjects whose families had problems and 33% of those who had experienced prenatal difficulties and a problem family presented no-risk in middle childhood.

Middle childhood to adolescence. The multiple developmental pathways from middle childhood to adolescence that were statistically significant are depicted in Figure 6.2. Again, most (81%) of the children not characterised by risk factors in middle childhood, continued to be free of such difficulties during adolescence when they constituted 82% of the no-risk group.

During middle childhood, as in the earlier period, family problems, either alone or in combination with other risk factors, dramatically increased the likelihood of difficulties during adolescence. Behaviour problems identified in middle childhood also greatly increased the risk of problems in adolescence but only if they had been accompanied in middle childhood by other risk factors.

In addition, family problems and poor intellectual performance and/or poor grades in early childhood greatly increased the risk of similar problems in adolescence, and also very greatly increased the risk of similar problems accompanied by behaviour problems.

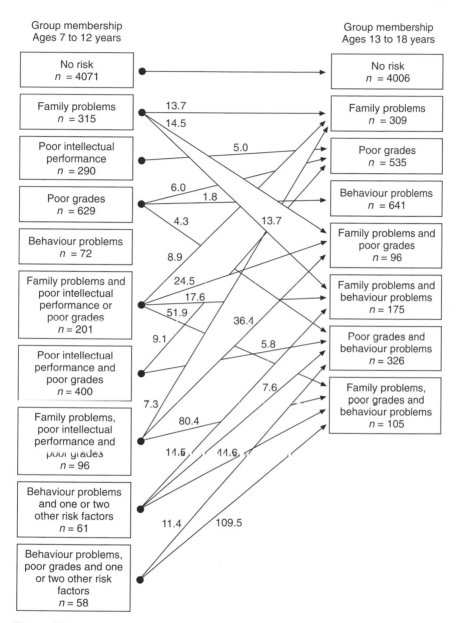

Figure 6.2 Developmental pathways from middle childhood to adolescence. The numbers on the arrows indicate how many times more likely it is for these subjects, as compared to those from the no-risk group, to follow this pathway.

If problems had been present during middle childhood, it was likely that they were also present in adolescence. Of those who had family problems in middle childhood, only 31% had no risk in adolescence. Of those who had family problems and low intelligence, 19% had no risk in adolescence. Of those who had family problems, low intelligence and poor grades in school, 12% had no risk in adolescence. These results demonstrate the persistence of family problems, and the likelihood that children from such families will develop additional problems which persist over time. They also demonstrate that it is not simply the number but the type of risk factor that is important. Family problems, alone or accompanied by other problems, were more likely to lead to problems in adolescence than either low intelligence test scores or poor grades. (Of those who obtained low scores on the intelligence test in middle childhood, 56% had no risk in adolescence. Of those who obtained low marks in school in middle childhood, 40% had no risk in adolescence.) Low intelligence test scores and poor academic performance in middle childhood, led to no-risk status in adolescence in only 28% of the cases. While almost half (47%) of those who had behaviour problems (only) in middle childhood had no-risk in adolescence, this was true of only 13% of those who had presented both behaviour problems and other risk factors in middle childhood.

Looking backwards in time, as depicted in Figure 6.3, more than half of the adolescents identified for behaviour problems (only), and a third of those who presented both behaviour problems and poor academic performance had not shown any risk in middle childhood. Similarly, 30% of the adolescents who obtained low marks in school (but who showed no other risk factor) had presented no-risk factor in middle childhood. However, as was noted from the early period to middle childhood, from middle childhood to adolescence, family problems persist and are likely to be associated with other problems.

Adolescence to adulthood. The statistically significant pathways from adolescence to adulthood are depicted in Figure 6.4. Once more, most (82%) of the subjects with no risk factors in adolescence have neither a mental illness nor a criminal record by age thirty. They constitute 78% of the non-mentally ill non-offender group at age thirty. Behaviour problems in adolescence were associated most strongly with early-start offending in adulthood. The addition of other risk factors to behaviour problems during adolescence did not significantly increase the risk of offending among those who did not develop a major mental disorder. However, among the mentally ill, the combination of behaviour problems and poor academic performance

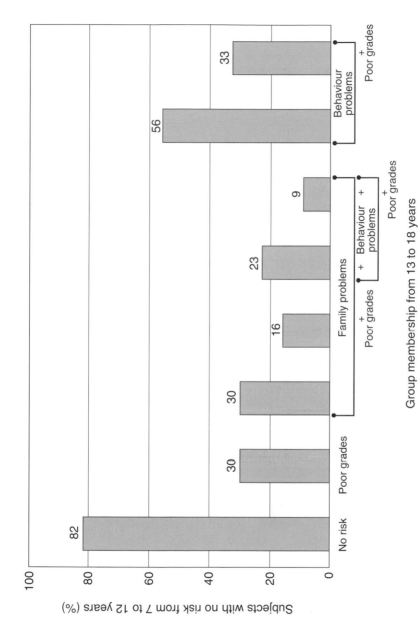

Figure 6.3. Group membership during adolescence of subjects with no risk factors during middle childhood.

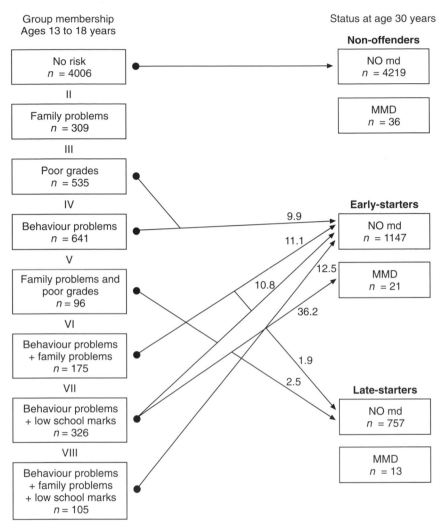

Figure 6.4 Developmental pathways from adolescence to adulthood. The numbers on the arrows indicate how many times more likely it is for those subjects, as compared to those from the no-risk group, to follow this pathway.

during adolescence dramatically increased the risk of early-start offending. Family problems, either in combination with only behaviour problems, or both behaviour problems and poor academic performance, increased the risk of offending only among those who did not develop a major mental disorder.

This powerful association between behaviour problems in adolescence and adult offending and the lack of association between family problems and offending and/or mental illness is also apparent when considering the percentages of subjects from each adolescent risk group who did not have negative adult outcomes. Three-quarters of those who had had family problems, 65% of those with poor grades, and 60% of those with both family problems and poor grades were non-mentally ill non-offenders at age thirty. By contrast, this was true of 27% of those who had had behaviour problems (only), 20% of those with behaviour problems and poor grades, 18% of those who had had behaviour problems and family problems, and 11% of those with behaviour problems accompanied by other risk factors.

From conception to adulthood. Behaviour problems in adolescence accompanied by other difficulties were found to lead to early-start offending. Subjects who presented such combinations of difficulties in adolescence, were characterised by multiple difficulties in middle childhood, most often including behaviour problems. Those whose families had problems in middle childhood were most likely to have had similar problems in their earliest years. Some had also experienced prenatal complications. As shown by our results, the antecedents of late-start offending remain obscure both among individuals who do and do not develop a mental illness.

Table 6.6 presents the percentages of subjects who were characterised by one or more of the risk factors during the various age periods. As can be seen, only eight per cent of the mentally ill and 16% of the non-mentally ill early-start offenders were *not* characterised by at least one of the risk factors during at least one age period. In fact, of these early-start offenders, 81% of those who developed a mental illness and 66% of those who did not, were characterised by risk before the age of thirteen. By contrast, among the late-start offenders, 40% of the mentally ill and 37% of the non-mentally ill never showed any of the risk factors. These proportions are similar to those observed for the non-offenders, both the mentally ill (43%) and the non-mentally ill (56%) who were never characterised by any of the risk factors. More than one-quarter of the mentally ill offenders, both early and late-starters, were characterised by risk during all three age periods. This was true of 22% of the non-mentally ill early-start offenders and 12% of the non-mentally ill late-starters. Conversely, only 5% of the non-mentally ill non-offenders were characterised by risk in all three age periods.

The early age at which many of the subjects who offended in adulthood began to show difficulties is further evident when examining the number of risk factors which characterised them (see Table 6.7). Consider first the non-mentally ill offenders: 64% of the early-starters and 39% of the late-starters

Table 6.6. *Percentages of subjects who presented risk factors at one or more age periods*

Patterns of risk by age periods	Early-starter		Late-starter		Non-offender	
	Major mental disorder (n = 26)	Non-disordered (n = 1324)	Major mental disorder (n = 15)	Non-disordered (n = 876)	Major mental disorder (n = 40)	Non-disordered (n = 4733)
No risk at all age periods	8%	16%	40%	37%	43%	56%
Risk at birth to 6 years	0%	3%	0%	8%	8%	11%
Risk at age 7 to 12 years	0%	6%	7%	13%	8%	10%
Risk at age 13 to 18 years	12%	19%	13%	10%	8%	6%
Risk at birth to 6 years and at 7 to 12 years	8%	4%	7%	5%	0%	5%
Risk at birth to 6 years and at 13 to 18 years	15%	7%	0%	3%	5%	2%
Risk at 7 to 12 years and at 13 to 18 years	31%	24%	7%	13%	15%	7%
Risk at all age periods	27%	22%	27%	12%	15%	5%

Table 6.7. *Percentages of subjects who presented one or more risk factors from birth to 18 years*

Number of risk factors from birth to 18 years	Early-starter		Late-starter		Non-offender	
	Major mental disorder (n = 26)	Non-disordered (n = 1324)	Major mental disorder (n = 15)	Non-disordered (n = 876)	Major mental disorder (n = 40)	Non-disordered (n = 4733)
None	8%	16%	40%	37%	43%	56%
One	4%	20%	13%	24%	23%	23%
Two	27%	22%	13%	17%	10%	11%
Three	23%	16%	7%	10%	10%	6%
Four	19%	12%	20%	6%	5%	2%
Five	8%	7%	7%	4%	8%	1.4%
Six	4%	5%	0%	2%	3%	0.5%
Seven	4%	2%	0%	1%	0%	0.2%
Eight	0%	1%	0%	0.2%	—	—
Nine	4%	0.2%	—	—	—	—
Ten	0%	0.1%	—	—	—	—

had two or more risk factors. Among the mentally ill offenders, 88% of the early-starters and 47% of the late-starters had two or more risk factors. By contrast, among the non-offenders, 21% of the non-mentally ill and 33% of the mentally ill subjects were characterised by two or more risk factors.

Conclusion

The first and most important conclusion is that almost all of the early-start offenders, both the non-disordered and the mentally ill, were characterised by one or more of the measured risk factors in childhood and adolescence. Among the non-mentally disordered early-start offenders, 84% had presented identifiable problems when growing up, 35% of them before age thirteen. Most presented behaviour problems, defined here as non-criminalised delinquency, and two-thirds of them presented other problems as well. These results concerning the non-disordered early-start offenders confirm those from many other longitudinal prospective investigations that are reviewed in Chapter 1. Among the early-start offenders who developed a mental illness, 92% were characterised by one or more risk factors. More than 80% were characterised by these risk factors before age thirteen. The proportion with multiple problems, 88%, is even higher than that for the non-disordered early-starters.

The second conclusion to be drawn from these results is that among the early-start offenders, both those who developed major mental disorders and those who did not, behaviour problems, either alone or in combination with other problems, almost always precede offending. By contrast, family problems and poor academic performance, either singly or in combination, are only infrequently precursors of offending or of mental illness. While behaviour problems appear to be necessary for the subsequent development of offending, they are not sufficient determinants, as indicated by the finding that 47% of those with behaviour problems in middle childhood did not present such problems in adolescence.

A third conclusion is that it is the accumulation and persistence of risk factors throughout childhood and adolescence that leads to negative outcomes. In fact, during middle childhood and adolescence, it was unlikely that a boy with one problem did not have at least one other problem. However, it was not simply the number of risk factors that increased the risk of later offending. The results strongly suggest that the combination of factors which act as determinants almost always includes behaviour problems. For example, three-quarters of the cohort members who had family problems, 65% of those who obtained low marks in school, and 60% who were characterised by both of these risk factors neither offended nor developed a mental illness. By contrast, 27% of those with behaviour problems only, and smaller proportions of those with behaviour problems and other problems had a positive outcome in adulthood.

The fourth conclusion is that we failed to identify the early childhood antecedents of behaviour problems. Of those cohort members with behaviour problems in adolescence, 56% had no risk in middle childhood, and of those with both behaviour problems and poor academic performance one-third had no antecedent risk factors. Similarly, of those with behaviour problems in middle childhood, 60% had no risk in early childhood.

The fifth conclusion that can be drawn from the results is that there is no evidence that the early antecedents of criminality differ for offenders who develop a major mental disorder and those who do not. However, this may be due to the relatively few subjects in the cohort who developed major mental disorders. Or, it could be that our risk factors did not include characteristics that would distinguish the children who developed major mental disorders in adulthood. Many of these children, for example, could likely be distinguished by the presence of first and second degree relatives who have a similar mental disorder. Research on the childhood precursors of the major mental disorders suggests that many such children would also be distinguished by their performance on neuropsychological tests and psychosocial functioning (see Hodgins, 1998). However, the findings from these analyses of the Metropolitan cohort confirm our hypothesis concerning the similarity of early-start offenders who do and who do not develop mental illness. The results demonstrate that among boys who present behaviour problems there are at least three sub-groups: (1) those who become non-disordered adult offenders; (2) those who develop a major mental disorder and offend; and (3) those who neither offend nor develop a mental illness.

Little was learned about the development of late-start offenders. The distinguishing characteristics of those with and without mental illness continue to elude us. Late-start offenders, both those who developed a major mental disorder and those who did not, were not more often characterised by risk factors in childhood and adolescence than were the non-offenders, nor did they accumulate more problems than the non-offenders.

Implications of the findings for future research and intervention

The conclusions drawn from our analyses have implications both for future research and for intervention. The high proportion of early-start offenders who are characterised by risk in childhood means that prevention of offending may be possible. The fact that behaviour problems appear to be necessary but insufficient precursors of offending further facilitates identification of potential offenders and provides the target for intervention. The fact that behaviour problems often occur singly before they combine with other risk factors increases the likelihood that a behavioural intervention aimed at eliminating such behaviours would be successful.

Our results leave many unanswered questions. Most notably, why are some children able to overcome difficulties and avoid the negative outcomes that were measured in adulthood, while others develop increasing difficulties with age? Some children who manifest problems do not grow up to offend or to develop mental illness. Single problems are more likely to lead to non-negative adult outcomes than are multiple problems. The younger the age at which the problem is identifiable, the more likely that it will be associated with a negative outcome. However, some children and adolescents with multiple problems which persisted over two age periods did avoid negative adult outcomes. The characteristics which distinguish such children deserve further investigation as this knowledge could be used in designing prevention programmes.

One of the few disadvantages of a longitudinal cohort study, like the Project Metropolitan, is that the measures are as old as the subjects. In other words, if we knew then (when the study was designed) what we know now, we would have added other information and measured certain factors differently. We would add for example, measures of antisocial personality disorder, alcohol abuse, and major mental disorders among the first degree relatives which are indicators, albeit it rather imprecise ones, of genetic vulnerabilities for these disorders (for further discussion, see Hodgins, 2000). In addition, we would add measures of mothers' behaviours during pregnancy. Recent studies have shown that maternal smoking during pregnancy increases the male offspring's risk for conduct disorder in childhood and adolescence (Fergusson, Woodward, and Horwood, 1998) and for violent offending in adulthood (Brennan, Grekin, and Mednick, 1999; Räsänen, Hakko, Isohanni, Hodgins, Järvelin, and Tiihonen, 1999). We would add measures of parenting skills that have been found to be lacking even among the parents of very young children who display behaviour problems (Patterson and Yoerger, 1993).

Based on current knowledge both from the Project Metropolitan and many other studies, we would hypothesise that early-start offenders develop as follows. Males who become early-start offenders may begin life with certain behavioural tendencies, for example, novelty-seeking, aggression, impulsivity, that they have inherited. If these tendencies are strengthened and reinforced by experiences subsequent to conception, they may become stable characteristics or traits. Such characteristics increase the likelihood of illegal behaviour. It is important to note that there is no evidence that such inherited characteristics in-and-of-themselves cause criminality. Rather, the evidence suggests that inherited vulnerabilities are strengthened or weakened by experience. (For a further discussion, see Hodgins, 2000).

Complications occurring during the pregnancy or at birth, either in interaction with hereditary factors or alone, may lead to subtle impairments of the central nervous system. Such impairment may be associated with a lack of self control expressed as conduct problems, and/or impaired performance on neuropsychological tests. Such impairments have been found to increase the likelihood of persistent aggressive behaviour among boys being raised in adverse home environments (Moffitt, 1990). Conduct problems and other deficits are exacerbated by the impoverished verbal abilities shown by most of these children. Just as inherited tendencies can be weakened or strengthened by experience, similarly the consequences of problems which occur during the pregnancy and birth can be worsened by events which follow. For example, the Danish Perinatal Project included all 9,125 individuals born at the university hospital in Copenhagen between 1959 and 1961 (Zachau-Christiansen and Mednick, 1981). When the subjects were eighteen years old, they were re-examined and the impact of perinatal complications combined with a stable family on intellectual skills and behaviour was measured. The subjects who had experienced difficult pregnancies or births obtained lower marks on reading and mathematics tests than those who had not experienced perinatal complications. However, among them (those who had experienced perinatal problems), many more of those from families that had split up, than those from intact families, evidenced deficits in reading and mathematics. Similarly, family status interacted with perinatal factors in predicting aggressive behaviour at age 18. Of those who had experienced no or few perinatal complications, 5 per cent of those raised in broken families and 9 per cent raised in intact families were rated as aggressive at age eighteen. However, of those who had experienced pregnancy and birth complications, 13% who came from an intact family as compared to 38% from a broken family were rated as aggressive at age eighteen. While intellectual skills and aggressive behaviour were found to be related to an interaction between perinatal complications and family status, this was not true of impulsive behaviour. Impulsivity at age eighteen was not related to the family stability variable, but only to perinatal factors. Among subjects who had experienced few or no perinatal complications, 10% were rated as impulsive at age eighteen as compared to more than half of those who had experienced difficulties during the pregnancy or at birth (Baker and Mednick, 1984a)[2]. In more detailed analyses of the pregnancy and birth records of the Metropolitan cohort, we have recently found that among the men who developed major mental disorders and who had experienced complications in the neonatal period, all but one committed at least one crime. Among those who developed a major mental disorder, this factor was found to be more powerful in determining adult outcome than were the characteristics of the family of origin. By contrast, among those who did not develop a mental disorder in adulthood, family characteristics were strongly associated with offending and neonatal complications were not (Hodgins, Kratzer, and McNeil, in press).

Children who are impulsive and/or disobedient present challenges to their parents. Many studies have shown that in order to overcome their problems, they require an especially rich and sympathetic learning environment and a structured and systematic set of responses to punish inappropriate behaviours while rewarding appropriate ones. Some parents may not be able to provide this type of environment which would allow the child to overcome his/her minor problems. Parents may themselves have problems, such as substance abuse, depression, have limited knowledge of what their child needs, and further, not know how to use community resources that could be helpful to the child. If addressed early in the child's life and appropriately, the lack of self-control and pursuant conduct problems may have no or few consequences. However, if not corrected, these difficulties may accumulate, affecting different spheres of functioning – behavioural, psychological, and intellectual – and manifesting themselves in different milieux – school and the community. As the child progresses in school and behaviour problems and poor academic achievement become apparent, the parents again fail to meet the challenge as does the child social welfare agency. In the case of the Metropolitan cohort members, both family problems and individual problems of the child were diagnosed by this agency, yet their interventions appear to have had little impact on the outcome. Once into adolescence, delinquency begins, is recognised by the child welfare agency, and develops and persists into adult criminality.

Our analyses indicated that from middle childhood on, behaviour problems accompanied by either academic difficulties and/or problems at home were very likely to lead to offending. Some of the male subjects who presented these problems may also have had attention deficit disorder. However, for the Metropolitan cohort we have no measure of this childhood disorder. Many studies have shown that boys with this disorder are at high risk for adult criminality (see for example, Achenbach, *et al.*,

1993; Farrington, Loeber, and Van Kammen, 1990). Behaviour problems in middle childhood merit corrective intervention for the findings suggest that they can easily develop into delinquency and criminality.

CLINICAL STUDIES OF EARLY AND LATE-START OFFENDERS

The existence and characteristics of early and late-starters among offenders with major mental disorders has been further explored by examining clinical samples. The disadvantage of this research strategy is that it depends on retrospective reports of childhood behaviour. Some of these reports are objective, for example records of juvenile offending or records of school achievement, while others are subjective, for example an adult subject's report of his/her own behaviour in childhood and adolescence. The advantage, of course, is that such clinical studies, as opposed to an investigation like the Project Metropolitan, can be completed in a relatively short period of time.

The findings from the Project Metropolitan suggested that factors associated with the offending of the early and late-starters with major mental disorders may be different. Certainly, among the mentally ill offenders, the early-starters had more varied and more severe childhood problems than did the late-starters. If further studies confirm the existence of the early and late-starter types, and as well the differences in the factors associated with their offending, then different treatment and management strategies are needed to prevent offending among the two types. Further, assessment procedures would have to be modified to take account of this distinction. Consequently, we judged it important to pursue clinical studies to confirm or refute this hypothesis. First, we wanted to know if both early and late-start offenders could be identified in clinical samples of offenders with major mental disorders. If they could be identified, we wanted to know if they are processed by the criminal justice and mental health systems of each country in the same way, and how they differ in terms of the primary disorder and symptomatology, the course of their disorders, the type of crimes that they commit, the frequency of offending, the conditions in which they offend, and their response to various treatments and services. This information could be critical for improving the accuracy of risk assessment and for treatment and management.

We first examined a representative sample of male penitentiary inmates in Quebec (Hodgins and Côté, 1990). These 495 men all had sentences of 2 years or longer. One-hundred and nine of them were diagnosed with a major mental disorder. The inmates were divided into early and late-starters based on self-reports of behaviour in childhood and adolescence. Those who reported a stable pattern of antisocial behaviour before the age of fifteen were categorised as early-starters, and the others as late-starters (for a more detailed description see Hodgins and Côté, 1993 a and b). Among the inmates with major mental disorders, the early-starters as compared to the late-starters were more likely to have been convicted of an offence while still a juvenile, to have been younger at the time of their first conviction in adult court, and to have been convicted of more non-violent crimes and a similar number of violent crimes. This confirmed the patterns of offending that we had observed with the subjects in the Metropolitan Project. More surprisingly, the early-starters with major mental disorders and those without these disorders had similar criminal histories, similar histories of antisocial behaviour in childhood and adolescence as did the non-mentally ill early-start offenders. Again, this was similar to what had been observed among the men in the Metropolitan cohort.

Next, we examined a sample of seventy-four men with schizophrenia who were recruited from a forensic hospital and a general psychiatric hospital. Early and late-starters were defined as in the previous study of penitentiary inmates using the patient's descriptions of the frequency, severity, and types of antisocial behaviour that they had presented during childhood and adolescence. As in the study of the penitentiary inmates, the early-starters as compared to the late-starters, were more likely to have been convicted of an offence while still a juvenile, to have been younger at the time of their first conviction in adult court, and to have been convicted of more non-violent crimes and similar numbers of violent crimes. In this study, we carefully examined the diagnoses, symptomatology, and psychosocial functioning of the early and late-starters using structured, validated, clinical instruments. These measures were taken two weeks prior to discharge from hospital when patients were functioning at their optimal levels. No differences could be detected in the schizophrenic symptomatology of the early and late-starters. More of the early than the late-starters had a history of alcohol and/or drug abuse or dependence. The early-starters obtained slightly higher scores for interpersonal social skills than did the late-starters. During the twenty-four months following discharge, 35% of the early-starters and seven per cent of the late-starters were convicted of a new offence. We concluded from this study that the clinical presentation of the major disorder is similar for early and late-starters, and that the differences between them are restricted to the age of onset of antisocial behaviour, the severity and frequency of these behaviours, the proportions who abuse (not use) alcohol and/or drugs, and their criminal histories (Hodgins, Côté, and Toupin, 1998).

A sub-group of thirty of the schizophrenic men from this study were compared to thirty non-disordered men on a test of neurological soft signs and a battery of neuropsychological tests. Scores on these tests differed depending on the history of antisocial behaviour. The schizophrenic men who had reported a stable pattern of antisocial behaviour in childhood and adolescence showed fewer neurological soft signs and less impairment on neuropsychological tests than did those with no history of childhood antisocial behaviour. Given the small number of subjects examined, these findings remain tentative. However, they concur with results from a Norwegian study, that unfortunately, like our own study, included only a small number of subjects (Rasmussen, Levander, and Sletvold, 1995) in suggesting that men who are both antisocial from a young age and schizophrenic evidence less brain damage than men with schizophrenia and no childhood or adolescent history of antisocial behaviour (but significantly more than non-disordered men). There is a good deal of evidence indicating that among men with schizophrenia, more severe brain abnormalities are associated with social withdrawal and fewer social contacts while less severe abnormalities are associated with a higher level of social functioning and more social contacts (Andreasen *et al.*, 1992). However, this higher level of social functioning is associated with antisocial behaviour, including both substance abuse (Laroche, Hodgins, and Toupin, 1995) and aggressive behaviour (Léveillée, 1994; Rasmussen *et al.*, 1995).

A group of Austrian researchers (Schanda, Födes, Topitz, and Knecht, 1992) have also compared early and late-start schizophrenic offenders. They found that early-starters, as compared to late-starters, scored higher on measures of sociability/withdrawal and social-sexual functioning in adolescence, performed more poorly at school, and scored higher on measures of sociability/withdrawal, peer relationships, and social-sexual adjustment in adulthood.

Côté, Lesage, Chawky and Loyer (1997) recruited a sample of men with major mental disorders in a penitentiary and matched them to men with similar disorders and age in a psychiatric hospital. This experimental design allowed us for the first time to compare early and late-start offenders among men with major mental disorders in a sample not biased by processing or the absence of processing by the criminal justice system. As we have described here, our first clinical study included only offenders sentenced to incarceration of two years or more. Our second study included men with similar disorders who had been excused from criminal responsibility because of their mental disorder or never even prosecuted. This third sample recruited in the penitentiary and hospital allowed us to compare early and late-starters regardless of their legal status.

We (Hodgins *et al.*, 1998) divided these men into two groups, early and late-starters. As in previous studies, early-starters were defined as those who displayed a stable pattern of antisocial behaviour from early adolescence through adulthood. The early-starters, as compared to the late-starters, were more likely to have been convicted in juvenile court and were a younger at first conviction in adult court. In contrast to our previous findings, the early and late-starters had been convicted, on average, of similar numbers of non-violent offences, but the early-starters had been convicted of more violent offences than the late starters. As in the Austrian study, the early-starters had a lower level of education than the late-starters. While both groups included significant proportions that had a history of alcohol and/or drug abuse or dependence, more of the early-starters than the late-starters met criteria for these substance use disorders. For the first time, a difference was identified in the diagnoses of the early and late-starters. Among the early-starters with a psychotic disorder, 25% suffered from schizophrenia and 50% from delusional disorder, while among the late-starters, 48% suffered from schizophrenia and 20% from delusional disorder.[3] Delusional disorder is extremely difficult to diagnose. Further, persons with this disorder, whether incarcerated or not, are unlikely to agree to participate in a research project. (In fact, we are perplexed as to why those in the penitentiaries did accept. It may be that once they have acted on their delusion by committing the crime that led to the incarceration, they are more willing to discuss their feelings and thoughts).

If diagnoses of delusional disorder are over-represented among early-start offenders, why didn't we identify this association in our previous studies? In the Project Metropolitan, diagnoses were extracted from hospital files. The proportion of persons with this disorder who require in-patient care is unknown, but it is likely to be much lower than that for the other major mental disorders. Further, this disorder seems to increase in severity with age and consequently would not often be identified before age thirty. The first violent offence often occurred when subjects were in their late thirties or early forties. In our first study of penitentiary inmates, inmates had to consent to participate. As delusional disorder is characterised by systematic paranoid delusions and beliefs, individuals with this disorder would be unlikely to agree to volunteer for such a project. Further, in this study, the DIS was used to make diagnoses. This instrument was developed for use by lay (non-clinically trained) interviewers in a community epidemiological investigation (the ECA) designed to measure all disorders, and not particularly major mental disorders (for a further discussion, see Hodgins, 1995). Consequently, subjects with delusional disorder, if they had agreed to complete the interview, would likely have been diagnosed as schizophrenic. In our study of patients being discharged from a forensic and a general psychiatric hospital, diagnoses were made by an experienced clinician using the Schedule for Schizophrenia and Affective Disorders (SADS) (Endicott and Spitzer, 1978) and the Research Diagnostic Criteria (Endicott and Spitzer, 1979; Spitzer, Endicott and Robins, 1978). These diagnoses differed little from diagnoses made by the clinicians who had known these patients for lengthy periods. Yet, we identified no case of delusional disorder. Again, it could be that such patients refused to participate. Or, it could be that these patients are not hospitalised and if they do commit an offence they are sentenced to the penitentiary rather than being excused from criminal responsibility because of a mental disorder.[4]

Thus the results from the Metropolitan Project and studies of samples of offenders with major mental disorders concurred in demonstrating that early as compared to late-starters commit more crimes and other studies have shown that they present more aggressive and violent behaviour (Stueve and Link, 1997). In addition, the studies concur in showing that the early-starters present more serious behaviour and academic problems in childhood and adolescence, a part of which is early onset substance abuse. Whether or not early-start offenders are distinguished by the primary disorder is still unresolved. The results of more recent studies concur.

Early and late-starters were examined in the Swedish cohort of violent offenders with schizophrenia (Tengström *et al.*, 2001). Early-starters were defined as those with a conviction before age eighteen. As in the previous studies, we found that the psychosocial functioning of the early-starters during childhood and adolescence was more impaired than that of the late-starters. The childhoods of most of the subjects were troubled, but those of the early-starters more so than those of the late-starters. Adding substantially to our knowledge was the finding that more than half of the parents of the early-start offenders and a quarter of the parents of the late-starters had a substance abuse problem. These figures are high, but similar to what has been recently reported for parents of patients with major mental disorders and antisocial behavior in the US (Mueser, Rosenberg, Drake, Miles, Wolford, Vidaver, and Carrieri, 1999). These results support our hypothesis about the role that inadequate and inappropriate parenting may play, particularly in the development of the early-start offenders. Further, the Swedish study found, as did the results of the investigation of the Metropolitan cohort, that significant proportions of early-starters could be identified in childhood.

Other recent findings open new questions about the early-start offenders with major mental disorders. Two studies, the one described above which included offenders with major mental disorders recruited in Canadian penitentiaries and hospitals (Hodgins *et al.*, 1998) and the Swedish cohort of violent male offenders with schizophrenia (Tengström *et al.*, 2001), have found that the early-starters show more of the personality traits of psychopathy than do the late-starters. In a US study, a sample of men with schizophrenia and a history of violence and crime from adolescence were also found to be characterised by the traits of psychopathy (Nolan, Volavka, Mohr, and Czobor, 1999). All of these studies used either the Psychopathy Checklist-Revised or the Psychopathy Checklist Screening Version to assess these traits. In addition, there is a large body of evidence showing that ratings of psychopathy (not a diagnosis but rather the total score on the items measuring both a history of antisocial behaviour and the personality traits of psychopathy) are the best predictor of violent behaviour among persons with major mental disorders (Douglas and Webster, 1999). This consistently replicated finding may be due entirely to early-start offenders. Within any sample of persons with major mental disorders, they are the most criminally active and likely to recidivate, they obtain the highest scores on the measure of psychopathy for their histories of antisocial behaviour which go back to early adolescence, and the highest scores for the personality traits associated with psychopathy.

A second attempt to further characterise the early-starters has recently been made. An investigation of a sample of persons with major mental disorders and antisocial behaviour identified two groups of early-starters, one who presented conduct disorder in childhood and the other substance abuse with no conduct disorder (Fulwiler, Grossman, Forbes, and Ruthazer, 1997; Fulwiler and Ruthazer, 1999).

CONCLUSION

The distinction between early and late-start offenders has been shown to be useful in understanding patterns of criminal offending and antecedents. This conclusion applies to both mentally ill and non-disordered offenders. The distinction may be of use in future investigations of the etiology of criminality among the mentally ill, and in the treatment, risk assessment, and management of mentally ill offenders.

Early and late-start offenders among the Metropolitan cohort members

The prevalence of early and late-start offenders differ by gender, both among the mentally ill and among the non-disordered. Among the men, early-starters, as compared to late-start offenders, were found to be more prevalent, while among the women the proportions of late-starters were greater than the proportions of early-starter offenders. Many other investigations have also found that antisocial behaviour or conduct disorder in childhood is much more prevalent among boys than among girls (Moffitt, 1993). The results from the present investigation demonstrate that among individuals who will develop a major mental disorder a greater proportion of the males than the females will have displayed a stable pattern of antisocial behaviour in childhood.

The frequency and types of offences committed by early and late-start offenders differ. Generally, these differences are greater among the mentally ill than the non-disordered subjects. Among the men, the early-starters, both mentally ill and non-disordered, had been convicted, on average, of more non-violent offences than the late-starters. Early and late-start offenders, both mentally ill and non-disordered, had similar histories of violent crime. Among the women, the patterns of crime did not differ to any great extent among early and late-start offenders, among either the mentally ill or the non-disordered. However, the few female mentally ill early-starters did tend to show the same excess of non-violent criminality evident among the male early-starters. Both among the men and the women, the mentally ill early-starters had accumulated more convictions than the non-disordered early-starters for both violent and non-violent offence. Gender differences again emerged in comparisons of the mentally ill and non-disordered late-starters. Among the men, the mentally ill late-starters had been convicted, on average, for more violent and non-violent offence. Among the women, only 8 per cent of the non-disordered late-starters had been convicted for a violent offence as compared to one-third of the mentally ill late-starters.

Previous research had succeeded in identifying some of the childhood antecedents of adult criminality. This research has been conducted almost exclusively with males and has focused primarily on those who displayed antisocial behaviour in childhood. The results of the present study confirmed and extended the findings from previous investigations in showing the importance of behaviour problems in childhood and adolescence as precursors of adult criminality. The subsequent addition of other problems which affected not only the child's behaviour, but also his/her psychological and intellectual functioning, and the persistence of these problems lead to offending. We interpret our findings as suggesting that this multiplicity of individual problems, which almost always included behaviour problems, in the context of a family unable to mobilise personal and/or professional resources to correct them eventually led to unofficial delinquency which escalated over time into persistent criminality.

The present investigation supported the utility of dividing mentally ill offenders into early and late-starters. The early-start offenders who develop mental illness differ little in childhood and adolescence from non-mentally ill early-start offenders. The findings from the present investigation support the hypothesis that the population of children who present conduct problems is very heterogeneous as to adult outcome. While most, if not all, grow up to be antisocial and to offend, some also develop mental illnesses (Hodgins, 2000), others early-onset alcoholism (Virkkunen *et al.*, 1994a and b), others organic brain syndromes as a result of reckless behaviour (Grekin, Brennan, Hodgins, and Mednick, in press), and in others, as would be expected, the intellectual impairment remains (Crocker and Hodgins, 1997). Given the multiple negative outcomes of this population, early interventions designed to prevent the development of an antisocial lifestyle are warranted. Cognitive and behavioural programmes designed to limit impulsive behaviour, to teach alternatives to physical aggression in conflict situations, to teach respect for rules and the rights of others, combined with educational programmes designed to help these children progress at normal rates in school, it is hypothesised, would have positive results. Such programmes exist and are being tested. The argument that such early childhood programmes are unethical or that they may even 'cause' delinquency is not supported by empirical fact. Children with conduct problems are readily identified by their peers, their teachers and their parents even by the beginning of elementary school (see for example, Ledingham, Younger, Schwartzman, and Bergeron, 1982). Further, children in elementary school often participate in different programmes depending on their individual needs and abilities. There is no evidence that providing a programme to children with behaviour problems which helps them learn prosocial behaviours would lead them to be labelled delinquents and thereby increase their risk of delinquency. If anything, such programmes would help them to develop positive relationships with peers and teachers and parents. Their new prosocial skills would allow them to benefit from many social and sports activities from which they are usually excluded. Ensuring that they can progress satisfactorily in school and acquire skills necessary for the job market is a further protection against the development of criminality.

The other objection to early childhood intervention programmes focuses on the inaccuracy of our identification of which children will become adult offenders. This is essentially a false issue as early intervention is not provided to prevent some problem in adulthood, but rather to overcome a problem in the present. The results of our studies with the Metropolitan cohort, and those of many other investigations, clearly indicate that children who present behaviour problems at a young age need help to overcome these problems so that they can enjoy their childhood and benefit from all the positive learning experiences, both academic and non-academic that are available to them. In other words, early intervention is designed to help children overcome the problems that they have presently. It is hypothesised, and hoped, that by-so-doing, difficulties will not cumulate nor persist.

Early and late-start offenders in clinical samples

Mentally ill early and late-start offenders were identified in four clinical samples. These studies included only men. The differences in the patterns of offending were similar to what had been observed among the mentally ill early and late-start offenders in the Metropolitan Project. One of our studies suggested that there was no difference in the clinical presentation of the symptoms of the major mental disorder by early and late-start offenders, while a second suggested that early-start offenders may be more likely to suffer from delusional disorder than are late-starters. While this finding is interesting, particularly in light of the results on TCO symptoms reviewed in Chapter 5, future research aimed at replicating it and furthering our understanding will, no doubt, be difficult. Individuals who have paranoid ideas, delusions, and/or hallucinations do not readily agree to participate in research projects. Consequently, studies which require consent of the participants may have samples biased by the absence of such subjects. (In other words, the population of mentally ill persons who offend would include a greater proportion of individuals who present paranoid symptomatology than samples recruited into studies.) Further, our findings suggest that individuals with delusional disorder, at least in Canada, may be more likely to be found in penitentiaries than in general psychiatric or forensic psychiatric hospitals. This confounding of type of mentally ill offender and legal processing, is not surprising but it may need to be considered in designing future studies. To conclude, data suggest that individuals with paranoid symptoms are at increased risk of committing crimes, but that they are reluctant to participate in research projects. One study suggests that they are likely to be sentenced to terms of incarceration if they do commit a crime. In most jurisdictions, consent is required from prisoners in order to include them in research projects. If this reasoning is correct, researchers are confronted with a formidable challenge.

Dividing mentally ill offenders into early and late-starters may be useful for treatment, management and risk assessment. Our findings suggest that early-starters commit more offences than do late-starters, and that their antisocial behaviour, which was present before the onset of the major disorder, will not be reduced by antipsychotic medications. They will be more likely than the late-starters to have had substance abuse problems from an early age. In general, they are, we think, less likely to comply with treatment. The factors associated with the criminality of the late-starters, we propose, are more likely related to symptomatology and current life situation.

NOTES

1. Among the non-disordered early-start offenders there are two groups: those (47.4%) whose criminality continues into adulthood and those (52.6%) who commit no new crime after the age of eighteen. Because we defined the early-starters to include all those convicted of an offence by age eighteen, we lumped together the early-starters and what have been called the adolescent-limited offenders. Subsequent analyses with the non-disordered subjects indicated important differences in the characteristics of those males that offend only in adolescence and those that begin their criminal careers early and persist throughout adulthood (see Kratzer and Hodgins, 1999).

2 The study of the role of pregnancy and birth complications in the development of antisocial behavior is only beginning, despite the positive findings of Litt in 1971. Two major obstacles block the field. First, little is known about normal foetal brain development, and consequently even less about development linked to impairments. Second, depending on how variables are coded and the source of information findings vary. Recent evidence underlines the importance of taking account of the time during development when the complication occurs and of using both obstetrical files and prospectively collected information from mothers about their behaviour during the pregnancy. The difficulty is well illustrated by contradictory results obtained in the Project Metropolitan on the association between pregnancy and birth complications and criminality. In the analyses presented here, pregnancy and birth complications were coded from medical records without taking account of the time during development when they occurred. Subsequently, we conducted other analyses in which the timing (first, second, third trimester, birth, neonatal period) of each complication was considered. These analyses showed that among the males who developed major mental disorders, 92.3% of those who had offended as compared

to 44.4% of those who did not offend had experienced neonatal complications $(X_2(N = 67) = 9.65, p < .002)$. While the offenders with major mental disorders showed no excess of complications during the three trimesters of pregnancy or at birth as compared to the mentally ill non-offenders, they did show a higher average number of neonatal complications ($M = 0.39, SD = 0.60; M = 0.32, SD = 0.18$) ($t = (42.26) = 3.40, p = <.001$), and a higher mean severity rating for neonatal complications ($M = 1.56, SD = 2.48; M = 0.16. SD = 0.90; t(45.36) = 3.14, p < .003$). Among the non-mentally ill men, complications which occurred in the neonatal period were not found to be associated with offending or with violence. However, in this latter population an association was observed between pregnancy complications occurring to a boy being raised in a family with problems and offending (Hodgins, Kratzer, and McNeil, forthcoming). This concurs with previous findings which have suggested that the consequences of obstetrical complications can be exacerbated by subsequent difficulties in the rearing environment. For example, in a recent study of a Danish birth cohort, obstetrical complications in interaction with maternal rejection were found to increase the risk of violent crime by the end of adolescence (Raine, Brennan, and Mednick, 1994).

3 Disorders featuring predominately paranoid symptomatology are common among the biological relatives of persons with schizophrenia (see for example, Kendler and Gruenberg, 1984; Kendler, McGuire, Gruenberg, O'Hare, Spellman, and Walsh, 1993). In addition, so is criminality and antisocial behaviour (Kraeplin, 1896; for a review see Hodgins, Toupin, and Côté, 1996).

4 The findings from this study may illustrate the difficulty inherent in using samples of mentally ill offenders recruited in different systems, for example correctional facilities, forensic hospitals, or general psychiatric hospitals, in attempting to further understanding of their characteristics. There may well be a confounding of the characteristics of these individuals and the type of facility where the individual is recruited into the study. If, for example, many early-starters suffer from delusional disorder, they are more likely to be found in correctional facilities than in hospitals. Consequently, investigations which aim to identify the characteristics of this type of mentally ill offender, must take account not only of the bias introduced by their suspiciousness and resulting reluctance to participate in research, but as well the unlikelihood of finding them within the mental health system.

CHAPTER 7

CONCLUSION

Mental disorder and crime have been examined in a birth cohort of metropolitan Swedes born in 1953 and followed to 1983. A number of conclusions can be drawn from this experience. Initially, we assess the usefulness of longitudinal, prospective cohort studies such as the Metropolitan Project. Next, we review the principal results of our study of criminality among persons with major mental disorders. From these results, we draw a number of conclusions regarding the assessment and treatment of offenders with major mental disorders and future research on this issue.

THE METROPOLITAN PROJECT

Like any longitudinal, prospective study, the Metropolitan Project required considerable investment of time and money during a period that spanned more than thirty years. However, as the findings described in this book and a perusal of the publications from this project demonstrate, it has contributed to advancing knowledge on a wide variety of important issues.

Like longitudinal prospective investigation of this type has a number of advantages. One, an unbiased cohort is examined. However, like any cohort, it is a sample with special characteristics determined by place and time. As described in Chapter 3, the society in which the cohort members were raised had many unique characteristics which must be taken into account in interpreting the results. As indicated in Chapter 5 and as will be further discussed in subsequent sections of this chapter, we propose that features of the society in which the cohort members were born and lived interacted with their own individual characteristics in determining the outcomes in adulthood that we have described. By proposing that there may be a cohort effect related to the findings of criminality among persons with major mental disorders, we are suggesting that the subjects in the Metropolitan Project were affected by factors related to the period and the place where they were born and lived. However, the factors related to period and place, which we hypothesise are associated with the illegal behaviours of those who developed major mental disorders, are not unique to Sweden in the era 1953 to 1983. At this time, they were common to many industrialised Western countries. Consequently, the similarity between findings from the present investigation and those from investigations with both similar and different experimental designs conducted in several countries suggests that our observations are generalisable, and that the time and place characteristics of the cohort can be used to understand why so many of the mentally ill cohort members were convicted of crimes. The only biases (time and place of birth) associated with the cohort are thus turned to our advantage.

A second advantage of a longitudinal investigation like the Metropolitan Project is that the data were collected, for the most part, prospectively. This means that the observations used to explain adult outcomes and behaviours have not been influenced by the outcomes or behaviours. Consider for example, the often repeated finding that juvenile delinquents as compared to adolescents of the same gender and age obtain lower scores on an IQ test. In order to understand if and how intelligence plays a role in the development of criminal behaviour, it is important to know if the lower levels of intelligence preceded the delinquent activity. Perhaps, the delinquents obtained lower IQ scores because they often fight and have been repeatedly hit on the head. If IQ was measured well before the criminal activity, as it was in the present project, then the relation between intelligence level and delinquency can be interpreted in a meaningful way. As noted in Chapter 2, some of the data included in the present project were collected retrospectively. But, as this was objective information extracted from records compiled for purposes other than this project, there is no reason to suspect a bias. For example, it is impossible to imagine how the notes made by the midwives, nurses, and obstetricians on the pregnancies and births of the cohort members could be biased by the knowledge that a cohort member would develop a mental illness or commit a crime in adulthood. While not biased, such record information is however limited. It was collected for clinical reasons and included information relevant to the medical care being provided to the mother and the foetus/newborn. It does not include information, for example, that researchers might have judged to be important. This record information is further limited by the fact that these notes were made in 1953. Knowledge of pregnancy and birth factors which are related to subsequent development of the child has advanced dramatically since then, and consequently relevant information that would be routinely recorded today was not included in the records in 1953.

The Metropolitan Project, like other such projects conducted in the Scandinavian countries includes much data from government registers. This is a very cost-effective way of conducting research. The government collects this information for other reasons, and then computerises it. As this project and many others demonstrate, it can be used to advance knowledge which contributes to the resolution of social problems. The information we have used on psychiatric hospitalisations and criminal convictions was extracted from such registers established and maintained by the state for other purposes. This information has allowed us to study a social problem, and hopefully to contribute some knowledge useful to finding a solution and reducing the associated suffering. Not only is this a cost-effective way of conducting research, it is also a procedure which provides objective information which is not biased or influenced by the questions being asked in the research project. Further, the use of this information in no way harmed the cohort members. As explained in Chapter 2, during the period of data collection it was necessary that the researchers collected identified data. This was the only way to link information from various sources and from different points in time. All information was kept strictly confidential. The analyses conducted after the end of the data collection period, like the ones reported here, were conducted with de-identified data.

The Metropolitan Project has yielded so many and such varied contributions, not only because of its design and the quality of the data that were collected, but also because of the foresight and openness of the project director. Initially, the project objectives were general questions of interest to sociologists in the 1960s, questions of social origins, families, attitudes, abilities and resources. However, social deviance and social stratification quickly became the focus. Yet, disciplinary boundaries were not allowed to limit the project. Empirical findings from methodologically sound investigations became the basis for adding new data. The importance of this attention to emerging findings, the flexibility of the project director in modifying the project in order to incorporate data which had not been included in the initial planning and that were not easily integrated into the theoretical orientation of the project, and the availability of funds for collecting such data, have all contributed to making this a unique project. Consider for example, the inclusion of data from pregnancy and birth records. The Metropolitan Project was set up by a sociologist in collaboration with other sociologists. As described in Chapter 2, the project was primarily concerned with social questions. Yet in the early 1970s, findings from a study conducted in

Copenhagen (Litt, 1971) indicated that pregnancy and birth complications played a role in criminality. Permission and funds were then sought to obtain the obstetrical records of the mothers' of the cohort members. This was a prophetic decision. In the subsequent decades, compelling evidence has accumulated demonstrating that pregnancy and birth complications which affect the developing foetal brain play a role in the etiology of schizophrenia, maybe also in the etiology of other major mental disorders, and that they are related to criminality, to violent behaviour, to intelligence, and probably to many other traits and behaviours.

At the time the Metropolitan Project was designed, there was no intention to study the relation between mental disorder and crime. However, this database and the Danish Metropolitan Project (Ortmann, 1981) were used to conduct the first epidemiological investigations of the relation between mental disorder and criminality. Doing so depended not only on the existence of the data, but also on the willingness of the project director to collaborate with another researcher, in this case a foreigner with funny ideas about mental illness, its causes and consequences. Hopefully, the advances in our understanding of the criminality of persons suffering from mental disorders described in this book, along with the numerous other publications based on this project, are sufficient evidence of the worth of such longitudinal prospective investigations.

CRIMINALITY AMONG PERSONS WHO DEVELOP MAJOR MENTAL DISORDERS

The subjects in the cohort were divided into five groups. Three of the groups had been admitted to a psychiatric ward before the age of thirty. The first group had at least one discharge diagnosis of a major mental disorder, a second group had no diagnoses of major mental disorders, but at least one principal diagnosis of an alcohol and/or drug use disorder, and the third group had neither a diagnosis of a major mental disorder, nor a principal diagnosis of an alcohol and/or drug use disorder, but a diagnosis of another mental disorder. Subjects who had been placed in special classes for mental retardates, in both elementary and high school, were assigned to a separate group. The comparison group included all those cohort members who were not placed in special classes at school due to low levels of intelligence, and who had not been admitted to a psychiatric ward prior to their thirtieth birthday.

In interpreting the findings from the present project, it is important to remember that subjects who had been admitted to a psychiatric hospital were assigned to a diagnostic group, regardless of when they developed the disorder. Criminal convictions were then examined. By this procedure we have examined criminal convictions of individuals who have been hospitalised for a major mental disorder before age thirty, without any reference to the time of onset of the major mental disorder. We have examined the co-occurrence of a major mental disorder and criminality in the same person. Underlying this approach is a presumption that persons who eventually develop a major mental disorder are different, in some way, from conception through adulthood, from persons who do not develop these disorders.

It was found that proportionately more of the men and women who developed major mental disorders than those with no mental disorder and no mental retardation were convicted of at least one criminal offence before the age of thirty. Half of the mentally ill men and one-in-five of the mentally ill women had a criminal record. Further, 19% of the men and 6 per cent of the women had been convicted for crimes of violence. Mentally ill men were twice as likely as non-disordered men to have been convicted of a crime, and almost five times as likely to have been convicted of a violent crime. The risks of criminality generally and of violent criminality were higher among mentally ill women than men. Mentally ill women were almost four times more likely than non-disordered women to be convicted of a criminal offence, and eleven times more likely to have been convicted of a violent offence. The importance of these findings is underlined by a recent report to the Swedish Ministry of Health noting that in September 1995 there were 2,500 persons incarcerated in Sweden for serious violent offences and 951 sentenced to psychiatric treatment for similar types of offences (Levander, 1996).

The risks of criminality and violence among the mentally ill observed in the present project are probably to some extent underestimates. This is likely because: (1) psychiatric hospitalisations which resulted from criminal court orders were not counted; and (2) no data were collected after the subjects' thirtieth birthdays. As the study of the Danish cohort (Hodgins *et al.*, 1996) illustrates, one-third of the mentally ill male offenders and two-thirds of the mentally ill female offenders were first convicted of an offence after the age of thirty.

Mental illness is associated with a higher risk of criminality and violence among women than among men. Among the non-disordered cohort members, there were approximately five-and-a-half male offenders for each female offender. By comparison, among the mentally ill, there were approximately two-and-a-half male offenders for each female offender. Among non-disordered offenders, women were much less likely than men to be convicted of violent crimes: there were approximately twelve violent male offenders for every violent female offender. However, among the mentally ill there were approximately four violent male offenders for every violent female offender. This finding, that mental illness is associated with a greater increase in the risk of offending generally and of violent offending particularly among women than among men, is consistent with results from other investigations (see for example, Eronen *et al.*, 1996 a and b; Hodgins *et al.*, 1996; Stueve and Link, 1998; Wallace *et al.*, 1998). It is true that many fewer women than men, both disordered and non-disordered, commit crimes. However, anti-social women have an impact on society that is disproportionate to their numbers because of the role they play in the reproduction and rearing of children.

The results of the present investigation concur with those from other studies of subjects born after World War II, and treated in the era when mental health services consisted of short periods of hospitalisation, antipsychotic and antidepressive medications, and services in the community of varying kinds and intensities. Three other Scandinavian birth cohort studies, an investigation of an Australian population cohort, of a representative sample of young Israelis, numerous follow-up studies of patients discharged from psychiatric wards into the community, and assessments of mental disorder among convicted offenders all support the conclusion that persons who will develop major mental disorders or who already have these disorders are more likely than non-disordered persons to commit crimes and crimes of violence. The fact that other investigations with similar experimental designs (the birth cohort studies) and with other designs (studies of samples of discharged patients and of convicted offenders) have all drawn similar conclusions increases confidence in the results of the present investigation. In addition, the rigorous methodologies employed in these studies further increase confidence in the results which have been obtained.

Estimates obtained in the different studies of the proportions of mentally ill subjects who are convicted of crimes vary for many reasons. The important conclusion which has implications for mental health and criminal justice policies and practices as well as for understanding the nature of these disorders, is that within each country, or region, the risk of criminality and of violence is higher among the mentally ill than among the non-disordered. However, it must be acknowledged that each type of study has methodological limitations. In the birth cohort studies, only those individuals who were admitted to hospital are included in the mentally ill groups. While some have argued (Monahan and Steadman, 1983) that aggressive mentally ill patients are more likely to be admitted to hospital than are more docile ones, mentally ill subjects with a history of antisocial behaviour and alcohol and/or drug abuse avoid mental health services (Hodgins and Côté, 1993b; Owen, Fischer, Booth, and Cuffel, 1996). Consequently, in both the birth cohort studies and the follow-up studies of discharged patients, the number of mentally ill subjects may be underestimated. In the studies of convicted offenders, the numbers of mentally ill may also be underestimated but for another reason. As participation in such diagnostic studies is voluntary and requires formal written consent, individuals who have paranoid or paranoid-type symptoms are unlikely to agree to participate. As it is suspected that they have a high risk of behaving violently, their refusal to participate in studies lessens the observed association between mental disorder and violence.

Offenders with major mental disorders were found to commit, on average, many offences, in fact proportionately more than the non-disordered offenders but fewer than the substance-abusing offenders. Their criminal careers often spanned many years. Some began offending as young adolescents while others began their criminal careers in adulthood. While most of the mentally ill male offenders committed their first offence before the age of eighteen years, most of the mentally ill female offenders committed their first offence after the age of eighteen.

EXPLANATIONS OF THE CRIMINALITY OBSERVED AMONG THE MENTALLY ILL

Three explanations of the criminality of the mentally ill were discussed. These explanations are not exclusive one of the other (they may all be right or some of them may be right), nor are they exhaustive.

Facilitated detection, arrest, and prosecution

There are some empirical data and much clinical lore to suggest that mentally ill offenders are more easily detected than are non-disordered offenders. In addition, there are empirical data suggesting that mentally ill offenders more often and more readily confess to the offences that they have committed than do non-disordered offenders. These findings suggest that for the same offence, a mentally ill offender is more likely to be prosecuted than a non-mentally ill offender. However, other findings suggest that persons with major mental disorders are less likely to be prosecuted than are non-disordered persons. In many jurisdictions, mentally ill persons suspected of crimes other than murder or attempted murder, are often diverted to the mental health system rather than being processed through the criminal justice system. Further, there is some evidence demonstrating that mentally ill persons are less likely to be arrested and charged for violent behaviour than are non-mentally ill persons. In the present investigation, as was described in Chapters 4 and 6, the offenders who developed or who had major mental disorders were convicted on average for many more offences than the non-disordered offenders. Even when the sub-groups of the early and late-start offenders were compared, the mentally ill had been convicted of more offences than the non-disordered offenders. These findings may be interpreted as suggesting either that offenders with major mental disorders are more easily detected or alternatively that they in fact commit more crimes than do non-disordered offenders.

However, the findings that greater proportions of persons with major mental disorders than persons without these disorders are convicted of crimes, and the findings that mentally ill offenders are convicted, on average, of more offences than non-disordered offenders may be partially explained by the fact that mentally ill offenders are more likely to stay at the scene of their crimes and then to admit to having committed the crime. This tendency on their part is insufficient to explain the existing findings. Other contributing factors, we hypothesise, include the greater risk of illegal behaviour among persons who suffer from major mental disorders and the inability of police in many countries to divert them to the health system rather than formally charge them within the criminal justice system.

The implementation of the policy of deinstitutionalisation

It is almost impossible to document criminality and violence among the mentally ill prior to the implementation of the policy of deinstitutionalising mental health care. Before this time, persons with these disorders spent their lives within asylums. They had few, if any, rights. Our own study of the records of such an institution in Montreal suggested that staff had enormous power over the patients, that treatments would today be considered as punishments, and that the so-called treatments were often used to control patients' behaviour (Hodgins and Lalonde, 1999). In studying the records from the turn of the century to the late 1950s, our impression was that aggressive behaviour was expected from the patients. In most countries during this period, discharging patients to the community was unusual, and involuntary rehospitalisation posed no problem if either the family or community complained of the patient's behaviour. Further, at this time, many patients with major mental disorders died at even younger ages than they do today. While almost no empirical data exist to document aggressive and other illegal behaviours in the pre-deinstitutionalisation era, there are compelling findings indicating that as soon as the policy of deinstitutionalising services for the mentally ill was implemented, the proportions of mentally ill persons convicted of crimes began to increase.

Evidence has accumulated in recent years suggesting that the lack of appropriate and adequate treatment and supervision explains part, if not all, of this criminality. The implementation of the policy of deinstitutionalisation, even in countries with universally accessible national health care programmes, led to a situation in which services for persons with major mental disorders were often limited to short hospital stays in which the goal was to reduce the acute symptomatology with medications and brief meetings with psychiatrists in out-patient clinics to renew prescriptions. Patients who did not attend the out-patient clinics were left to their own devices. A situation often referred to as the revolving door soon developed in which patients were frequently rehospitalised in a full blown psychotic episode a couple of weeks after they had stopped taking medications. In many instances, the staff of out-patient clinics changed often so that there was no one person who knew the patient (see for example, Hodgins, 1994c). Treatment was limited to medications.

Since mental health services were deinstitutionalised, many persons with major mental disorders live in the community, are offered little treatment or refuse to comply with the available treatment, and abuse alcohol and/or drugs. Studies have demonstrated that the presence of agitated, psychotic and TCO symptoms increases the risk of violent behaviour. One of these studies also suggests that this association is strengthened in the presence of substance abuse problems. As we and others have shown, not all persons with major mental disorders who behave violently evidence such symptoms. While rates of substance abuse among the mentally ill vary from country to country, from region to region, and from one time period to another, within each place and time period the rates among the mentally ill are higher than among the non-mentally ill subjects. Further, as we found, subjects who developed major mental disorders were more likely to have abused alcohol and/or drugs as children or young adolescents than were subjects who did not develop a mental illness. These data suggest that persons who develop major mental disorders have a vulnerability which increases the likelihood that they will develop substance abuse problems and that this vulnerability is realised when they live in a society where they receive little supervision and care for their mental disorder and where alcohol and drugs are readily available. As in non-mentally ill persons, for many reasons too numerous to discuss here, the abuse of alcohol and drugs is associated with criminality and violence. However, as we documented, not all persons with major mental disorders who commit crimes have a co-morbid alcohol or drug use disorder or are intoxicated at the time of the offence.

Three changes in mental health policy and practice – deinstitutionalisation of services, increased patients' rights to refuse treatment, strictly limited involuntary treatment – were quickly followed in time by an increase in criminality and substance abuse among men and women who would develop or who already had developed a major mental disorder. Mental health services, for persons with major mental disorders in many countries even today, are limited to short voluntary hospital stays and visits to an out-patient clinic to renew prescriptions. The problems such as alcohol and drug abuse, a lack of life skills, antisocial behaviour, which add to and complicate the symptomatology of the major mental disorders are not addressed by specific treatments. Further, persons with multiple problems tend to avoid mental health services when they are not mandatory, as do patients with paranoid symptoms. Given that such individuals are not in regular contact with a mental health professional who can assess symptomatology and the risk of illegal behaviour, and that they have a right not to be treated except if assessed and found to present an imminent danger to self or others, many of those with a history of antisocial behaviour and/or substance abuse problems and many who are actively psychotic receive little or no treatment. Findings from the present investigation and from numerous other rigorous studies suggest that this situation is contributing to criminality and violence among persons with major mental disorders. This conclusion is supported by the results of evaluations of specialised after-care programmes (in which attendance was mandated by a court order and treatment was multifaceted) which proved to be successful in preventing criminality even among high risk cases.

Two types of mentally disordered offenders

We hypothesise that the increased risk of criminality and violence among persons with major mental disorders cannot be entirely explained by either an increased risk of detection or inadequate and/or inappropriate treatment. These factors add to, and in some cases enhance, personal difficulties of individuals who will develop major mental disorders or who already have these disorders. These difficulties in turn lead to behaviours that are generally defined as illegal. In other words, the findings of an increased risk of criminality and substance abuse among persons with major mental disorders result from an interaction between contextual factors, such as inadequate and inappropriate treatment services, availability of alcohol and drugs, and individual characteristics. Our findings identify two different combinations of individual characteristics among offenders with major mental disorders. These two types of offenders, we hypothesise, are affected by and affect their environments differently. As each type follows a different developmental trajectory, both the distal and proximal factors associated with their illegal behaviours differ. The first type, the early-starters, display a stable pattern of antisocial behaviour from a young age. The second type, the late-starters, begin to offend at the end of adolescence or in adulthood when the symptoms of the major mental disorder become manifest. Early-starters are more prevalent among mentally ill males, while late-starters are more prevalent among mentally ill women. Early-starter mentally ill men, resemble, in many ways, antisocial boys who grow up to be recidivistic offenders. Not only have early-starters been identified in investigations of criminality and violence among the mentally ill, they have also been identified in epidemiological studies of mental disorders among children (Angold and Costello, 1993) and in investigations of children at high risk from one or other of the major mental disorders (Asarnow, 1988; Cannon, Mednick, and Parnas, 1990; Carlson and Weintraub, 1993). Some proportion, as yet not well specified, of individuals who develop schizophrenia, recurrent major depressions, and bipolar disorder, display aggressive behaviour and/or conduct disorder as children. Presently, it is not clear if the differences between these two types of mentally ill offenders are limited to their history of antisocial behaviour or whether aspects (sub-types, symptom presentation) of the major disorder also differ. (For a further discussion, see Hodgins, 2000).

A cohort effect

We cannot rule out the possibility that the increased prevalence of criminality among the men and women who developed major mental disorders is a cohort effect. A cohort effect would mean that the increased risk of criminality identified among the mentally ill is limited to subjects born in the late 1940s and early 1950s. There may be both individual and contextual characteristics of these birth cohorts that explain the increased prevalence of criminality among those who developed major mental disorders. Individuals born in the late 1940s and early 1950s may have experienced certain specific pregnancy and birth complications more often than persons born prior or subsequent to this period. For example, certain behaviours of their mothers that were more common then than in preceding or subsequent generations, like smoking and drinking, have been found to be associated with individual characteristics such as impulsivity, concentration problems, attention difficulties, that are associated with criminality and with conduct problems and violent crime. The subjects in these cohorts may have developed certain problems which increased their risk of illegal behaviour, not only because of their mothers' behaviour during their pregnancies, but also because of obstetrical practices current at the time they were born. For example, men whose mothers were given phenobarbital while they were in-utero have been found to have lower verbal intelligence than the norm. The effect of the phenobarbital on adult verbal intelligence scores was found to be increased among men whose mothers had a low socioeconomic status and who did not want to be pregnant (Reinisch, Sanders, Mortensen, Rubin, 1995).

Subjects born in the mid 1940s and early 1950s may be distinctive not only because of the factors which affected their development in the peri-natal period, but also because of those factors that affected them during early childhood. They may have been exposed more than previous genera-tions to certain environmental pollutants which damage the central nervous system in such a way as to limit self-control. For example, a cumulation of lead in the bones of young boys has been found to be associated with ag-gressive behaviour and delinquency (Needleman, Riess, Tobin, Biesecker, and Greenhouse, 1996). Subjects in the Metropolitan study and in other studies which have shown an increased risk of criminality and violent be-haviour among the mentally ill were the first generation to grow up with automobiles. Until recent environmental controls were made mandatory, cars, trucks and buses which, during the early years of their lives became common in urban centres, emitted fumes full of lead. We hypothesise that such perinatal factors and environmental pollutants may have increased the prevalence of antisocial behaviour in these cohorts, generally. This propo-sition is consistent with findings from the ECA study in the US which found an increase in antisocial behaviour during this century and with the in-crease in crime rates in the same period in most countries. Consequently, as the prevalence of persistent antisocial behaviour increased generally, so did the proportion of mentally ill persons who were also antisocial. However, it could also be that such factors differentially affected individuals at genetic risk from a major mental disorder.[1] Either way, the individual characteristics of some proportion of subjects with major mental disorders in these cohorts increased their risk of antisocial and violent behaviour.

In a context where mental health care was largely voluntary and lim-ited to antipsychotic medications and where alcohol and drugs were read-ily accessible, they committed crimes. If the factors, such as, mother's behaviour during pregnancy, obstetrical practices, environmental pollu-tants (which could lead to the development of the distinctive individual characteristics that are associated with their criminal behaviour or the contextual factors), and inadequate and inappropriate treatment, have changed or are changed, the increased risk of criminality among persons with major mental disorders may diminish or even disappear. This speculative hypothesis applies most clearly to those we have called early-starters. The context – deinstitutionalisation of services, increased patients' rights to refuse treatment, strictly limited involuntary care – and the consequences of the context – substance use and psychotic symptoms – may well be sufficient to explain the criminality of the late-starters.

There is most certainly a cohort effect related to the lack of exposure of the cohort members to violence on television and in films. During the period in which the subjects in the Metropolitan study (and those in the large Danish cohort) were growing up, there was television transmission for only a few hours a day. Programming was restricted and programmes depicting violence were not shown. Further, it was not customary at the time for families to go to movies, except on occasion to see special children's films.

While the aggressive behaviours of the cohort members in the Metropolitan Project were not influenced by having viewed violence on television or in the movies, other longitudinal investigations concur in demonstrating that aggressive children who grow up to be aggressive adults, watch violent television programmes. Low social class, low IQ, and mother working outside the home are factors that have been found to be correlated with this increased viewing of violence (Huesmann and Eron, 1986), as is the fact that most of these aggressive children grow up to be aggressive adults. It also seems reasonable to speculate that children who are at genetic risk from one of the major mental disorders might be susceptible to modelling what they see on television or in the movies and may misinterpret scenes of violence.

If, as noted previously, there are more antisocial children, some of whom will develop major mental disorders in adulthood, violence on television and in movies may be acting to consolidate or reinforce their aggressive behaviour. Consequently, given the consistent results of the effects of violent films on aggressive behaviour, this factor merits, in our opinion, further investigation.

IMPLICATIONS FOR MENTAL HEALTH AND CRIMINAL JUSTICE POLICY

The results from our analyses of the Project Metropolitan data, as well as those from numerous other investigations conducted in several different countries, all concur in demonstrating that individuals born since the mid-1940s who develop major mental disorders in adulthood are at increased risk of criminality and violence. Persons suffering from major mental disorders require care throughout their lives. In order to be effective, that is to allow these individuals to live in the community without causing harm to themselves or to others and with a reasonable quality of life, research findings indicate that an array of treatments and services must be available. An individual treatment plan would include a combination of these treatment components and services based on the individual patient's needs. These components would include medications, support provided by a stable person who knows the patient well and with whom the patient develops a relationship, supervision, treatment for substance abuse, specialised behavioural training programmes to improve life skills, social skills, to learn to cope with stress, anger and with frustrating situations, and specialised housing with varying levels of supervision. Demands for such intensive, multifaceted services for the mentally ill are not new. However, they are based on empirical data and not acceding to them has led to the current situation in which seriously ill individuals are not only suffering from a major mental disorder, and often one or two other disorders as well, but they are also committing crimes. While money might be being saved in the health budget under the current policy of limited services, the data would suggest that a great deal more is being spent to pay for police, courts, expert witnesses and correctional facilities, and for the mentally ill offender, as well as for mental health and social services for the victims of their crimes. The human suffering resulting from the situation is not often considered. (This call for adequate and appropriate care for the mentally ill as a strategy to prevent violence is not original. See for example, Coid, 1996; Monahan and Arnold, 1996; Müller-Isberner, 2000.)

Mental health policy then, must be based on the real needs of individuals with major mental disorders and on empirical data about their behaviours. Given our present knowledge, this implies coordinating both criminal and civil law to take account of crime committed by persons with major mental disorders. Civil law must provide for the possibility of rehospitalising persons with major mental disorders, quickly and efficiently, if they are assessed in a rigorous manner by experienced mental health professionals as presenting a significant risk of committing a crime. Civil law must also provide for the possibility of long-term compulsory treatment in the community for the mentally ill individual with a long history of antisocial behaviour who fails to comply with treatment. If, however, the law makes treatment compulsory, it must also ensure that effective treatment is provided. Further, criminal law and practice must make provision for the assessment of mental disorder among individuals accused of crimes. (This is not necessarily an easy task. For a discussion, see Hodgins, 1995). Correctional facilities have to be organised to provide care for inmates with major mental disorders and the law amended so that care continues once the offender is released into the community (for a discussion, see Hodgins and Côté, 1995).

IMPLICATIONS FOR ASSESSMENT AND TREATMENT

The data described herein provide compelling evidence for the necessity of assessing the risk of aggressive behaviour and criminality among persons suffering from major mental disorders. Mental health professionals in general psychiatric settings can no longer limit their assessments of patients to an examination of symptomatology and suicide risk. Routine mental health work-ups need to include an assessment of the risk of illegal behaviours. Procedures for risk assessment have been greatly improved in recent years and will continue to be improved in the coming years. (Borum, 1996; Douglas and Webster, 1999). These procedures which have been developed and validated in collaboration with clinicians are practical tools for use in clinical settings.

The data from the Metropolitan Project and from our clinical studies suggest further, that in order to prevent illegal behaviours on the part of patients with major mental disorders, it is necessary to take account of their history of antisocial behaviour in childhood and early adolescence. Patients who displayed a stable pattern of antisocial behaviour from a young age are at high risk of persisting in all forms of antisocial behaviour, but they most frequently commit non-violent crimes. It is unlikely that the use of medications to reduce symptoms in an acute episode will end their antisocial behaviour. However, as we noted, the type of disorder and symptomatology presented by the early-starters is still unclear. The assessment of the risk of criminality, and especially of violence, among patients who have no history of antisocial behaviour until the onset of the major disorder, the late-starters, is much more difficult. Information on the disorder – schizophrenia versus delusional disorder, symptomatology – paranoid and threat-control-overide symptoms, and alcohol and drug abuse and behaviour when intoxicated – are essential for an assessment of risk.

As noted above, treatment programmes for persons with major mental disorders must be long-term with stable staff. They must include multi-component treatment programmes, both in-patient and out-patient, which specifically address the numerous problems presented by individuals with major mental disorders. Further, the clinicians staffing these programmes require the legal authority to rehospitalise patients quickly, against their will if necessary, in order to prevent criminal recidivism. If the changes to mental health policy, laws, police and judicial practice, assessment and treatment outlined above were implemented, we hypothesise that the proportions of mentally ill persons committing crimes would be reduced. The extent of the reduction remains an empirical question. However, the evaluations of the obligatory after-care programmes for offenders with major mental disorders suggest that criminality can be prevented even among the most high risk cases. (For further discussion, see Hodgins and Müller-Isberner, 2000).

IMPLICATIONS FOR FUTURE RESEARCH

Measuring the prevalence of criminality among persons who develop major mental disorders

The first study we conducted with the data from the Metropolitan Project examined the criminality of persons who developed a major mental disorder by age thirty as compared to persons of the same gender and age who did not develop a serious mental disorder and whose intelligence test scores fell within normal limits. These findings demonstrated that more of the male and female cohort members who had developed a major mental disorder had been convicted of criminal offences than the non-disordered subjects. These epidemiological findings are consistent with those from other similar studies and with those from follow-up studies of patients with major disorders who were discharged to the community and with those from investigations of the mental health of convicted offenders. Almost all of these studies have been conducted with subjects born since the mid-1940s.

The research presented and reviewed in this volume suggests that the criminality of persons who suffer from major mental disorders or who will develop these disorders in adulthood, varies from place to place and from one time period to another. Depending on the laws, especially those relating to obligatory in-patient and out-patient treatment, and the intensity and type of out-patient care available, rates of criminality among the mentally ill vary. The more effective treatment is in limiting psychotic symptoms, particularly what have been called threat-control/override symptoms and other paranoid symptoms and in limiting abuse of alcohol and other drugs, the lower the rate of crime in this population will be. Consequently, the results of studies conducted in different places and at different time periods may not be directly comparable. Future epidemiological investigations that measure criminality and violence among the mentally ill need to take account of, or at least describe, the context in which the subjects are living and the types of treatment that they are receiving. This practice would go a long way towards explaining different rates of criminality and violence among the mentally ill documented in different places and time periods.

Clarifying the sub-types of persons who develop major mental disorders and commit crimes

Examination of the age-related patterns of offending of the cohort members who developed major mental disorders, indicated that there were two distinctive types, the early and late-starters. The early-starter males appear to resemble in many ways conduct-disordered boys whose antisocial behaviour escalates in frequency and severity throughout childhood and adolescence, and culminates in repetitive adult criminality. Clinical studies of adult offenders from major mental disorders confirmed the existence of the two types, but contributed somewhat contradictory evidence about the specificity of the disorder and symptomatology of the early-starters. Future research, in our view, needs to clarify the characteristics which distinguish these two types of offenders from those with major mental disorders. This is necessary because existing data suggest that not only do they differ as to etiology, but they require different types of treatment and management to prevent criminal activity and that different proximal factors influence their criminal behaviours.

To conduct studies aimed at identifying homogeneous sub-groups of persons who will develop a major mental disorder and commit crimes is a challenge. First, but thankfully, such persons are not so numerous and consequently sample sizes are usually small. Second, existing data indicate that it is important to examine men and women separately, thereby further limiting the sample size. Third, and probably most important, is the difficulty of recruiting samples that are representative of the population of persons who develop major mental disorders and commit crimes. This difficulty, in our view, is currently a major obstacle to furthering our understanding of the offending of this population.

As we have noted, certain subgroups of individuals with major mental disorders often fail to use available treatment services. In particular, those who have a history of antisocial behaviour and/or substance abuse typically refuse to attend out-patient treatment unless it is imposed on them by a court order. Similarly, persons with paranoid and/or TCO symptoms may avoid treatment. As samples for research projects are usually drawn from patient populations, they will be biased in that they may include smaller proportions of these two sub-groups than actually exist. Consequently, the associations identified between certain characteristics or symptoms and violence will be weaker than may actually be the case. This will be important in studies attempting to understand the long-term antecedents of criminality among the mentally ill, the proximal factors associated with violence, and those studies evaluating the effects of treatment on criminality and violence in this population.

Samples of offenders with major mental disorders who are recruited in different types of facilities, for example prisons as compared to forensic hospitals, may include the different sub-groups in varying proportions. This point was illustrated by the finding from Canada (Côté, Lesage, Chawky, and Loyer, 1997) that subjects with delusional disorder were more often found in a penitentiary than in a psychiatric hospital. In addition, different sub-groups of offenders with major mental disorders may be processed differentially by the courts of different countries.

The composition of samples of persons with major mental disorders will also vary depending on whether or not informed consent is required. Studies of samples in which informed consent is not required, for example, all the persons declared not guilty by reason of insanity in a certain state at a certain period of time, or all the persons remanded by the criminal court in a certain province over a certain period of time, will include different proportions of sub-groups of patients at differential risk for criminality than studies which require informed consent of the participants. Thus, depending on the country in which the study is conducted, the setting in which subjects are recruited (remand centre, forensic hospital, general psychiatric hospital, prison and community), and how samples for study are recruited (with or without informed consent), the sub-groups of subjects composing the samples will vary. It will not be surprising then, that the results of such investigations will also vary.

The importance of prenatal and early childhood factors

Most research on violence and criminality among persons with major mental disorders is conducted on samples of adults. For the most part, this research focuses on identifying the correlates of violence, particularly the proximal factors. Some retrospective, self-report information on distal precursors is included in these studies. We have tried to demonstrate the advantages of studying the development of criminality in persons who present major mental disorders in adulthood. In so doing, we have used objective data collected prospectively. By tracking the development of these persons over the life-span we compared their development to that of persons who did not develop either a major mental disorder nor a record of criminality, and to persons who developed only a major mental disorder, and to persons who developed only criminality. The study presented here was conducted in the context of research on the development of each of the major mental disorders and on the development of criminality. The results demonstrate the relevance of these two bodies of knowledge to understanding the criminality and violence of persons who will develop or who already present a major mental disorder.

We hope that we have demonstrated the contribution that such investigations can make to advancing knowledge about the criminality and violence of persons who develop major mental disorders. There is now a great deal of evidence to suggest that these individuals are different from the moment of conception than others and that they respond differently to their environments than do others. As we found, they are vulnerable to alcohol and drug abuse at a young age, have conduct problems, and in some cases, achieve poor academic performance. In addition, their families often seem unable to provide the help they need to overcome what in the beginning may be relatively minor problems. A developmental perspective not only allows us to identify the distal antecedents of criminality and violence among the mentally ill, it allows us to begin to think about early identification and prevention. How do children at risk from major mental disorders and criminality differ from conduct-disordered children, or from children at risk for a major disorder but not for criminality? Would they and their families respond positively to interventions of the same kind as in conduct-disordered are aimed at reducing the risk of antisocial and/or aggressive behaviour children? Much remains to be learned.

In order to advance however, longitudinal research on the development of criminality and violence among the mentally ill, must identify children at risk for the different disorders, principally schizophrenia, major depression, bipolar disorder, and delusional disorder. Presently, it is not known whether the factors associated with the development of antisocial and/or aggressive behaviour in persons at risk for one or other of these disorders are similar. There are hints in the literature suggesting that the frequency and types of crime may differ by diagnosis. What is clear however, is that significant subgroups of children who grow up to develop major mental disorders display stable patterns of antisocial and/or aggressive behaviour.

NOTE

1. In March 1997, *Science* (Kaiser, 1997) reported that the National Institute of Environmental Health Sciences would invest over $60 million in an effort to identify genes that confer vulnerability to chemicals.

References

Abram, K. M. and Teplin, L. A. (1991). Co-occurring disorders among mentally ill jail detainees: Implications for public policy. *American Psychologist*, 46, 1036–45.

Abramson, M. F. (1972). The criminalization of mentally disordered behavior: Possible side-effect of a new mental health law. *Hospital and Community Psychiatry*, 23, 101–5.

Achenbach, T. M. (1993). Taxonomy and comorbidity of conduct problems: Evidence from empirically based approaches. *Development and Psychopathology*, 5, 51–64.

Achenbach, T. M., Klinteberg, B., Andersson, T., Magnusson, D., and Stattin, H. (1993). Hyperactive behavior in childhood as related to subsequent alcohol problems and violent offending: A longitudinal study of male subjects. *Personality and Individual Differences*, 15(4), 381–8.

Ågren, G. (1996). Personal communication based on calculations made from statistics of the Stockholm läns landsting.

Ahlberg, J. (ed.) (1992). *Brottsutvecklingen* 1991. BRÅ rapport 1992: 2. Stockholm: BRÅ.

Alin-Åkerman, B. and Fischbein, S. (1990). *Tvillingar – en riskgrupp*. Project Metropolitan Research Report no. 29. Stockholm.

Allodi, F. A., Robertson, M., and Kedward, H. B. (1974). Insane but Guilty: Psychiatric Patients in Jail. Paper presented at the Annual Meeting of the Canadian Psychiatric Association, Ottawa.

American Psychiatric Association (1987). *Diagnostic and Statistical Manual of Mental Disorders* (3rd edn. revised). Washington, DC: Author.

American Psychiatric Association (1994). *Diagnostic and Statistical Manual of Mental Disorders* (4th edn. revised). Washington, DC: Author.

Andenaes, J. (1952). General prevention – illusion or reality? *Journal of Criminal Law, Criminality, and Police Science*, 43, 176–98.

Andersson, J. (1993). *A Longitudinal Simulation Model of Incapacitation Effects*. Project Metropolitan Research Report no. 38. Stockholm.

Andersson, J. (1994). Rån. In J. Ahlberg (ed.), *Brotts-utvecklingen 1992 och 1993*. BRÅ rapport 1994: 2. Stockholm: BRÅ.

Andreasen, N. C. *et al.* (1992). Hypofrontality in neuroleptic-naive patients and inpatients with chronic schizophrenia. *Archives of General Psychiatry*, 49, 943–58.

Angold, A. (1988). Childhood and adolescent depression. I. Epidemiological and aetiological aspects. *British Journal of Psychiatry*, 152, 601–17.

Angold, A., and Costello, E. J. (1993). Depressive comorbidity in children and adolescents: Empirical, theoretical, and methodological issues. *American Journal of Psychiatry*, 150, 1779–91.

Angst, J. (1985). Switch from depression to mania: A record study over decades between 1920 and 1982. *Psychopathology*, 18, 140–54.

Anonymous (1984). Manic-depressive illness. *Lancet*, 8414, 1268.

Appelbaum, P. S., Robbins, P. C., and Monahan, J. (2000). Violence and delusions: Data from the MacArthur Violence Risk Assessment Study. *American Journal of Psychiatry*, 157, 566–572.

Asarnow, J. R. (1988). Children at risk for schizophrenia: Converging lines of evidence. *Schizophrenia Bulletin*, 14, 613–31.

Axelsson, C. (1992). *Hemmafrun som försvann*. Stockholm: Institute for Social Research, Stockholm University.

Baker, R. L., and Mednick, B. R. (1984a). Long-term consequences for adolescent identified as at-risk at birth. In S. A. Mednick (ed.), *Influences on Human Development: A Longitudinal Perspective*. Boston: Nijhoff Publishing, 143–79.

Baldwin, J. A. (1979). Schizophrenia and physical disease. *Psychological Medicine*, 9, 611–18.

Bank, L., and Patterson, G. R. (1992). The use of structural equation modelling in combining data from different types of assessment. In J. C. Rosen and P. McReynolds (eds.), *Advances in Psychological Assessment*: vol. 8. New York, NY: Plenum.

Barnes, G. E., and Toews, J. (1983). Deinstitutionalization of chronic mental patients in the Canadian context. *Canadian Psychology*, 24, 22–36.

Beaudoin, M. N., Hodgins, S., and Lavoie, F. (1993). Homicide, schizophrenia and substance abuse or dependency. *Canadian Journal of Psychiatry*, 38, 1–7.

Bejerot, N. (1975). *Drug abuse and drug policy*. Copenhagen: Munksgaard. *Acta Psychiatrica Scandinavia*, Suppl. 256.

Belcher, J. R. (1989). On becoming homeless. *Journal of Community Psychology*, 17, 173–85.

Belfrage, H. (1998). A ten-year follow-up of criminality in Stockholm mental patients: New evidence for a relation between mental disorder and crime. *British Journal of Criminology*, 38(1), 145–55.

Bergman, L. R., and El-Khouri, B. M. (1992). M-REP: A fortran 77 computer program for the preparatory analysis of multivariate data (Report no. 1). Stockholm University, Department of Psychology.

Bergman, L. R., and El-Khouri, B. M. (1995). SLEIPNER. A computer package for person oriented analyses of developmental data. Version A (Manual). Stockholm University, Department of Psychology.

Bergman, L. R., and Magnusson, D. (1997). A person-oriented approach in research on developmental psychopathology. *Development and Psychopathology*, 9, 291–319.

Bergryd, U., Boalt, G., and Janson, C.-G. (1988). Selection to higher education. In C.-G. Janson (ed.), *Research Notes*. Project Metropolitan Research Report no. 22.

Bernstein, D. P., Cohen, P., Skodol, A., Bezirganian, S., and Brook, J. S. (1996). Childhood antecedents of adolescent personality disorders. *American Journal of Psychiatry*, 153, 907–13.

Black, D. W., Winokur, G., and Nasrallah, A. (1987a). Is death from natural causes still excessive in psychiatric patients? A follow-up of 1593 patients with major affective disorder. *Journal of Nervous and Mental Disease*, 175, 674–80.

Black, D. W., Winokur, G., and Nasrallah, A. (1987b). Suicide in subtypes of major affective disorder. A comparison with general population suicide mortality. *Archives of General Psychiatry*, 44, 878–80.

Blackburn, R. (1968). Personality in relation to extreme aggression in psychiatric offenders. *British Journal of Psychiatry*, 114, 821–8.

Bland, R. C. (1997). Epidemiology of affective disorders: A review. *Canadian Journal of Psychiatry*, 42(4), 367–77.

Bloom, J. D., Williams, M. H., and Bigelow, D. A. (1991). Monitored conditional release of persons found not guilty by reason of insanity. *American Journal of Psychiatry*, 148, 444–8.

Blumenthal, S., and Wessely, S. (1992). National survey of current arrangements for diversion from custody in England and Wales. *British Medical Journal*, 305, 1322–5.

Blumstein, A., Farrington, D. P., and Moitra, S. (1985). Delinquency careers: Innocents, desisters, and persisters. In M. Tonry and N. Morris (eds.), *Crime and Justice: An Annual Review of Research*, vol. 6. Chicago, IL: University of Chicago Press.

Boalt, G. (1947). *Skolutbildning och skolresultat*. Stockholm: Norstedts.

Borum, R. (1996). Improving the clinical practice of violence risk assessment. *American Psychologist*, 51, 945–56.

Brennan, P. A., Grekin, E. R., and Mednick, S. A. (1999). Maternal smoking during pregnancy and adult male criminal outcomes. *Archives of General Psychiatry*, 56, 215–19.

Brennan, P. A., Mednick, S. A., and Hodgins, S. (2000). Psychotic disorders and criminal violence in a total birth cohort. *Archives of General Psychiatry*, 56, 215–219.

Brent, D. A., Perper, J. A., Goldstein, C. E., Kolko, D. J., Allan, M. J., Allman, C. J., and Zelenak, J. P. (1988). Risk factors for adolescent suicide: A comparison of adolescent suicide victims with suicidal in-patients. *Archives of General Psychiatry*, 45, 581–8.

Brooke, D., Taylor, C., Gunn, J., and Maden, A. (1996). Point prevalence of mental disorder in unconvicted male prisoners in England and Wales. *British Medical Journal*, 313, 1524–7.

Bruun, K. and Frånberg, P. (1985). *Den svenska supen*. Stockholm: Prisma.

Bryant, K. J., Rounsaville, B., Spitzer, R. L., and Williams, J. B. W. (1992). Reliability of dual diagnosis. Substance dependence and psychiatric disorders. *Journal of Nervous and Mental Disease*, 180, 251–7.

Burke, K. C., Burke, J. D. Jr., Rae, D. S., and Regier, D. A. (1990). Age at onset of selected mental disorders in five community populations. *Archives of General Psychiatry*, 47, 511–18.

Burke, K. C., Burke, J. D. Jr., Rae, D. S., and Regier, D. A. (1991). Comparing age at onset of major depression and other psychiatric disorders by birth cohorts in five US community populations. *Archives of General Psychiatry*, 48, 789–95.

Cadoret, R. J., Yates, W. R., Troughton, E., Woodworth, G., and Stewart, M. A. (1995). Genetic-environmental interaction in the genesis of aggressivity and conduct disorders. *Archives of General Psychiatry*, 52, 916–24.

CAN and Folkhälsoinstitutet. (1995). *Alkohol- och narkotika-utvecklingen i Sverige.* Rapport 95. Stockholm: CAN och Folkhälsoinstitutet.

Cannon, T. D., Mednick, S., and Parnas, J. (1990). Antecedents of predominantly negative and predominantly positive symptom schizophrenia in a high risk population. *Archives of General Psychiatry*, 47, 622–32.

Carlson, G. A., and Weintraub, S. (1993). Childhood behavior problems and bipolar disorder – relationship or coincidence? *Journal of Affective Disorders*, 28, 143–53.

Carpelan, K. S. (1992). *Unga narkotikamissbrukare i en vårdkedja.* School of Social Work, Stockholm University.

Carpenter, W. T., Heinrichs, D. W., and Wagman, A. M. I. (1988). Deficit and non-deficit forms of schizophrenia. *American Journal of Psychiatry*, 145, 578–83.

Charney, D. S., Nelson, J. C., and Quinlan, D. M. (1981). Personality traits and disorder in depression. *American Journal of Psychiatry*, 138, 1601–04.

Cicchetti, D. and Toth, S. L. (1998). The development of depression in children and adolescents. *American Psychologist*, 53(2), 221–41.

Cline, H. F. (1980). Criminal behavior over the life span. In O. G. Brim, Jr. and J. Kagan (eds.), *Constancy and Change in Human Development.* Cambridge, MA: Harvard University Press, 641–74.

Cohen, C. I. (1980). Crime among mental patients: A critical analysis. *Psychiatry Quarterly*, 52, 100–07.

Coid, J. W. (1996). Dangerous patients with mental illness: Increased risks warrant new policies, adequate resources, and appropriate legislation. *British Medical Journal*, 312, 965–9.

Coid, B., Lewis, S. W., and Reveley, A. M. (1993). A twin study of psychosis and criminality. *British Journal of Psychiatry*, 162, 87–92.

Collins, J. J. and Schlenger, W. E. (1983). *The Prevalence of Psychiatric Disorder Among Admissions to Prison.* Paper presented at the 35th Annual Meeting of the American Society of Criminology, Denver.

Cooke, D. J. (1992). Reconviction following referral to a forensic clinic: The criminal justice outcome of diversion. *Medical Science and Law*, 32, 325–30.

Cooke, D. J. (1994). *Psychological Disturbance in the Scottish Prison System: Prevalence, Precipitants and Policy.* Scottish Prison Service Occasional Papers.

Cooke, D. J. (2000). Major mental disorder and violence in correctional settings. In S. Hodgins (ed.), *Violence among the Mentally Ill: Effective Treatment and Management Strategies.* Dordrecht, The Netherlands: Kluwer.

Coryell, W., Scheftner, W., Keller, M., Endicott, J., Maser, J., and Klerman, G. L. (1993). The enduring psychosocial consequences of mania and depression. *American Journal of Psychiatry*, 150, 720–7.

Côté, G. and Hodgins, S. (1990). Co-occurring mental disorders among criminal offenders. *Bulletin of the American Academy of Psychiatry and the Law*, 18, 271–83.

Côté, G. and Hodgins, S. (1992). The prevalence of major mental disorders among homicide offenders. *International Journal of Law and Psychiatry*, 15, 89–99.

Côté, G., Hodgins, S., Toupin, J., and Proulx, J. (1995). Les problèmes toxicomaniaques et la conduite antisociale chez les sujets en demande d'aide psychologique dans une salle d'urgence générale. In J. M. Léger (ed.), *Compte-rendu du congrès de psychiatrie et neurologie de langue française* tome IVB Paris: Masson, 95–110.

Côté, G., Lesage, A., Chawky, N., and Loyer, M. (1997). Clinical specificity of prison inmates with severe mental disorders: A case-control study. *British Journal of Psychiatry*, 170, 571–7.

Crocker, A. G. and Hodgins, S. (1997). The criminality of noninstitutionalized mentally retarded persons: Evidence from a birth cohort followed to age 30. *Criminal Justice and Behavior*, 24, 432–54.

Dahlberg, G.-B. and Ödmann, E. (1969). *Stadsutveckling och planering i Sverige*. Stockholm: Läromedelsforlägen.

Daniel, A. E., Robins, A. J., Reid, J. C., and Wilfley, D. E. (1988). Lifetime and six-month prevalence of psychiatric disorders among sentenced female offenders. *Bulletin of the American Academy Psychiatry and Law*, 16, 333–42.

DiLalla, L. F. and Gottesman, I. I. (1989). Heterogeneity of causes for delinquency and criminality: Lifespan perspectives. *Development and Psychopathology*, 1, 339–49.

Douglas, K. S. and Webster, C. D. (1999). Predicting violence in mentally and personality disordered individuals. In R. Roesch, S. D. Hart, and J. R. P. Ogloff (eds.), *Psychology and Law: The State of the Discipline*. New York: Kluwer/Plenum, 175–239.

Douglas, K. S. and Webster, C. D. (1999). The HCR-20 violence risk assessment scheme: Concurrent validity in a sample of incarcerated offenders. *Criminal Justice and Behavior*, 26, 3–19.

Drake, R. E., Osher, F. C., Noordsy, D. L., Hurlbut, S. C., Teague, G. B., and Beaudett, M. S. (1990). Diagnosis of alcohol use disorders in schizophrenia. *Schizophrenia Bulletin*, 16, 51–67.

Drake, R. E., Osher, T. C., and Wallach, M. A. (1989). Alcohol use and abuse in schizophrenia: A prospective community study. *Journal of Nervous and Mental Disease*, 177, 408–14.

Dubé, M. (1992). *Une comparaison entre l'histoire des comportements d'agression des hommes et des femmes souffrant de schizophrénie et ceux et celles ne manifestant aucun trouble mental grave*. Unpublished master's thesis, Université de Montréal.

Duncan, O. D. and Duncan, B. (1955). Residential distribution and occupational stratification. *American Journal of Sociology*, 60, 493–503.

Elliott, D. S. and Ageton, S. S. (1980). Reconciling differences in estimates of delinquency. *American Sociological Review*, 45, 95–110.

Elliott, D. S., Huizinga, D., and Menard, S. (1989). *Multiple Problem Youth*. New York, NY: Springer-Verlag.

Endicott, J. and Spitzer, R. L. (1978). A diagnostic interview: The schedule for affective disorders and schizophrenia. *Archives of General Psychiatry*, 35, 837–44.

Endicott, J. and Spitzer, R. L. (1979). Use of the RDC and SADS in the study of affective disorders. *American Journal of Psychiatry*, 136, 52–6.

Endler, N. S. (1982). *Holiday of Darkness: A Psychologist's Personal Journey out of his Depression*. Toronto: Wall and Thompson.

Erb, M., Hodgins, S., Freese, R., Müller-Isberner, R., and Jöckel, D. (2001). *Homicide and schizophrenia: Maybe treatment does have a preventive effect. Criminal Behaviour and Mental Health*, 11, 6–26.

Erb, M., Freese, R., and Müller-Isberner, R. (1996). Personal communication.

Eronen, M. (1995). Mental disorders and homicidal behavior in female subjects. *American Journal of Psychiatry*, 152, 1216–18.

Eronen, M., Hakola, P., and Tiihonen, J. (1996a). Mental disorders and homicidal behavior in Finland. *Archives of General Psychiatry*, 53, 497–501.

Eronen, M., Hakola, P., and Tiihonen, J. (1996b). Schizophrenia and homicidal behavior. *Schizophrenia Bulletin*, 22, 83–9.

Estroff, T. W., Dackis, C. A., Gold, M. S., and Pottash, A. L. C. (1985). Drug abuse and bipolar disorders. *International Journal of Psychiatry and Medicine*, 15, 37–40.

Estroff, S. E., Zimmer, C., Lachicotte, W. S., and Benoit, J. (1994). The influence of social networks and social support on violence by persons with serious mental illness. *Hospital and Community Psychiatry*, 45, 669–79.

Farrington, D. P. (1983). Offending from 10 to 25 years of age. In K. T. Van Dusen and S. A. Mednick (eds.), *Prospective Studies of Crime and Delinquency*. The Hague: Kluwer-Nijhoff, 17–37.

Farrington, D. P., Loeber, R., and Van Kammen, W. B. (1990). Long-term criminal outcomes of hyperactivity–impulsivity–attention deficit and conduct problems in childhood. In L. N. Robins and M. Rutter (eds.), *Straight and Devious Pathways from Childhood to Adulthood*. Cambridge University Press, 62–81.

Farrington, D. P. and Wikström, P.-O. H. (1994). Criminal careers in London and Stockholm. In E. G. M. Weitekamp and H.-J. Kerner (eds.), *Cross-National Longitudinal Research on Human Development and Criminal Behavior*. Dordrecht, The Netherlands: Kluwer Academic Publishers, 65–90.

Ferdinand, R. F. and Verhulst, F. C. (1995). Psychopathology from adolescence into young adulthood: An 8-year follow-up study. *American Journal of Psychiatry*, 152, 1586–94.

Fergusson, D. M., Woodward, L. J., and Horwood, J. (1998). Maternal smoking during pregnancy and psychiatric adjustment in late adolescence. *Archives of General Psychiatry*, 55, 721–7.

Fischbein, S. and Alin-Åkerman, B. (1993). Within-pair similarity in MZ and DZ twins from birth to eighteen years of age. *Acta Geneticae Medicae et Gemellologiae*, 41, 2–3.

Frändén, O. (1992). *Early Mortality and Morbidity in a Stockholm Cohort*. Project Metropolitan Research Report no. 36. Stockholm.

Freed, E. X. (1969). Alcohol abuse by manic patients. *Psychological Reports*, 25, 280.

Fritzell, J. (1991). *Icke av marknaden allena*. Institute for Social Research, Stockholm University.

Fulwiler, C., Grossman, H., Forbes, C., and Ruthazer, R. (1997). Early-onset substance abuse and community violence by outpatients with chronic mental illness. *Psychiatric Services*, 48, 1181–5.

Fulwiler, C. and Ruthazer, R. (1999). Premorbid risk factors for violence in adult mental illness. *Comprehensive Psychiatry*, 40(2), 96–100.

Gelberg, L., Linne, L. S., and Leake, B. D. (1988). Mental health, alcohol and drug use, and criminal history among homeless adults. *American Journal of Psychiatry*, 145, 191–6.

Geller, B., Cooper, T. B., Watts, H. E., Cosby, C. M., and Fox, L. W. (1992). Early findings from a pharmacokinetically designed double-blind and placebo-controlled study of lithium for adolescents comorbid with bipolar and substance dependency disorders. *Progress in Neuro-psychopharmacology and Biological Psychiatry* 16, 281–99.

Gershon, E. S., Hamovit, J. H., Guroff, J. J., and Nurnberger, J. I. (1987). Birth cohort changes in manic and depressive disorders in relatives of bipolar and schizoaffective patients. *Archives of General Psychiatry*, 44, 314–19.

Gibbens, T. C. and Robertson, G. (1983). A survey of the criminal careers of hospital order patients. *British Journal of Psychiatry*, 143, 362–9.

Giovanni, J. M. and Gurel, L. (1967). Socially disruptive behaviour of ex-mental patients. *Archives of General Psychiatry*, 17, 146–53.

Glueck, B. (1918). A study of 608 admissions to Sing Sing Prison. *Mental Hygiene*, 2, 85–151.

Goldstein, J. M. (1988). Gender differences in the course of schizophrenia. *American Journal of Psychiatry*, 145, 684–9.

Goodman, N. (1983). *Fact, Fiction, and Forecast.* [Fourth edn.]. Cambridge, MA: Harvard University Press.

Goodwin, F. D. and Jamison, K. R. (1990). *Manic-Depressive Illness.* New York, NY: Oxford University Press.

Gottesman, I. I. and Shields, J. (1982). The social biology of schizophrenia. *The Epigenetic Puzzle.* Cambridge University Press, 187–94.

Gottlieb, P., Gabrielsen, G., and Kramp, P. (1987). Psychotic homicides in Copenhagen from 1959 to 1983. *Acta Psychiatrica Scandinavica*, 76, 285–92.

Grekin, E. R., Brennan, P., Hodgins, S., and Mednick, S.(in press). Organic brain syndrome and criminal arrests: Two types of offenders. *American Journal of Psychiatry.*

Grunberg, F., Klinger, B. I., and Grumet, B. R. (1978). Homicide and community-based psychiatry. *Journal of Nervous and Mental Disease*, 166, 868–74.

Gunn, J., Maden, A., and Swinton, M. (1992). *The Number of Psychiatric Cases Among Sentenced Prisoners.* London: Home Office.

Guze, S. B. (1976). *Criminality and Psychiatric Disorders.* London: Oxford University Press.

Häfner, H. and Böker, W. (1982). *Crimes of Violence by Mentally Abnormal Offenders.* Cambridge University Press. (Originally published in Germany in 1973 as *Gewalttaten Geistesgestörter*, Berlin: Springer-Verlag).

Hagnell, O., Lanke, J., Rorsman, B., and Öjesjö, L. (1982). Are we entering an age of melancholy? Depressive illnesses in a prospective epidemiological study over 25 years: The Lundby Study, Sweden. *Psychological Medicine*, 12, 279–89.

Hakola, P. (1979). The profile of Finnish offender patients. *Lakimies*, 4, 303–05. (Author's translation).

Harding, C. (1988). Course types in schizophrenia: Converging lines of evidence. *Schizophrenia Bulletin*, 14, 613–32.

Harrington, R., Rutter, M., and Fombonne, E. (1996). Developmental pathways in depression: Multiple meanings, antecedents, and endpoints. *Development and Psychopathology*, 8, 601–16.

Harrow, M., Goldberg, J. F., Grossman, L. S., and Meltzer, H. Y. (1990). Outcome in manic disorders. *Archives of General Psychiatry*, 47, 665–71.

Hart, S. D. (1987). *Diagnosis of Psychopathy in a Forensic Psychiatric Population.* Unpublished master's thesis, The University of British Columbia, Canada.

Hegarty, J. D., Baldessarini, R. J., Tohen, M., Waternaux, C., and Oepen, G. (1994). One hundred years of schizophrenia: A meta-analysis of the outcome literature. *American Journal of Psychiatry*, 151, 1409–16.

Heilbrun, K. and Peters, L. (2000). The efficacy of community treatment programmes in preventing crime and violence. In S. Hodgins and R. Müller-Isberner (eds.), *Violence, Crime, and Mentally Disordered Offenders: Concepts and Methods for Effective Treatment and Prevention.* Chichester, United Kingdom: Wiley.

Helzer, J. E. and Przybeck, T. R. (1988). The co-occurrence of alcoholism with other psychiatric disorders in the general population and its impact on treatment. *Journal of Studies on Alcohol*, 49, 219–24.

Henriksson, M. M., Aro, H. M., Marttunen, M. J., Heikkinen, M. E., Isometsä, E. T., Kuoppasalmi, K. I., and Lönnqvist, J. K. (1993). Mental disorders and comorbidity in suicide. *American Journal of Psychiatry*, 150, 935–40.

Hindelang, M. J. (1981). Variations in rates of offending. *American Sociological Review*, 46, 461–74.

Hindelang, M. S., Hirschi, T., and Weis, J. G. (1979). Correlates of delinquency: The illusion of discrepancy between self-report and official measures, *American Sociological Review*, 44, 995–1014.

Hodgins, S. (1992). Mental disorder, intellectual deficiency and crime: Evidence from a birth cohort. *Archives of General Psychiatry*, 49, 476–83.

Hodgins, S. (1993). The criminality of mentally disordered persons. In S. Hodgins (ed.), *Mental Disorder and Crime.* Newbury Park, CA: Sage, 1–21.

Hodgins, S. (1994a). Letter to the Editor. *Archives of General Psychiatry*, 51, 71–2.

Hodgins, S. (1994b). Status at age 30 of children with conduct problems. *Studies on Crime and Crime Prevention*, 3, 41–62.

Hodgins, S. (1994c). Schizophrenia and violence: Are new mental health policies needed? *Journal of Forensic Psychiatry*, 5, 473–7.

Hodgins, S. (1995). Assessing mental disorder in the criminal justice system: Feasibility versus clinical accuracy. *International Journal of Law and Psychiatry*, 18, 15–28.

Hodgins, S. (1996). The major mental disorders: New evidence requires new policy and practice. *Canadian Psychology*, 37, 95–111.

Hodgins, S. (1998). Epidemiological investigations of the associations between major mental disorders and crime: Methodological limitations and validity of the conclusions. *Social Psychiatry and Epidemiology*, 33(1), 29–37.

Hodgins, S. (2000). The etiology and development of offending among persons with major mental disorders: Some preliminary findings. In S. Hodgins (ed.) *Effective Prevention of Crime and Violence among the Mentally Ill.* Dordrecht, The Netherlands: Kluwer Academic Publishers.

Hodgins, S. and Côté, G. (1990). The prevalence of mental disorders among penitentiary inmates. *Canada's Mental Health*, 38, 1–5.

Hodgins, S. and Côté, G. (1993a). The criminality of mentally disordered offenders. *Criminal Justice and Behavior*, 28, 115–29.

Hodgins, S. and Côté, G. (1993b). Major mental disorder and APD: A criminal combination. *Bulletin of the American Academy of Psychiatry and the Law*, 21, 155–60.

Hodgins, S. and Côté, G. (1995). Major mental disorder among Canadian peniten-
tiary inmates. In L. Stewart, L. Stermac and C. Webster (eds.), *Clinical Criminology: Toward Effective Correctional Treatment*. Toronto: Ministry of the Solicitor General and Correctional Services of Canada, 6–20.

Hodgins, S., Coté, G., and Toupin, J. (1998). Major mental disorders and crime: An etiological hypothesis. In D. Cooke, A. Forth and R. D. Hare (eds.), *Psychopathy: Theory, Research and Implications for Society*. Dordrecht, The Netherlands: Kluwer Academic Publishers, 231–56.

Hodgins, S. and Gaston, L. (1987a). Les programmes communautaires pour patients chroniques: L'élaboration d'un cadre conceptuel. *Santé mentale au Canada*, 35, 7–10.

Hodgins, S. and Gaston, L. (1987b). Composantes d'efficacité des programmes de traitement communautaires destinés aux personnes souffrant de désordres mentaux. *Santé mentale au Québec*, 12, 124–34.

Hodgins, S. and Hébert, J. (1984). Une étude de relance auprès de malades mentaux ayant commis des actes criminels. *Revue canadienne de Psychiatrie*, 29, 669–75.

Hodgins, S., Hébert, J., and Baraldi, R. (1986). Women declared insane: A follow-up study. *International Journal of Law and Psychiatry*, 8, 203–16.

Hodgins, S., Kratzer, L., and McNeil, T. F. (2001). Obstetrical complications, parenting, and risk of criminal behavior. *Archives of General Psychiatry*, 58, 746–52.

Hodgins, S., Kratzer, L., and McNeil, T. F. (forthcoming). Obstetrical complications, parenting practices and risk of criminal behavior among persons who develop major mental disorders. *Acta Psychiatrica Scandinavica*.

Hodgins, S. and Lalonde, N. (1999). Major mental disorders and crime: Changes over time? In P. Cohen, L. Robins and C. Slomkowski (eds.), *Where and When: Geographical and Historical Aspects of Psychopathology*. Mahwah, NJ: Lawrence Erlbaum Associates.

Hodgins, S., Lapalme, M., and Toupin, J. (1999). Criminal activities and substance use of patients with major affective disorders and schizophrenia: A two year follow-
up. *Journal of Affective Disorders*, 55, 187–202.

Hodgins, S., Mednick, S. A., Brennan, P., Schulsinger, F., and Engberg, M. (1996). Mental disorder and crime: Evidence from a Danish birth cohort. *Archives of General Psychiatry*, 53, 489–96.

Hodgins, S. and Müller-Isberner, J. R. (eds.) (2000). *Violence, Crime and Mentally Disor-
dered Offenders: Concepts and Methods for effective Treatment and Prevention*. Chichester, United Kingdom: John Wiley and Sons.

Hodgins, S., Toupin, J., and Côté, G. (1996). Schizophrenia and antisocial person-
ality disorder: A criminal combination. In L. B. Schlesinger (ed.), *Explorations in Criminal Psychopathology: Clinical Syndromes with Forensic Implication*. Springfield, Il: Charles C. Thomas Publisher, 217–37.

Hodgins, S. and Webster, C. D. (1985). *Establishing a Canadian Data Base for Forensic Patients Under Warrants of the Lieutenant Governor: Rationale and Feasibility*. Report commissioned by the Minister of Justice of Canada.

Hodgins, S. and Webster, C. D. (1992). *The Canadian Data Base: Patients Held on Lieutenant-Governors' Warrants*. Ottawa: Department of Justice of Canada.

Hodgins, S., Webster, C. and Paquet, J. (1990). *Annual Report Year-2 Canadian Data Base: Patients Held on Lieutenant-Governors' Warrant.* Report commissioned by the Department of Justice of Canada.

Hodgins, S., Webster, C. and Paquet, J. (1991). *Annual Report Year-3 Canadian Data Base: Patients Held on Lieutenant-Governors' Warrant.* Report commissioned by the Department of Justice of Canada.

Hodgins, S., Webster, C., Paquet, J., and Zellerer, E. (1989). *Annual report Year-I Canadian Data Base: Patients Held on Lieutenant Governor's Warrants.* Report commissioned by the Minister of the Justice of Canada.

Høgh, E. and Wolf, P. (1981). Project Metropolitan: A longitudinal study of 12,270 boys from the metropolitan area of Copenhagen, Denmark (1953–1977). In S. A. Mednick and A. E. Baert (eds.), *Prospective Longitudinal Research: An Empirical Basis for the Primary Prevention of Psychological Disorders* Oxford: Oxford University Press, 99–103.

Høgh, E. and Wolf, P. (1983). Violent crime in a birth cohort: Copenhagen 1953–1977. In K. T. Van Dusen and S. A. Mednick (eds.), *Prospective Studies of Crime and Delinquency.* The Hague: Kluwer-Nijhoff, 249–67.

Holmberg, G. (1994). *Forensic Psychiatric Investigations in Sweden – A brief introduction.* Stockholm: The National Board of Forensic Medicine.

Hoyt, H. (1939). *The Structure and Growth of Residential Neighborhood in American Cities.* Washington, DC: FHA.

Huesmann, L. R., Eron, L. D. (1986). The development of aggression in American children as a consequence of television violence viewing. In L. R. Huessman and L. D. Eron (eds.), *Television and the Aggressive Child: A Cross-National Comparison.* Hillsdale, NJ: Lawrence Erlbaum Associates, 45–80.

Huesmann, L. R., Lefkowitz, M. M., Eron, L. D., and Walder, L. O. (1984). Stability of aggression over time and generations. *Developmental Psychology,* 20, 1120–34.

Hyde, P. S. and Seiter, R. P. (1987). *The Prevalence of Mental Illness Among Inmates in the Ohio Prison System.* The Department of Mental Health and the Ohio Departments of Rehabilitation and Correction. Interdepartmental Planning and Oversight Committee for Psychiatric Services to Corrections.

Inghe, G. (1961). Mental abnormalities among criminals. *Acta Psychiatrica and Neurological,* 16, 28–457.

Jahn, J., Schmid, C. F., and Schrag, C. (1947). The measurement of ecological segregation. *American Sociological Review,* 12, 293–303.

Janson, C.-G. (1970). Juvenile delinquency in Sweden. *Youth and Society,* 2, 207–31.

Janson, C.-G. (1971). A preliminary report on Swedish urban spatial structure. *Economic Geography,* 47, 249–57 (suppl.).

Janson, C.-G. (1981). Some problems of longitudinal research in the social sciences. In F. Schulsinger, S. A. Mednick and J. Knop (eds.), *Longitudinal Research.* Boston, MA: Martinus Nijhoff, 19–55.

Janson, C.-G. (1982). *Delinquency Among Metropolitan Boys.* Project Metropolitan Research Report no. 17. Stockholm.

Janson, C.-G. (1987). Working-class segregation in Stockholm and some other Swedish cities. In U. Bergryd and C.-G. Janson (eds.), *Sociological Miscellany.* Department of Sociology, Stockholm University.

Janson, C.-G. (1990). Retrospective data, undesirable behaviour, and the longitudinal perspective. In D. Magnusson and L. R. Bergman (eds.), *Data Quality in Longitudinal Research.* Cambridge University Press, 100–21.

Janson, C.-G. (1994). A case for a longitudinal study. In E. G. M. Weitekamp and H.-J. Kerner (eds.), *Cross-National Longitudinal Research on Human Development and Criminal Behavior.* Dordrecht, The Netherlands: Kluwer Academic Publishers, 409–22.

Janson, C.-G. (1996). *Social Class and Gender – Selection to Higher Education in a Stockholm Cohort.* (manuscript).

Janson, C.-G. and Torstensson, M. (1984). Sweden. In M. Klein (ed.), *Western Systems of Juvenile Justice.* Beverly Hills, CA: Sage, 191–211.

Janson, C.-G. and Wikström, P.-O. H. (1995). Growing up in a welfare state: The social class–offending relationship. In J. Hagan (ed.), *Delinquency and Disrepute in the Life Course: Current Perspectives on Aging and the Life Cycle.* Greenwich, CT.: Jai Press, 4, 191–215.

Jöckel, D. (1996). Personal communication.

Johns, C. A., Stanley, M., and Stanley, B. (1986). Suicide in schizophrenia. *Annals of the New York Academy of Science,* 487, 294–9.

Kaiser, J. (1997). NIEHS to study genes for environmental risk. *Science,* 275, 1407.

Kallmann, F. J. (1938). *The Genetics of Schizophrenia.* New York, NY: Augustin.

Keller, M. B., Lavori, P. W., Mueller, T. I., Endicott, J., Coryell, W., Hirschfeld, R. M. A., and Shea, T. (1992). Time to recovery, chronicity, and levels of psychopathology in major depression. *Archives of General Psychiatry,* 49, 809–16.

Kendler, K. S. and Gruenberg, A. M. (1984). An independent analysis of the Danish Adoption Study of schizophrenia. *Archives of General Psychiatry,* 41, 555–64.

Kendler, K. S., McGuire, M., Gruenberg, A. M., O'Hare, A., Spellman, M., and Walsh, D. (1993). The Roscommon family study. III. Schizophrenia-related personality disorders in relatives. *Archives of General Psychiatry,* 50, 781–8.

Kerr, M., Tremblay, R. E., Pagani, L., and Vitaro, F. (1997). Boys' behavioral inhibition and the risk of later delinquency. *Archives of General Psychiatry,* 54, 809–16.

Kessing, L. V., Andersen, P. K., Mortensen, P. B., and Bolwig, T. G. (1998). Recurrence in affective disorder: 1. Case register study. *British Journal of Psychiatry,* 172, 23–8.

Kessler *et al.* (1994). Lifetime and 12-month prevalence of DSM-III-R psychiatric disorders in the United States. *Archives of General Psychiatry,* 51, 8–19.

Kety, S. F., Rosenthal, D., Wender, P. H., and Schulsinger, F. (1968). The types and prevalences of mental illness in the biological and adoptive families of adopted schizophrenics. In D. Rosenthal and S. S. Kety (eds.), *The Transmission of Schizophrenia.* London: Pergamon Press, 345–62.

Klein, M. W. (1995). *The American Street Gang.* New York: Oxford University Press.

Klerman, G. L. (1976). Age and clinical depression today's youth in Twenty-First Century. *Journal of Gerontology,* 31(3), 318–23.

Klerman, G. L. and Weissman, M. M. (1989). Increasing rates of depression. *Journal of the American Medical Association,* 261, 2229–35.

Klerman, G. L. and Weissman, M. M. (1992). The course, morbidity, and costs of depression. *Archives of General Psychiatry*, 49, 831–4.

Kovacs, M. and Pollock, M. (1995). Bipolar disorder and comorbid conduct disorder in childhood and adolescence. *Journal of the American Academy of Child and Adolescence Psychiatry*, 34(6), 715–23.

Kramp, A. J. and Gabrielsen, G. (1994). Udviklingen i antallet af tilsynsklienter idømt psykiatriske særforanstaltninger fra 1977 til 1993. *Nordisk Tidsskrift for kriminalvidenskab*.

Kraeplin, E. (1896). *Psychiatrie, Ein Lehrbuch für Studierende und Aerzte*. Leipzig: 5 Aufl., Barth.

Kratzer, L. and Hodgins, S. (1997). Adult outcomes of child conduct problems: A cohort study. *Journal of Abnormal Child Psychology*, 25, 65–81.

Kratzer, L. and Hodgins, S. (1999). A typology of offenders: A test of Moffitt's theory among males and females from childhood to age 30. *Criminal Behaviour and Mental Health*.

Krauth, J. and Lienert, G. A. (1982). Fundamentals and modifications of configural frequency analysis (CFA). *Interdisciplinaria*, 3.

Kristjansson, E., Allebeck, P., and Wistedt, B. (1987). Validity of the diagnosis schizophrenia in a psychiatric inpatient register. *Nordisk Psykiatrisk Tidsskrift*, 41, 229–34.

Lagerström, M., Bremme, K., Eneroth, P., and Janson, C.-G. (1991). School marks and IQ-test scores for low birth weight children at the age of 13. *European Journal of Obstetrics and Gynecology and Reproductive Biology* 40, 129–36.

Lagerström, M., Bremme, K., Eneroth, P., and Janson, C.-G. (1994). Long-term development for girls and boys at age 16–18 as related to birth weight and gestation age. *International Journal of Psychophysiology*, 17, 175–80.

Lahey, B. B., Piacentini, J. C., McBurnett, K., Stone, P., Hartdagen, S., and Hynd, G. (1988). Psychopathology in the parents of children with conduct disorder and hyperactivity. *Journal of the American Academy of Child and Adolescence Psychiatry*, 27, 163–70.

Landau, R., Harth, P., Othnay, N., and Sharthertz, C. (1972). The influence of psychotic parents on their children's development. *American Journal of Psychiatry*, 129, 38–43.

Laniard, G. A. and Bergman, L. R. (1985). Longisectional interaction structure analysis (LISA) in psychopharmacology and developmental psychopathology. *Neuropsychobiology*, 14, 27–34.

Laroche, I., Hodgins, S., and Toupin, J. (1995). Liens entre les symptômes et le fonctionnement social chez des personnes souffrant de schizophrénie ou de trouble affectif majeur. *Canadian Journal of Psychiatry*, 40, 27–34.

Lavori, P. W., Klerman, G. L., Keller, M. B., Reich, T., Rice, J., and Endicott, J. (1987). Age-period-cohort analysis of secular trends in onset of major depression: Findings in siblings of patients with major affective disorder. *Journal of Psychiatric Research*, 21, 23–5.

Leary, J., Johnstone, E. C., and Owens, D. G. C. (1991). Social outcome. *British Journal of Psychiatry*, 159 (suppl. 13), 13–20.

Ledingham, J., Younger, A., Schwartzman, A., and Bergeron, G. (1982). Agreement among teacher, peer and self-ratings of children's aggression, withdrawal and likability. *Journal of Abnormal Child Psychology*, 55, 109–10.

Levander, S. (1996). Report to the Swedish Ministry of Health.

Léveillée, S. (1994). *Évaluation multidimensionnelle du support social des sujets schizophrènes.* Unpublished doctoral thesis, Université de Montréal.

Lewinsohn, P. M., Zeiss, A. M., and Duncan, E. M. (1989). Probability of relapse after recovery from an episode of depression. *Journal of Abnormal Psychology*, 98, 107–16.

Lewis, D. O. and Bälla, D. A. (1970). *Delinquency and Psychopathology.* New York, NY: Grune Stratton.

Leygraf, N. (1988). *Psychisch kranka Straftäter.* Berlin: Springer-Verlag.

Lidberg, L., Wiklund, N., and Jakobsson, S. W. (1988). Mortality among criminals with suspected mental disturbance. *Scandinavian Journal of Social and Medicine*, 17, 59–65.

Lindelius, R. (ed.) (1970). A study of schizophrenia: A clinical, prognostic, and family investigation. *Acta Psychiatrica Scandinavica*, Supplement 216.

Lindqvist, P. (1986). Criminal homicide in Northern Sweden 1970. In 1981: Alcohol intoxication, alcohol abuse and mental disease. *International Journal of Law and Psychiatry*, 8, 19–37.

Lindqvist, P. (1989). *Violence against a person: The role of mental disorder and abuse.* Sweden: Umeå University Medical Dissertations.

Lindqvist, P. and Allebeck, P. (1989). Schizophrenia and assaultive behaviour: The role of alcohol and drug abuse. *Acta Psychiatrica Scandinavica*, 82, 191–5.

Lindqvist, P. and Allebeck, P. (1990). Schizophrenia and crime: A longitudinal follow-up of 644 schizophrenics in Stockholm. *British Journal of Psychiatry*, 157, 345–50.

Lindström, P. (1995). *School Context and Delinquency.* Project Metropolitan Research Report no. 41. Stockholm.

Link, B. G., Andrews, H., and Cullen, F. T. (1992). The violent and illegal behaviour of mental patients reconsidered. *American Sociological Review*, 57, 275–92.

Link, B. G. and Stueve, A. (1994). Psychotic symptoms and the violent/illegal behavior of mental patients compared to community control. In J. Monahan and H. Steadman (eds.), *Violence and Mental Disorder. Developments in Risk Assessment.* University of Chicago Press, 137–59.

Linkowski, P., de Maertelaer, V., and Mendlewicz, J. (1985). Suicidal behaviour in major depressive illness. *Acta Psychiatrica Scandinavica*, 72, 233–8.

Litt, S. M. (1971). *Perinatal Complications and Criminality.* Unpublished doctoral dissertation, University of Michigan.

Loeber, R. (1988). Behavioural precursors and accelerators of delinquency. In W. Buikhuisen and S. Mednick (eds.), *Explaining Crime.* London: Brill, 51–67.

Logan, J. (1976). *Josh: My Up and Down, In and Out Life.* New York, NY: Delacorte Press.

Lowell, R. (1977). *Day by Day.* New York, NY: Farrar, Strauss and Giroux.

Lynam, D., Moffitt, T., and Stouthamer-Loeber, M. (1993). Explaining the relation between IQ and delinquency: Class, race, test motivation, school failure, or self-control? *Journal of Abnormal Psychology*, 102, 187–96.

Lyons, M. J., True, W. R., Eisen, S. A., Goldberg, J., Meyer, J. M., Faraone, S. V., Eaves, L. J., and Tsuang, M. T. (1995). Differential heritability of adult and juvenile antisocial traits. *Archives of General Psychiatry*, 52, 906–15.

Machon, R. A., Mednick, S. A., and Huttenen, M. O. (1997). Adult major affective disorder following prenatal exposure to an influenza epidemic. *Archives of General Psychiatry*, 54, 322–8.

Magnusson, D. and Stattin, H. (1998). Person context interaction theories. In W. Damon and R. M. Lerner (eds.), *Handbook of child psychology. Volume 1: Theoretical Models of Human Development.* New York, NY: Wiley, 685–759.

Manzano, J. and Salvador, A. (1993). Antecedents of severe affective (mood) disorders. Patients examined as children or adolescents and as adults. *Acta Paedopsychiatrica*, 56, 11–8.

Marengo, J. (1994). Classifying the courses of schizophrenia. *Schizophrenia Bulletin*, 20, 519–36.

Martens, P. L. (1981). *Socioeconomic Status, Family Structure, and Socialization of Early Adolescent Children.* Project Metropolitan Research Report no. 16. Stockholm.

Martens, P. L. (1982). *Achievement-Related Behavior of Early Adolescents.* Project Metropolitan Research Report no. 18. Stockholm.

Marttunen, M. J., Aro, H. M., Henriksson, M. M., and Lönnqvist, J. K. (1991). Mental disorders in adolescent suicide. DSM-III-R axes I and II diagnoses in suicides among 13- to 19-year-olds in Finland. *Archives of General Psychiatry*, 48, 834–9.

McGlashan, T. H. (1988). A selective review of recent North American long-term follow-up studies of schizophrenia. *Schizophrenia Bulletin*, 14, 515–42.

McGlashan, T. H. and Carpenter, W. T. (1988). Long-term follow-up studies of schizophrenia. Editors' introduction. *Schizophrenia Bulletin*, 14, 497–500.

McNeil, T. F., Cantor-Graae, E., and Ismail, B. (2000). Obstetric complications and congenital malformation. *Brain Research Reviews*, 31, 166–178.

Mednick, S. A., Parnas, J. and Schulsinger, F. (1987). The Copenhagen high-risk project, 1962–1986. *Schizophrenia Bulletin*, 13, 485–95.

Meller, W. H. and Borchardt, C. M. (1996). Comorbidity of major depression and conduct disorder (Research report). *Journal of Affective Disorders*, 39, 123–6.

Menzies, R. and Webster, C. D. (1995). Construction and validation of risk assessments in a six-year follow-up of forensic patients: A tridimensional analysis. *Journal of Consulting and Clinical Psychology*, 63, 766–78.

Mesnikoff, A. M. and Lauterbach, C. G. (1975). The association of violent dangerous behaviour with psychiatric disorders: A review of the research literature. *Journal of Psychiatry and the Law*, 3, 415–45.

Moberg, S. (1951). *Vem blev student och vad blev studenten? (Who Graduated and What Became of the Student?)* Lund: Gleerups.

Modestin, J. and Ammann, R. (1995). Mental disorders and criminal behaviour. *British Journal of Psychiatry*, 166, 667–75.

Moffitt, T. E. (1990). The neuropsychology of delinquency: A critical review of theory and research. In N. Morris and M. Tonry (eds.), *Crime and Justice.* University of Chicago Press, 12, 99–169.

Moffitt, T. E. (1992). Natural histories of delinquency. In E. G. M. Weitekamp and H. J. Kerner (eds.), *Cross National Longitudinal Research on Human Developmental Criminal Behavior.* Dordrecht, The Netherlands: Kluwer Academic Publishers, 3–61.

Moffitt, T. E. (1993). Adolescence-limited and life-course-persistent antisocial behavior: A developmental taxonomy. *Psychological Review*, 100, 674–701.

Moffitt, T. E. (1994). Natural histories of delinquency. In E. G. M. Weitekamp and H. J. Kerner (eds.), *Cross-National Longitudinal Research on Human Development and Criminal Behavior.* The Netherlands: Kluwer Academic Press, 3–61.

Moffitt, T. E., Caspi, A., Dickson, N., Silva, P., and Stanton, W. (1996). Childhood-onset versus adolescent-onset antisocial conduct problems in males: Natural history from ages 3 to 18 years. *Development and Psychopathology,* 8, 399–424.

Monahan, J. (1999). Implications of findings from the MacArthur Risk Assessment Project for treatment designed to prevent violence among the mentally ill. Presented at the NATO Advanced Study Institute on the Prevention of Crime and Violence among the Mentally Ill, Italy, May, 1999.

Monahan, J. and Arnold, J. (1996). Violence by people with mental illness: A consensus statement by advocates and researchers. *Psychiatric Rehabilitation Journal,* 19, 67–70.

Monahan, J. and Steadman, H. J. (1983). Crime and mental disorder: An epidemiological approach. In M. Tonry and R. Morris (eds.), *Crimes and Justice: An Annual Review of Research,* 4, 145–89.

Monahan, J. and Steadman, H. J. (1994). *Violence and Mental Disorder – Developments in Risk Assessment.* University of Chicago Press.

Morrison, J. R. (1974). Bipolar affective disorder and alcoholism. *American Journal of Psychiatry,* 131, 1130–3.

Morrissey, J. P. and Goldman, H. H. (1986). Care and treatment of the mentally ill in the United States: Historical developments and reforms. *The Annals of the American Academy of Political and Social Science,* 484, 12–27.

Motiuk, L. and Poporino, F. (1991). *The Prevalence, Nature and Severity of Mental Health Problems Among Federal Male Inmates in Canadian Penitentiaries.* Correctional Services of Canada Research Report, no. 24.

Mueser, K. T., Rosenberg, S. D., Drake, R. E., Miles, K. M., Wolford, G., Vidager, R., and Carrieri, K. (1999). Conduct disorder, antisocial personality disorder, and substance use disorders. *Journal of Studies on Alcohol,* 60, 278–84

Mueser, K. T., Yarnold, P. R., Levinson, D. F., Singh, H., Bellack, A. S., Kee, K., Morrison, R. L., and Yadalam, K. G. (1990). Prevalence of substance abuse in schizophrenia. *Schizophrenia Bulletin,* 16, 31–56.

Mullen, P. E., Burgess, P., Wallace, C., Palmer, S., and Ruschena, D. (2000). Community care and criminal offending in schizophrenia. *The Lancet,* 355, 614–17.

Mullen, P., Taylor, P. J., and Wessely, S. (1993). Psychosis, violence and crime. In J. Gunn and P. J. Taylor (eds.), *Forensic Psychiatry: Clinical, Legal and Ethical Issues.* Oxford: Butterworth-Heinemann Ltd, 329–72.

Müller-Isberner, J. R. (1996). Forensic psychiatric aftercare following hospital order treatment. *International Journal of Law and Psychiatry,* 19, 81–6.

Müller-Isberner, R. and Hodgins, S. (2000). Evidence based treatment for mentally disordered offenders. In S. Hodgins and R. Müller-Isberner (eds.), *Violence, Crime and Mentally Disordered Offenders: Concepts and Methods for Effective Treatment and Prevention.* Chichester, United Kingdom: John Wiley and Sons.

Munk-Jørgensen, P., Kastrup, M., and Mortensen, P. B. (1993). The Danish psychiatric case register as a tool in epidemiology. *Acta Psychiatrica Scandinavica,* 370, 27–32.

Munk-Jørgensen, P., Lehtinen, V., Helgason, T., Dalgard, O. S., and Westrin, C. G. (1995). Psychiatry in the five Nordic countries. *European Psychiatry*, 10, 197–206.

Murray, C. J. L. and Lopez, A. D. (1996). Evidence-based health policy – Lessons from the global burden of disease study. *Science*, 274, 740–3.

National Institute of Mental Health/National Institutes of Health (NIMH/NIH) Consensus Development Conference Statement. (1985). Mood disorders: Pharmalogical prevention of recurrences. *American Journal of Psychiatry*, 142, 469–76.

Nedopil, N. (1996). Personal communication.

Needleman, H. L., Riess, J. A., Tobin, M. J., Biesecker, G. E., and Greenhouse, J. B. (1996). Bone lead levels and delinquent behavior. *Journal of American Medical Association*, 275, 363–9.

Neighbors, H. W., Williams, D. H., Gunnings, T. S., Lipscomb, W. D., Broman, C., and Lepkowski, J. (1987). *The Prevalence of Mental Disorder in Michigan Prisons*. Final report submitted to the Michigan Department of Corrections, MI.

Newman, D. L., Moffitt, T. E., Caspi, A., Magdol, L., Silva, P. A., and Stanton, W. R. (1996). Psychiatric disorder in a birth cohort of young adults: Prevalence, comorbidity, clinical significance, and new case incidence from ages 11 to 21. *Journal of Consulting and Clinical Psychology*, 64, 552–62.

Nolan, K. A., Volavka, J., Mohr, P., and Czobor, P. (1999). Psychopathy and violent behavior among patients with schizophrenia or schizoaffective disorder. *Psychiatric Services*, 50, 787–800.

Ohlin, S., John, R. S., and Mednick, S. A. (1995). Assessing the predictive value of teacher reports in a high risk sample for schizophrenia: A ROC analysis. *Schizophrenia Research*, 16, 53–66.

O'Leary, D. A. and Lee, A. S. (1996). Seven years prognosis, depression mortality and readmission risk in the Nottingham ECT cohort. *British Journal of Psychiatry*, 169, 423–9.

Olson, H. S. E. (1993). *Social Policy and Welfare State in Sweden*. Lund: Arkiv.

Olsson, B. (1994). *Narkotikaproblemets bakgrund*. Stockholm: CAN.

Olweus, D. (1991). Bully/victim problems among schoolchildren: Basic facts and effects of a school based intervention program. In K. Rubin and D. Pepler (eds.), *The Development and Treatment of Childhood Aggression* Hillsdale, NJ: Erlbaum, 411–48.

Olweus, D. (1993). Bully/victim problems among schoolchildren: Long-term consequences and an effective intervention program. In S. Hodgins (ed.), *Mental Disorder and Crime*. Newbury Park, CA: Sage, 317–49.

Ortmann, J. (1981). Psykisk ofvigelse og kriminel adfaerd en under sogelse af 11533 maend fodt i 1953 i det metropolitane omrade kobenhaun. *Forksningsrapport*, 17.

Owen, R. R., Fischer, E. P., Booth, B. M., and Cuffel, B. J. (1996). Medication non-compliance and substance abuse among patients with schizophrenia. *Psychiatric Services*, 47, 853–8.

Pasewark, R. A. (1982). Insanity plea: A review of the research literature. *Journal of Psychiatry and the Law*, 9, 357–402.

Patterson, G. R. (1982). *A Social Learning Approach: III. Coercive Family Process*. Eugene, OR: Castalia.

Patterson, G. R. (1984). Siblings: Fellow travellers in coercive family processes. In R. J. Blanchand and D.C. Blanchard (eds.), *Advances in the Study of Aggression.* Orlando, FL: Academic Press, 1, 173–215.

Patterson, G. R., Capaldi, D. M., and Bank, L. (1991). An early starter model for predicting delinquency. In D. Pepler and K. H. Rubin (eds.), *The Development and Treatment of Childhood Aggression.* Hillsdale, NJ: Lawrence Erlbaum, 139–68.

Patterson, G. R. and Reid, J. B. (1984). Social interactional processes within the family: The study of moment-by-moment family transactions in which human social development is imbedded. *Journal of Applied Developmental Psychology,* 5, 237–62.

Patterson, G. R. and Yoerger, K. (1993). Developmental models for delinquent behavior. In S. Hodgins (ed.), *Mental Disorder and Crime.* Newbury Park, CA: Sage, 140–72.

Petursson, H. and Gudjonsson, G. H. (1981). Psychiatric aspects of homicide. *Acta Psychiatrica Scandinavica,* 64, 363–72.

Popenoe, D. (1977). *The Suburban Environment.* University of Chicago Press.

Post, R. M., Weiss, S. R. B., and Leverich, G. S. (1994). Recurrent affective disorder: Roots in developmental neurobiology and illness progression based on changes in gene expression. *Development and Psychopathology,* 6, 781–813.

Pulkkinen, L. (1988). Delinquent development: Theoretical and empirical considerations. In M. Rutter (ed.), *Studies of Psychosocial Risk. The Power of Longitudinal Data.* Cambridge University Press, 184–99.

Quinsey, V. L. (1995). The prediction and explanation of criminal violence. *International Journal of Law and Psychiatry,* 18, 117–27.

Quinsey, V. L. (2000). Institutional violence among the mentally ill. In S. Hodgins (ed.), *Violence among the Mentally Ill: Effective Treatment and Management Strategies.* Dordrecht, The Netherlands: Kluwer.

Quinsey, V. L., Coleman, G., Jones, B., and Altrows, I. F. (1997). Proximal antecedent of eloping and reoffending among supervised mentally disordered offenders. *Journal of Interpersonal Violence,* 12, 794–813.

Quinsey, V. L., Harris, G. T., Rice, M. E., and Cormier, C. (1998). *Violent Offenders: Appraising and Managing Risk.* Washington, DC: American Psychological Association.

Rabkin, J. G. (1979). Criminal behaviour of discharged mental patients. A critical appraisal of the research. *Psychological Bulletin,* 86, 1–29.

Raine, A., Brennan, P., and Mednick, S. A. (1994). Birth complications combined with early maternal rejection at age 1 year predisposed to violent crime at age 18 years. *Archives of General Psychiatry,* 51, 984–8.

Rappeport, J. R. and Lassen, G. (1966). The dangerousness of female patients. A comparison of the arrest rate of discharged psychiatric patients and the general population. *American Journal of Psychiatry,* 123, 413–19.

Räsänen, P., Hakko, H., Isohanni, M., Hodgins, S., Järvelin, M.-R., and Tiihonen, J. (1999). Maternal smoking during pregnancy and risk of criminal behavior in the Northern Finland 1966 birth cohort. *The American Journal of Psychiatry,* 156(6), 857–62.

Rasmussen, K., Levander, S., and Sletvold, H. (1995). Aggressive and non-aggressive schizophrenics: Symptom profile and neuropsychological differences. *Psychology, Crime, and Law,* 15, 119–29.

Reed, J. (1995). Personal Communication. NHS Executive, Department of Health, London.

Regier, D. A., Farmer, M. E., Rae, D. S., Locke, B. Z., Keith, S. J., Judd, L. L., Goodwin, F. K. (1990). Comorbidity of mental disorders with alcohol and other drug abuse. *Journal of the American Medical Association*, 264, 2511–18.

Regionplanekontoret. (1983). *Områdesdata 1983* (Data by district). Report 1983: 1.

Regionplanekontoret. (1984). *Invandrare i Stockholms län 1* (Immigrants in Stockholm County 1). Report 1984: 5.

Reinisch, J. M., Sanders, S. A., Mortensen, E. L., and Rubin, D. B. (1995). In utero exposure to phenobarbital and intelligence deficits in adult men. *Journal of American Medical Association*, 274, 1518–25.

Ridgely, M. S., Goldman, H. H., and Talbott, J. A. (1986). *Chronic Mentally Ill Young Adults with Substance Abuse Problems: A Review of Relevant Literature and Creation of a Research Agenda*. Baltimore, MD: University of Maryland School of Medicine. Mental Health Policy Studies.

Riley, M. W. (1992). Cohort perspectives. In E. F. Borgatta and M. L. Borgatta (eds.), *Encyclopedia of Sociology*. New York, NY: Macmillan, 1, 231–7.

Riley, M. W., Johnson, M., and Foner, A. (1972). *Aging and Society: A Sociology of Age Stratification*, vol. 3. New York, NY: Russell Sage Foundation.

Robertson, G. (1988). Arrest patterns among mentally disordered offenders. *British Journal of Psychiatry*, 153, 313–16.

Robins, L. (1966). *Deviant Children Grown Up*. Baltimore, MD: Williams and Wilkins.

Robins, L. N., Helzer, J. E., Weissman, M. M., Orvaschel, H., Gruenberg, E., Burke, J. D., and Regier, D. A. Jr. (1984). Lifetime prevalence of specific psychiatric disorders in three sites. *Archives of General Psychiatry*, 41, 949–58.

Robins, L. N. and McEvoy, L. (1990). Conduct problems as predictors of substance abuse. In L. N. Robins and M. Rutter (eds.), *Straight and Deviant Pathways from Childhood to Adulthood*. Cambridge University Press, 182–204.

Robins, E., Murphy, G. E., Wilkinson, R. H., Gassner, S., and Kayes, J. (1959). Some clinical considerations in the prevention of suicide based on a study of 134 successful suicides. *American Journal of Public Health*, 49, 888–99.

Robins, L. N. and Ratcliff, K. S. (1979). Risk factors in the continuation of childhood antisocial behavior into adulthood. *International Journal of Mental Health*, 7, 96–116.

Robins, L. N. and Regier, D. A. (1991). *Psychiatric Disorders in America: The Epidemiologic Catchment Area Study*. New York, NY: The Free Press.

Rosenfeld, R. A. and Kalleberg, A. L. (1990). A cross-national comparison of the gender gap in income. *American Journal of Sociology*, 96, 69–106.

Rowe, J. B., Sullivan, P. F., Mulder, R. T., and Joyce, P. R. (1996). The effect of a history of conduct disorder in adult major depression. *Journal of Affective Disorders*, 37, 51–63.

Rutter, M. (1996). Introduction: Concepts of antisocial behaviour, of cause, and of genetic influences. In Ciba Foundation Symposium 194 (ed.), *Genetics of Criminal and Antisocial Behaviour*. Chichester: John Wiley and Sons Ltd, 1–15.

Satsumi, Y., Inada, T., and Yamauchi, T. (1998). Criminal offenses among discharged mentally ill individuals. *International Journal of Law and Psychiatry*, 21, 197–207.

Schanda, H., Födes, P., Topitz, A., and Knecht, G. (1992). Premorbid adjustment of schizophrenic criminal offenders. *Acta Psychiatrica Scandinavica*, 86, 121–6.

Scott, J. (1988). Chronic depression. *British Journal of Psychiatry*, 153, 287–97.

Seeman, M. V. (1985). Symposium: Gender and schizophrenia. *Canadian Journal of Psychiatry*, 30, 311–12.

Shepherd, M., Watt, D., Falloon, D., and Smeeton, N. (1989). The natural history of schizophrenia: A five year follow-up study of outcome and prediction in a representative sample of schizophrenics. *Psychological Medicine*, Monograph Supplement 15.

Shevky, E. and Bell, W. (1955). *Social Area Analysis*. Stanford University Press.

Silverton, L. (1985). *Crime and the Schizophrenia Spectrum: A Study of Two Danish Cohorts*. Unpublished thesis, University of Southern California.

Slater, E., Hare, E. H., and Price, J. (1971). Marriage and fertility of psychotic patients compared with national data. In I. I. Gottesman and L. Erlenmeyer-Kimling (eds.), Fertility and reproduction in physically and mentally disordered individuals. *Social Biology*, Supplement.

Smith, W. R. (1991). *Social Structure, Family Structure, Child Rearing, and Delinquency: Another Look*. Project Metropolitan Research Report no. 33. Stockholm.

Smith, W. R. (1994). Moderation in life and in regression models. *Studies of a Stockholm Cohort*. Project Metropolitan Research Report no. 39. Stockholm, 131–55.

Snyder, J. J. and Patterson, G. R. (1986). The effects of consequences on patterns of social interaction: A quasi experimental approach to reinforcement in natural interaction. *Child Development*, 57, 1257–68.

Snyder, J. J. and Patterson, G. R. (1992). *Covariation of the relative rate of child behavior and the relative rate of maternal reinforcement in natural family interactions.* (manuscript).

Söderqvist, L. (1999). *Rekordår och miljonprogram*. University of Chicago Press.

SOS (1984). *Tema Invandrare*. (Theme Immigrants). Report 38.

SOU (1992). *Psykiatriutredningen*. Välfärd och valfrihet-service, stöd och vård för psykiskt störda, 73.

Spitzer, R. L., Endicott, J., and Robins, E. (1978). Research diagnostic criteria: Rationale and reliability. *Archives of General Psychiatry*, 35, 773–82.

Statistics Sweden. *Statistisk årsbok för Sverige*.

Stattin, H. and Klackenberg-Larsson, I. (1993). Early language and intelligence development and their relationship to future criminal behavior. *Journal of Abnormal Psychology*, 102, 369–78.

Stattin, H. and Magnusson, D. (1991). Stability and change in criminal behaviour up to age 30: Findings from a prospective, longitudinal study in Sweden. *British Journal of Criminology*, 31, 327–46.

Stattin, H. and Magnusson, D. (1993, March). *Convergence in time of age at onset of official delinquency and educational and behavioral problems.* Paper presented at the Society for Research in Child Development (SRCD) Conference in New Orleans.

Stattin, H. and Magnusson, D. (1996). Antisocial development: A holistic approach. *Development and Psychopathology*, 8(4), 617–45.

Steadman, H. J. and Cocozza, J. J. (1974). *Careers of the Criminally Insane*. Lexington, Mass.: Lexington Books, D.C. Heath.

Steadman, H. J., Cocozza, J. J., and Veysey, B. M. (1999). Comparing outcomes for diverted and nondiverted jail detainees with mental illnesses. *Law and Human Behavior*, 23, 615–27.

Steadman, H. J. and Felson, R. B. (1984). Self-reports of violence. Ex-mental patients, ex-offenders, and the general population. *Criminology*, 22, 321–42.

Steadman, H. J., Monahan, J., Duffee, B., Hartstone, E., and Robbins, P. C. (1984). The impact of state mental hospital deinstitutionalization on United States prison populations, 1968–1978. *The Journal of Criminal Law and Criminology*, 75, 474–90.

Steadman, H. J., Mulvey, E. P., Monahan, J., Robbins, P. C., Appelbaum, P. S., Grisso, T., and Roth, L. H. (1998). Violence by people discharged from acute psychiatric inpatient facilities and by others in the same neighborhoods. *Archives of General Psychiatry*, 55, 393–401.

Stenberg, S.-Å. (1994). Family structure and the inheritance of welfare dependence. *Studies of a Stockholm Cohort*. Project Metropolitan Research Report no. 39. Stockholm, 157–83.

Stoll, A. L., Tohen, M., Baldessarini, R. J., Goodwin, D. C., Stein, S., Katz, S. Geenens, D., Swinson, R., Goethe, J. W., and Glashan, T. (1993). Shifts in diagnostic frequencies of schizophrenia and major affective disorders at six North American psychiatric hospitals. *American Journal Psychiatry*, 150, 1668–73.

Strauss, J. S., Carpenter, W. T. Jr., and Bartko, J. J. (1974). An approach to the diagnosis and understanding of schizophrenia: Part III. Speculations on the processes that underlie schizophrenic symptoms. *Schizophrenia Bulletin*, 1, 61–70.

Stueve, A. and Link, B. G. (1997). Violence and psychiatric disorders: Results from an epidemiological study of young adults in Israel. *Psychiatric Quarterly*, 68, 327–42.

Swanson, J. W. (1993). Alcohol abuse, mental disorder, and violent behavior. *Alcohol, Health and Research World*, 17, 123–32.

Swanson, J. W., Borum, R., Swartz, M., and Monahan, J. (1996). Psychotic symptoms and disorders and the risk of violent behavior in the community. *Criminal Behaviour and Mental Health*, 6, 309–29.

Swanson, J. W., Holzer, C. E., Ganju, V. K., and Jono, R. T. (1990). Violence and psychiatric disorder in the community: Evidence from the epidemiologic catchment area surveys. *Hospital and Community Psychiatry*, 41, 761–70.

Swartz, M. S., Swanson, J. W., Hiday, V. A., Borum, R., Wagner, R., and Burns, B. J. (1998a). Taking the wrong drugs: The role of substance abuse and medication noncompliance in violence among severely mentally ill individuals. *Social Psychiatry and Psychiatric Epidemiology*, 33 (suppl. 1), S75–S81.

Swartz, M. S., Swanson, J. W., Hiday, V. A., Borum, R., Wagner, R., and Burns, B. J. (1998b). Violence and severe mental illness: The effects of substance abuse and non adherence to medication. *American Journal of Psychiatry*, 155, 226–31.

Sweetser, F. L. (1965). Factorial ecology: Helsinki. *Demography*, 2, 372–86.

Taylor, P. J. (1985). Motives for offending among violent and psychotic men. *British Journal of Psychiatry*, 147, 491–8.

Taylor, P. J. (1995). Schizophrenia and the risk of violence. In S. R. Hirsch and D. R. Weinberger (eds.), *Schizophrenia*. Oxford: Blackwell Science, 163–83.

Taylor, P. J. and Gunn, J. (1984). Violence and psychosis. II: Effect of psychiatric diagnosis on conviction and sentencing of offenders. *British Medical Journal Clinical Research* ed., 289 (6436), 9–12.

Taylor, P. J. and Gunn, J. (1984). Violence and psychosis. I. Risk of violence among psychotic men. *British Medical Journal Clinical Research* ed., 288 (6435), 1945–9.

Tengström, A., Hodgins, S., and Kullgren, G. (2001). *Men with schizophrenia who behave violently: The usefulness of an early versus late starters typology.* Schizophrenia Bulletin, 27, 205–218.

Teplin, L. A. (1983). The criminalization of the mentally ill: Speculation in search of data. *Psychological Bulletin*, 94, 54–67.

Teplin, L. A. (1984). Criminalizing mental disorder: The comparative arrest rate of the mentally ill. *American Psychologist*, 39, 794–803.

Tessler, R. C. and Dennis, D. L. (1989). *A Synthesis of Nimh-Funded Research Concerning Persons Who Are Homeless and Mentally Ill.* Bethesda, Maryland: National Institute of Mental Health.

Thase, M. (1994). *What's Become of this Good Prognosis Illness?* First International Conference on Bipolar Disorder.

Thompson, C. B. (1937). A psychiatric study of recidivists. *American Journal of Psychiatry*, 94, 591–604.

Thornberry, T. P. and Jacoby, J. E. (1979). *The Criminally Insane.* University of Chicago Press.

Tiihonen, J., Hakola, P., Eronen, M., Vartiainen, H., and Ryynänen, O.-P. (1996). Risk of homicidal behavior among discharged forensic psychiatric patients. *Forensic Science International*, 79, 123–9.

Tiihonen, J., Isohanni, M., Räsänen, P., Koiranen, M., and Moring, J. (1997). Specific major mental disorders and criminality: A 26-year prospective study of the 1966 Northern Finland birth cohort. *American Journal of Psychiatry*, 154(6), 840–5.

Timms, D. W. G. (1991a). *Family Structure in Childhood and Mental Health in Adolescence.* Project Metropolitan Research Report no. 32. Stockholm.

Timms, D. W. G. (1991b). *Individual Characteristics, Parental Ideology and Mental Health in Adolescence.* Project Metropolitan Research Report no. 34. Stockholm.

Timms, D. W. G. (1995). *Mental Health, Mental Illness and Family Background.* Project Metropolitan Research Report no. 42. Stockholm.

Timms, D. W. G. (1996). Teenage mothers and the adult mental health of their sons. *Journal of Adolescence*, 19, 545–56.

Tittle, C. R., Villemez, W. J., and Smith, D. A. (1978). The myth of social class and criminality. *American Sociological Review*, 43, 643–56.

Tohen, M., Hennen, J., Zarate, C.M., Baldessarini, R. J., Strakowski, S. M., Stoll, A. L., Faedda, G. L., Suppes, T., Gebre-Medhin, P., and Cohen, B. M. (2000). Two-year syndromal and functional recovery in 219 cases of first-episode major affective disorder with psychotic features. *American Journal of Psychiatry*, 157, 220–8.

Tohen, M., Waternaux, C. M., Tsuang, M. T. (1990). Outcome in mania. *Archives of General Psychiatry*, 47, 1106–11.

Torrey, E. F. (1994). *Schizophrenia and Manic-Depressive Disorder*, New York: Basic Books.

Torstensson, M. (1987). *Drug-Abusers in a Metropolitan Cohort.* Project Metropolitan Research Report no. 25. Stockholm.

Tremblay, R. E., Loeber, R., Gagnon, C., Charlebois, P., Larivée, S., and LeBlanc, M. (1991). Disruptive boys with stable and unstable high fighting behavior patterns during junior elementary school. *Journal of Abnormal Child Psychology*, 19, 285–300.

Tuovinen, M. (1973). Offender patients. *Duodecim*, 89, 950–4. (Author's translation.)

Vartiainen, H. and Hakola, H. P. A. (1992). How changes in mental health law adversely affect offenders discharged from a security hospital. *Journal of Forensic Psychiatry*, 3, 564–70.

Verba, S. *et al.* (1987). *Elites and the Idea of Equality.* Cambridge, MA: Harvard University Press.

Virkkunen, M. (1974). Observations on violence in schizophrenia. *Acta Psychiatrica Scandinavica*, 50, 145–51.

Virkkunen, M., Rawlings, R., Tokola, R., Poland, R. E., Guidotti, A., Nemeroff, C., Bissette, G., Kalogeras, K., Karonen, S.-L., and Linnoila, M. (1994a). CSF biochemistries, glucose metabolism, and diurnal activity rhythms in alcoholic, violent offenders, fire setters, and healthy volunteers. *Archives of General Psychiatry*, 51, 20–27.

Virkkunen, M., Kallio, E., Rawlings, R., Tokola, R., Poland, R. E., Guidotti, A., Nemeroff, C., Bissette, G., Kalogeras, K., Karonen, S.-L., and Linnoila, M. (1994b). Personality profiles and state aggressiveness in Finnish alcoholic, violent offenders, fire setters, and health volunteers. *Archives of General Psychiatry*, 51, 28–33.

Walker, R. D. and Howard, M. O. (1996). Letter to the Editor. *Science*, 274.

Walker, E. F., Lewine, R. R. J., and Nemann, C. (1996). Childhood behavioral characteristics and adult brain morphology in schizophrenia. *Schizophrenia Research*, 22, 93–101.

Walker, N. and McCabe, S. (1973). *Crime and Insanity in England, II.* Scotland: Edinburgh University Press.

Wallace, C., Mullen, P., Burgess, P., Palmer, S., Ruschena, D., and Browne, C. (1998). Serious criminal offending and mental disorder. *British Journal of Psychiatry*, 172, 477–84.

Walldén, M. (1990). *Sibling Position and Mental Capacity – Reconsidered.* Project Metropolitan Research Report no. 31. Stockholm.

Walldén, M. (1992). *Sibling Position and Educational Career.* Project Metropolitan Research Report no. 37. Stockholm.

Walldén, M. (1994). Sibling position and the educational process. *Studies of a Stockholm Cohort.* Project Metropolitan Research Report no. 39. Stockholm, 155–219.

Warshaw, M. G., Klerman, G. L., and Lavori, P. W. (1991). The use of conditional probabilities to examine age-period-cohort data: Further evidence for a period effect in major depressive disorder. *Journal of Affective Disorders*, 23, 119–29.

Watson, J. B., Mednick, S. A., Huttenen, M. O., and Wang, X. (1999). Prenatal teratogens and the development of adult mental illness. *Psychopathology and Development*, 11, 457–66.

Webster, C. D. and Eaves, D. (1995). *The HCR–20 Scheme: The Assessment of Dangerousness and Risk.* British Columbia, Canada: Simon Fraser University and Forensic Psychiatric Services Commission.

Webster, C. D., Harris, G. T., Rice, M. E., Cormier, C., and Quinsey, V. L. (1994). *The Violence Prediction Scheme: Assessing Dangerousness in High Risk Men.* Toronto, Canada: Centre of Criminology.

Weissman, M. M., Livingston Bruce, M. L., Leaf, P. J., Florio, L. P., and Holzer, C. (1991). Affective disorders. In L. N. Robins and D. Regier (eds.), *Psychiatric Disorder in America.* New York, NY: Macmillan/Free Press, 53–80.

Wessely, S., Castle, D., Douglas, A., and Taylor, P. (1994). The criminal careers of incident cases of schizophrenia. *Psychological Medicine*, 24, 483–502.

Wetterberg, L. and Farmer, A. E. (1990). Clinical polydiagnostic studies in a large Swedish pedigree with schizophrenia. *European Archives of Psychiatry and Clinical Neuroscience*, 240, 188–90.

Whyte, W. F. (1943). *Street Corner Society*. University of Chicago Press.

Wickramaratne, P. J., Weissman, M. M., Leaf, P. J., and Holford, T. R. (1989). Age, period and cohort effects on the risk of major depression: Results from five United States communities. *Journal of Clinical Epidemiology*, 42, 333–43.

Wikström, P.-O. H. (1987). *Patterns of Crime in a Birth Cohort*. Project Metropolitan Research Report no. 24. Stockholm.

Wikström, P.-O. H. (1989). Age and crime in a Stockholm cohort. *Crime and Delinquency in a Metropolitan Cohort*. Project Metropolitan Research Report no. 26. Stockholm, 85–116.

Wilcox, D. E. (1985). The relationship of mental illness to homicide. *American Journal of Forensic Psychiatry*, vi, 3–15.

Wills, G. (1996). A tale of two cities. *The New York Review of Books*, 3 October, 16–22.

Wilson, D., Tien, G., and Eaves, D. (1995). Increasing the community tenure of mentally disordered offenders: An assertive case management program. *International Journal of Law and Psychiatry*, 18, 61–9.

Wolf-Seibel, H. R. (1980). *Sex Differences in Determinants of Educational and Occupational Goal Orientation*. Project Metropolitan Research Report no. 13. Stockholm.

World Health Organization (ed.). (1967). *International Classification of Diseases*, vol. 1, version 8. Geneva.

Zabczynska, E. (1977). A longitudinal study of development of juvenile delinquency. *Polish Psychological Bulletin*, 8, 239–45.

Zachau-Cristiansen, B. and Mednick, B. R. (1981). Twelve-year follow-up status of low birthweight infants. In F. Schulsinger, S. A. Mednick and J. Knop (eds.), *Longitudinal Research: Methods and Uses in Behavioral Science*, Boston: Martinus Nijhoff Publishing, 162–75.

Index

Note: Page numbers in *italics* refer to tables.